Outsourcing

A Practical Guide

Consulting Editor **Kit Burden**

Consulting editor
Kit Burden

Managing director
Sian O'Neill

Commissioning editor
Katherine Cowdrey

Editorial services director
Carolyn Boyle

Production manager
Neal Honney

Group publishing director
Tony Harriss

Outsourcing: A Practical Guide
is published by
Globe Law and Business
Globe Business Publishing Ltd
New Hibernia House
Winchester Walk
London SE1 9AG
United Kingdom

Tel +44 20 7234 0606
Fax +44 20 7234 0808
Web www.globelawandbusiness.com

Printed and bound by Gomer Press, Llandysul, Ceredigion, SA44 4JL

ISBN 9781909416659

Table of contents

Part 1: Preparing to outsource

Introduction 5
Kit Burden

State of the outsourcing market 9
John McKinlay
Jan Pohle

Overview of the procurement, negotiation and delivery process 15
Gareth Stokes
Kristof de Vulder

Part 2: Practical guidance and risks

Role of the client 37
Paul Allen
Gregory Manter

Practical perils and pitfalls – or why do projects fail? 53
Stéphane Lemarchand
Scott Thiel

Multi-jurisdictional deals 63
Kit Burden
Joris Willems

Service integration and management/multi-vendor projects 71
Callum Sinclair

Different types of outsourced services 85
Peter Jones
Stéphane Lemarchand

Part 3: Key provisions and issues

Due diligence and transition 97
Kit Burden
Tim Lyons

Services and service levels 107
Kit Burden
Peter Jones

Charges and charging models 139
Kit Burden
Joris Willems

Warranties and delivery commitments 151
Paul Allen
Jonathan Rofé

Confidentiality, intellectual property and data 167
Jan Geert Meents
Duncan Pithouse

Liability and indemnities 189
Anne Friedman
John McKinlay

Human resources and Acquired Rights Directive/ Transfer of Undertakings (Protection of Employment) 203
Kai Bodenstedt
Tom Kerr-Williams

Termination and step-in rights 217
Sharon Rowe
Anthony Willis

Assets and third-party contracts 233
Gareth Stokes

Governance, vendor management and dispute resolution 251
Peter Brook
Gregory Tulquois

Renegotiations, retenders and termination assistance 265
Tim Lyons
Jan Pohle

About the authors 279

Introduction

Kit Burden

There has probably never been a better time to write a book about outsourcing and the associated process of negotiating and drafting an outsourcing agreement.

Outsourcing agreements are inevitably substantial and complex contracts. They can be likened to business sale/acquisition-related contracts because of the size of the deal itself (outsourcing contracts will frequently be valued in the millions of dollars/euros, and the so-called 'mega deals' can get into the hundreds of millions or even billions), and the fact that they need to address a wide variety of issues – including the treatment of employees, transfers of assets and/or premises, tax and third-party contracts. However, it can also be argued that they are more complex than a business sale contract, because while a business sale looks only at a relatively short snapshot in time (ie, when the sale actually occurs, after which the parties would ideally have as little to do with each other as possible), an outsourcing contract needs to allow for the continuation of the relationship and the services over a prolonged period of time. Moreover, while the description of the required services and the associated model may be a good fit for the circumstances as they exist at the point of signature, the reality is that the business environment and the circumstances of the parties (and the customer in particular) will be highly likely to change during the term of the envisaged outsourcing engagement, and the contract will accordingly need to create a significant degree of flexibility to allow for this – which is far easier to say than it is to achieve in practice!

In the background, however, the size of the outsourcing market continues to grow; Gartner estimated it to hit $288 billion in 2013/14 and to grow by 4% in the period immediately thereafter up to the start of 2015. Fellow consultant and data gatherer ISG likewise cited record deal volumes and aggregate deal values in 2014. The scope of services being outsourced has also continued to extend, as more and more 'non-core' services are handed across to outside service providers, for reasons of cost and also because of the enhanced impression that organisations should concentrate on what they do best and outsource the rest. Once functions have been outsourced, while it is possible that they could be brought back in-house (and such insourcing happens), in practice it is relatively rare and so second-, third- and fourth-generation deals then provide a continuing flow of outsourcing project work.

At the same time, the process and thinking behind the negotiation of contract provisions for outsourcing engagements has also developed, perhaps at a faster pace than ever before. The reinvigoration of multi-sourcing (often, but not always, under the Service Integration and Management banner) has given rise to new contract structures and provisions geared to securing collaboration between historic competitors, while the continuing fall-out from the financial crisis and subsequent recession has manifested itself in new forms of wording for outsourcing in the financial services market in particular vis-à-vis forced divestments and, more generally, in respect of anticipatory breach and termination rights associated with declines in financial condition falling short of actual insolvency. As a result, traditional forms of contract drafting and precedent language has been re-thought and adapted, and the service provider community has likewise sought to reconsider the way in which it balances out the risks and rewards associated with such large-scale engagements, and their willingness therefore to accept certain forms of wording proposed by their customers.

As an equally important driver to changes and developments in contract drafting, technology changes are also affecting significantly outsourced services – in particular the dramatic growth in cloud service solutions (forecast to account for the majority of IT spending by 2016). Where not replacing outsourced solutions entirely, cloud solutions and services are increasingly forming a part of a wider outsource service, but on the basis of the imposition by the cloud service provider of contract clauses that are often not subject to much negotiation and that will bear little – if any – resemblance to the 'prime' contract terms that the outsource service provider will have had to sign up to with the ultimate customer. As a result, buyers of cloud-based services that would traditionally have been outsourced on a more labour-intensive basis are facing challenges in negotiating terms that are nothing like what their past corporate norms may have led them to expect, while providers of outsourced services that are broad in scope but rely on elements of cloud-related third-party services can find themselves squeezed in terms of their inability to flow down fully aspects of their prime contract commitments and risks. We expect this to be a fertile area for negotiation and developments in contract drafting during the course of 2015 and 2016, in particular.

The global DLA Piper technology and sourcing group have been right at the heart of these developments in the outsourcing market, negotiating on behalf of both customers and service providers on major outsourcing projects all around the world, in a multitude of different market sectors, and covering just about every flavour of outsource service imaginable (eg, desktop, networks, finance and accounting, human resources and payroll, application development and maintenance, data centres, call centres, document management services, facilities management and temporary/permanent recruitment services – to name but a few). With a shared knowledge base of what is – and is not – being agreed in such contract negotiations, we are accordingly uniquely placed to provide a comprehensive view of outsourcing contracts and best practice. The authors of each of the chapters of this book are drawn from the DLA Piper team, covering jurisdictions from all over the world.

In this book, you will accordingly find an A to Z of the process of producing an outsourcing agreement, from an analysis of the state of the market as a whole, through to a description of the roles of the customer and service provider in the procurement process and the key perils and pitfalls associated with it, through to a detailed summary of the key issues and points of drafting associated with the primary constituent parts of an outsourcing agreement. Recognising that customers and service providers have different perspectives as to what would be appropriate (or even reasonable) to include in such an agreement, we have endeavoured to set out some of the key options for negotiation and types of compromise drafting that we have seen in the market (allowing for the fact that each contract must ultimately be a product of its own unique facts, such that what might be appropriate for one contract/project may be inappropriate for another, even if it involves much the same kind of services, and even before taking into account the regional and cultural variations that we see having an effect on the contract drafting, depending on the core jurisdiction in which the outsourcing contract is being negotiated).

In pulling together the contributing authors of the various chapters contained in this book, we have deliberately provided for inputs from partners who are genuine outsource specialists in their relevant jurisdictions, so as to ensure also that we can provide a view that is truly global, and not merely tied to the circumstances and norms of a single country (not least because we find that approaches to negotiations and typical contract end points reached in negotiations will vary from country to country).

We hope that you will find this book insightful and useful. While it can never be a substitute for specific legal advice for a particular engagement, we aim to provide a sufficient level of understanding to enable the reader to navigate his way through a typical outsourcing contract and to appreciate the key provisions and why they are drafted in the way that they are. No doubt the legal market for such negotiations will continue to grow and mature such that in any future edition, there will be even more to say.

Kit Burden
Editor and co-author
Partner, DLA Piper

State of the outsourcing market

John McKinlay
Jan Pohle

1. Introduction

Outsourcing of services is now big business – a $6 trillion-a-year industry operating on a worldwide basis. Indeed, 2014 is said to have been the best ever for outsourcing, both in terms of total deal value and the number of separate deals entered into. How did a market of this size emerge, and what does the future hold?

2. Why outsource?

Engaging third parties to provide services is as old as history (as witnessed by the 'outsourcing' of the constructions of the Pyramids), but the idea of a specific industry that takes the delivery of entire business processes from an internal function to an outside service is much more recent.

Fundamentally, outsourcing is about better use of resources. In economic theory, the concept of specialisation is one of the core building blocks of an efficient business sector. So the theory goes, organisations are at their most efficient when they concentrate on specific tasks for which their particular combination of people, location, skills and financial resources is best suited. If all parts of the economy work in this way, everyone benefits since goods and services are produced cheaper, faster and better.

These high-level principles can be broken down into a number of more specific justifications for outsourcing, such as:

- reducing overall cost;
- obtaining a better, more technologically advanced and/or more reliable service;
- rebalancing fixed and variable costs;
- introducing greater flexibility;
- improving staff quality, motivation and career prospects;
- meeting regulatory requirements;
- improving controls/information;
- streamlining and standardising processes; and
- sharing the risk of delivery between the customer and service provider.

Depending on the nature of the outsourcing in question, one or more of these justifications will be paramount, which will then dictate the nature of the outsourcing and the service providers that are likely to be able to respond. In the past, the driving force for outsourcing tended to be the reduction of headcount and cost. However, as outsourcing offerings have become more sophisticated, any of the above strategic concerns could encourage or mandate a business to outsource.

3. Industry players

Outsourcing as a business has grown out of the IT services industry, and initially the major players were IT companies based in the United States and Europe. Large international accounting and consultancy companies followed suit, although again these were largely US and European based.

More recently, Tier-1 players in the outsourcing industry have included a series of Indian service providers that have made a major impact on the market by offering services from lower-cost locations, offering significant labour cost savings over and above any process efficiencies, particularly with regard to IT-led outsourcing, but more recently in respect of the business process outsourcing market as well. The market entrance of Indian service providers further urged the existing market participants not only to establish large delivery centres themselves in India (where IBM, among others, now has more employees than in the United States), but to look for even lower-cost operations in locations including, for example, Thailand and Vietnam.

The outsourcing market has also experienced a growth of industry-specific outsourcing service providers – for example, those offering services such as HR outsourcing, facilities management and payment processing. Harking back to the concept of specialisation, these dedicated service providers have the specialist skills to inherit a particular function from the customer's in-house team and deliver this to a better standard.

Lastly, it is worth noting that certain organisations operate 'captive entities', which are wholly owned subsidiaries (typically in offshore locations) that provide services as if they were independent third parties. The captive entity offers cost savings and process improvements, while the service recipient still retains overall control. Historically, this has been particularly appealing to regulated organisations, such as those in the financial services sector, as it enables the customer to exercise a higher degree of control and flexibility over the service than if it outsourced to a wholly independent service provider. The drawback to this is that the customer bears a higher degree of risk, as there is no 'true' third party with which to share the burden of any problems associated with the service. Establishing a captive entity can also be a lengthy process and requires a substantial up-front investment from the customer.

4. Recent developments

Over the past five to 10 years, three things have increased the size and scale of outsourcing. We will examine each in turn.

4.1 Customers' desire to manage costs

Companies face increasing pressure to manage their costs due to relentless worldwide competition across a wide range of industries. This has forced organisations to consider outsourcing, or risk falling behind in the market due to their cost base being too high or too inflexible. The push to outsourcing has increasingly come from global operations as they can most easily gain the benefits of cost savings and streamlined processes, but it has also come from purely national customers. The global financial crisis from 2008 onwards added further impetus and necessity in this regard.

This has been important because there is a natural inertia to overcome and costs to consider before any decision to outsource is taken. An organisation may be largely comfortable with the existing processes that are run internally. It may have limited appetite to investigate in detail what else the market can offer. It may be concerned with the organisational risk (and risk to individual careers) if outsourcing does not go well or does not deliver its stated goals. In addition, outsourcing any process requires considerable investment, both in time and resources. Preparation and execution of the contract can be a lengthy process and the customer will often incur a considerable up-front cost (eg, investment in new technology, redundancy costs for staff, etc), which will be recouped over a period of years. Taken together, these can act as a considerable drag on any decision to outsource, and the financial savings may accordingly need to be compelling – and/or the customer's need very great – in order to make the case for outsourcing work from the customer's perspective.

4.2 Technological development

Rapid growth in the speed and availability of computing and communications power, matched by an equally rapid decrease in its real cost, has assisted outsourcing gain popularity among businesses. With the development of technology comes increased automation of processes, which lowers labour costs and thus the overall cost to the customer. Technological developments have enabled a further surge in growth in the nature, location and complexity of the services that can be offered. In practice, this has been particularly important in the rise of offshoring as a distinct feature of the outsourcing market. Most outsourcing procurements now include at least one potential service provider that is proposing that a component of the services be offered overseas, whether core services like application development or payment processing, or ancillary services such as telephone support or account management. The fact that this can be offered is largely down to improvements in technology that allow rapid and real-time communication at an affordable cost, which have reduced or eliminated any issues with locating service or call centres in locations that are remote from the customer or users.

4.3 Increased choice of outsourcing providers

Lastly, the number of organisations able to deliver the services has grown rapidly. Initially largely based in the United States and Europe, they now operate on a worldwide basis, with a particular focus on low-cost regions of the world such as India and Asia-Pacific. These organisations take advantage of the ability to offer attractive careers in an organisation that is an industry leader, and so can attract the level of talent required to provide a specialised and effective outsourcing service. The fact that the majority of these staff can be located anywhere in the world brings advantages in relation to recruitment and lower-cost base, but has also increased the need for sophisticated quality management.

With this growth come other factors that reinforce the outsourcing market. A support industry of advisers and consultants has grown up ready to offer assistance in structuring and delivering outsourcing arrangements. Case studies by industry peers naturally act as an encouragement to others, as does the experience of staff who move from one organisation to another, bringing experience and examples of efficiencies and benefits. Culturally, outsourcing has become more normal and less in need of special justification beyond a normal business case, and organisations are more aware of the benefits of outsourcing and some of the pitfalls to avoid to give their project the best chance of success.

5. Issues facing the outsourcing market

Despite the sound economic basis for outsourcing and its growth and maturity, no one can be unaware of the issues that the industry has faced in delivering tangible customer benefits. It is estimated that between half and three-quarters of all outsourcing deals are renegotiated in some form or other during their lifetime, and in many cases companies would have saved more money if they had kept their operations in-house.

There are also examples of blue-chip organisations bringing operations back in-house, often due to problems with their end-customer experiences. Often the problems that customers report are down to the expectation gap. After signing, there can be disparity and confusion between what the customer expects and what the service provider delivers. This can stem from a lack of understanding of both parties regarding how the contract will be implemented post-signing. Customers that are looking for innovation and continual improvement are more likely to be disappointed than those whose main focus is immediate cost savings. Further cultural issues might result in significant problems for the outsourcing project after signing, especially in an international delivery environment.

What do these issues tell us about the state of the outsourcing market? In many ways they are symptomatic of a more mature industry. Customers' expectations and requirements are high, and the marketing and sales operations of service providers have become more sophisticated in response. As outsourcings become more complex and easy wins fewer to find, it is natural that issues will arise with delivery. In addition, the recent economic difficulties felt across most of the developed world has left a permanent legacy of cost control, which means that customers are more likely to raise issues than in the past with an outsourcing that is failing to deliver to expectations.

6. Outsourcing trends

6.1 Strategic partnerships between customers and service providers

Historically, businesses have limited their use of outsourcing service providers for those functions that are ancillary to their core business (eg, data processing, IT support, etc). These functions, while necessary to run an efficient business, were not the services that the company provided to its customers. However, outsourcing is now being used for more direct customer-facing operations, rather than simply for back-office functions. As most of the cost has been taken out of the back-office functions and the skill base of the outsourcing organisations increases, it has been natural to seek to move further up the value chain in the services that are being offered.

This is linked to the move towards using outsourcing for more sophisticated operations, often involving a strategic element. Examples may be HR recruitment, asset and estate strategy, procurement of goods and services, and financial planning. This is a natural progression from first outsourcing commodity and easily replicable services, and then continuing to move to greater levels of complexity.

This move has been accompanied by greater complexity of the contracting models used, with some outsourcings now being structured as joint ventures rather than the more traditional customer/service provider contract. The distinguishing feature of the joint-venture structure is a different approach to risk sharing, whereby the customer and staff provide the services benefits in a share of the profits generated by the outsourcing itself.

6.2 Stricter regulation

Another trend to note at this point is the increased scrutiny and sophistication of regulators. A complex set of rules exist in the major jurisdictions, coupled with diligent regulators that want to be assured that the outsourcing is not an attempt to transfer responsibility for compliance, and want to know that contingency measures are in place to secure continuity of service in material areas. Examples of regulatory structures that apply to outsourcing include:

- the EU Markets in Financial Instruments Directive (2004/39/EC), which requires businesses operating in the financial services sector to implement policies and procedures that are adequate to manage the risks involved in outsourcing functions or investment activities that are critical or important to the business;
- the Sarbanes-Oxley Act, which increases the disclosure and reporting requirements on public companies doing business in the United States; and
- EU Directive 95/46/EC on the protection of individuals, which provides the basic regulatory framework for the processing of personal data of individuals in the European Union and the transfer of such data offshore. This directive is to be replaced be a completely revised directive in the near future.

Regulators are increasingly less likely to be satisfied with vague reassurances from businesses regarding compliance and business continuity, and are looking for both specific contractual protections and the need to retain some capability in-house to act as a safeguard. Outsourcing services offshore presents distinct regulatory challenges. Specific rules exist in various jurisdictions in relation to offshoring, and recent trends have seen difficulties in securing regulatory approval for areas such as managed security where the risks offshore are seen as too difficult to manage.

7. Looking beyond offshoring

As the customer-service provider relationship becomes more integrated, the services to be outsourced grow more complex, and service providers become more diverse and sophisticated, mixed outsourcing models are likely to become more common.

Businesses are increasingly aware of the subtleties of their different outsourcing requirements and will invest more in global business service models that are a combination of onsite, offshore and nearshore outsourcing (each bringing its own advantages).

Offshoring might be unsuitable for some customers, or for some specific business functions, for reasons such as political sensitivity, cultural misalignment, regulatory issues or end-customer antipathy for the offshore model. The customer might therefore choose to base its operations in a country that is not only closer in terms of location, but that also shares values and legal/regulatory structures.

For this reason, countries in Central and Eastern Europe have strengthened their offerings to the European market, and are providing increasing competition to the traditional cost favourites such as India and Asia-Pacific. In addition, certain countries have developed a number of outsourcing hubs in regional cities, which can give customers the safety of a base within the European Union, while offering relatively reduced costs, highly skilled staff, support that is close at hand and legal compliance.

Similarly, for businesses operating in the United States, the Americas are growing in popularity as a destination for outsourcing. As the gap in cost between offshoring and nearshoring continues to narrow, US companies can enjoy benefits such as shared time zones, closer cultural connections and attractive tax incentives by outsourcing their operations to locations in the Americas. As a result, we have seen a visible boost to the outsourcing industries of countries such as Brazil, Colombia, Chile and Costa Rica.

Overview of the procurement, negotiation and delivery process

Gareth Stokes
Kristof de Vulder

1. The ultimate aim: successful delivery

Outsourcing projects do not start off with the aim of failing to deliver the service. However, key to the successful delivery of the service is a contract that accurately reflects the service to be delivered, and provides a framework within which issues (eg, change, service failures, *force majeure* (unforeseen) events) can be accommodated.

If the contract represents a plan for successful delivery of the service, the procurement and negotiation process should then represent a plan for successful delivery of that contract. Although this seems a simple enough statement, the reality is that the complexity and time taken to ensure the success of a procurement/negotiation process for an outsourcing project is commonly underestimated.

The customer will, in most cases, be able to dictate the terms and timing of the process. The more sophisticated customer will use this to drive a considerable advantage for itself, from ensuring that the initial draft of the contract issued at the request-for-proposal (RFP) stage matches its needs, to preserving competitive tension between competing bidders for as long as possible. However, customers can often over or underplay their hand in this regard. Making a process look too harsh will scare off suppliers, resulting in a much narrower range of bids to take forward. Rushing to appoint a single preferred bidder wastes a golden opportunity to apply competitive commercial pressure, not just with regard to pricing, but in relation to the contract terms as well.

By contrast, service providers should familiarise themselves with the rules of the process as soon as possible, identifying areas where they can play to their strengths, or where they might seek to bend the rules to overcome weaker aspects of their offering. Suppliers often lose out during a competitive process due to simple and avoidable errors. When looked at in the context of the service provider's costs of bidding for each major project, these apparently minor errors can result in significant wasted bid costs, and even greater lost opportunity costs. Again, the more experienced service providers tend to have more sophisticated bid and risk-management processes in place, such that they will either decline to bid for work or withdraw from bidding processes if they perceive that the risk/reward balance is getting unduly skewed, or if they sense that they are simply a 'stalking horse' in the bid process.

2. End to end – from RFP to exit assistance

The diagram below provides an outline of the lifecycle of a typical outsourcing project. The black sections show pre-contractual activities, while the grey sections describe the various post-contractual phases. The activities that typically take place during each phase are described further below.

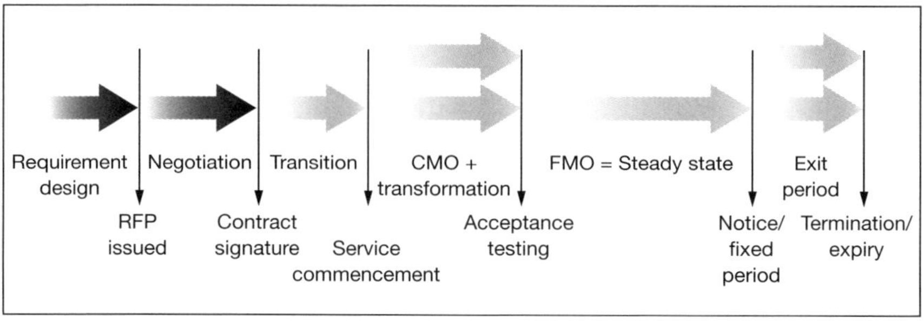

Requirement design: This marks the very start of the process, where the requirement for a service to be outsourced is identified, the business case verified and the RFP document drafted. In addition to a description of the customer's requirements for the services, the RFP will usually include materials describing how the procurement process will be run, and a draft of the contract that bidders will be asked to mark up and submit as part of their bid response (although in some cases a set of key terms or principles will be sent out in lieu of a full contract, albeit often set out in quite exhaustive detail). The phase ends when the RFP is issued to prospective bidders, with a deadline to submit responses.

Negotiation: This is the period between RFP issuance and final signature of the contract with the selected supplier(s). As detailed below, negotiation often proceeds in several distinct sub-phases. What (hopefully) starts out as a relatively large field of providers is first whittled down to a smaller pool for more detailed negotiations based on an initial assessment of the high-level merits of the bids. From there, it is perhaps narrowed to two potential suppliers. That phase will often then conclude in a best-and-final-offer (BAFO) down-selection point before a single supplier is appointed as preferred bidder. That then leads to final contract signature when any outstanding matters have been settled. See section 4 below for more detail.

Transition: This is the period after signature but before service commencement. It usually sees the service provider undertaking knowledge transfer activities, readying systems and interfaces for the commencement of delivery, and both the customer and service provider undertaking any staff-transfer activities (see the chapter on HR and ARD/TUPE for more detail). Transition usually ends with service commencement, although in some cases transition activity might continue after that (eg, if the service transfer is to take place in phases, as opposed to a single 'big bang' cut over).

Current mode of operation (CMO)/business as usual (BAU): This period starts with service commencement, where the service provider takes on delivery of the service from the customer (or previous supplier in a second-generation outsourcing), but is delivering the services in an essentially identical manner to that employed by the customer (or previous supplier) before service commencement. This will persist until any transformation-related activities result in changes to the services.

Transformation: One of the aims of many significant outsourcing projects is to improve services (even if – during the time of the recession from 2008/09 onwards at least – cost reduction seem to take an even more prominent role in the justification for short outsourcing projects). The customer must test and accept the improved method of delivering the services before it is implemented within the production/business environment, with the end of such testing process signifying the end of the transformation phase. The transformation might involve reducing the headcount required to deliver services, sending services offshore, introducing new technologies or methods of operation, improving the service levels against which the services are delivered, or finding improvements and/or cost savings via other means. Occasionally, the transformation will be a single 'big bang' change at service commencement, in which case there may be no CMO/BAU phase.

Future mode of operation (FMO)/steady state services: The services after the transformation has been completed and any acceptance or service commencement tests have been passed will then generally reach a new steady state of operation (subject to any change control procedures/continuous improvement obligations that might apply) for the remainder of the term of the contract. The service provider will remain under an obligation to deliver these transformed services until either handback of the services to the customer, or handover to a replacement supplier.

Exit period/exit assistance: Towards the end of the term, in addition to the continued provision of the FMO/steady state services, the service provider will be obliged to implement the exit obligations set out in a pre-agreed exit plan. Ideally, the exit plan will have been formalised early in the engagement (eg, within 60 days of contract signature) and then kept up to date throughout the term. The exit plan will cover matters including knowledge transfer to the entity that will have responsibility for service delivery after the term (the customer in insourcing cases, or otherwise a replacement supplier). These typically include transfer of any staff, novation/assignment of contracts, transfer of assets, migration of data, handover of premises, etc. See the chapter on assets and third-party contracts for more detail in this regard.

Different suppliers will use different terminology to describe the pre-transformed 'as was' services, and the post-transformed services. 'CMO' and 'FMO', or 'BAU' and 'steady state' are reasonably common terms within the industry, but other suppliers may have their own preferred jargon for these phases. Whatever the terminology used, the phases will generally map onto the block diagram above, with initial service commencement being an end point for transition activities, and final acceptance of transformation activities being a secondary end point.

Similarly, some regulated processes will have their own terminology for particular elements within the process. A good example is the European Union's regulated procurement process, where public authority customers will generally issue an invitation to tender rather than an RFP, and (depending on the regulated process used) the initial sifting of bidder responses might be done via a pre-qualification questionnaire stage within strict legal limitations rather than a more commercial sifting of initial responses.

In some cases, the complexity of the outsourcing might require multiple iterations of both transition and transformation. For example, it is not uncommon for an outsourcing with a phased transition of services where those services were historically provided onshore within a higher-labour cost area (Western Europe, the United States) and are to be transitioned offshore to lower labour cost areas (Eastern Europe or Brazil, Russia, India and China). That type of arrangement might see multiple instances of transition occurring, with delivery of the relevant service line from the offshore location signalling the successful completion of each transition phase. Similarly, a broad-spectrum outsourcing of an enterprise IT function might see multiple individual transformation projects within a transformation programme. In that context, the successful upgrade of the network, or hardware refresh of a mainframe, might be individual transformation projects with their own acceptance criteria and milestones. It is only when the entire transformation programme is complete and all projects fully accepted that the FMO or steady state is reached.

3. Request for proposal

3.1 So tell me what you want – what you really, really want

Fables abound in which a fool is granted three wishes and the story then relates how each of the wishes then results in misery for the unlucky fellow, rather than a life of ease and luxury. We need no mischievous genies, malevolent faerie-folk or the devil himself to be involved for an unwary customer to find that what it thought it wanted has not only failed to solve its existing problems, but has created a heap of new ones. "Be careful what you wish for" is as true in outsourcing as it is in the pages of Grimm, Aesop or Goethe.

The RFP needs to specify what the customer is seeking to purchase. In some cases that will be relatively easy, in the sense that a working system already exists which can be described and documented. We do not wish to understate the complexity involved in documenting how an existing business process works – in itself, properly documenting how something is done can be challenging – but it is less of a challenge than drafting a description from scratch for a service not currently provided. In any event, documenting an existing process presents the procurement team with a good starting point, even where new or transformed services are the ultimate aim of the procurement exercise.

Documenting how an existing business process currently operates may or may not be an effective starting point depending on the rationale for the outsourcing. If the rationale is primarily cost driven, with any improvement in service quality or transformational aspects a secondary concern, then it can be very useful. In that case, the customer is likely to achieve its aims as a result of the service provider being able to leverage volume savings and/or reduce staff costs (via either headcount reduction or labour arbitrage by offshoring). The service provider will be best able to identify these opportunities, and how the current service levels are achieved, if it has a detailed understanding of the methods by which the services are delivered.

If the rationale is more dependent upon realising the benefits of the transformation phase (eg, by upgrading platforms, moving to a 'best of breed' technology, significantly increasing service quality, or re-engineering systems), then the minutiae of how the service is currently delivered is less relevant to how it will look in a post-transformation steady state. It is still worth including information about how the service operates, but the detail may be less critical to the various potential suppliers' bids.

All of this is even easier in a second-generation outsourcing, where the existing service provider should have process flows, manuals and documentation on standard operating procedures describing exactly what is done. If the customer drafted its original outsourcing contract properly such that it can use the content of those documents within its RFP without worrying about any IP or confidentiality claims from the supplier, then that can short-cut the need to document separately the services for the RFP.

The risk is that the customer inadvertently locks in stale processes and methods. By being overly prescriptive about the services that it wishes the potential suppliers to provide, the customer is less likely to receive bids for potentially better methods of delivering equivalent outcomes, on the basis that such bids would be non-compliant with the customer's stated requirements. Service providers are justifiably nervous about submitting non-compliant bids, and while it is not unheard of for suppliers to submit multiple bids, with both a compliant and non-compliant submission for the same RFP (especially if this has been flagged in the RFP as something that the customer is prepared to consider), it adds to the service provider's cost of sale.

3.2 Dealing with uncertainty

Increasingly often, the customer will wish to rely on the various potential suppliers' market knowledge, expertise and proprietary methodologies or software to obtain a 'best of breed' service. To a greater or lesser extent, in such circumstances the customer does not know exactly what it wishes to buy.

Where this is the case, the customer needs to be very clear about the outcomes that it seeks to achieve. These should be specified both in terms of positive outcomes that are to be delivered (eg, achievement of specific service levels, availability of support during particular hours) and negative outcomes that are to be avoided (eg, high staff turnover within the supplier, poor knowledge of the customer). If a customer simply specifies the positive outcomes sought without considering what negative effects these could have, the mischievous supplier could grant the customer's wish at the cost of those negative outcomes without having breached any aspect of the requirement.

The customer should consider what level of detail it wishes to use when describing the outcome. While the outcome needs to be defined properly, too much detail about how it is to be achieved risks missing the point of why it is desirable. A trick frequently used in training salespeople is to describe a product not just in terms of features (what it can do), but also in term of benefits (what problems it solves, and how it provides an advantage to the customer's operations). The same approach is useful when creating an outcome-based requirements document: the customer should think not just in terms of what it wants the supplier to do, but also in terms of what benefit the supplier delivers for the customer. For the customer, it is useful to set out the benefits to be delivered explicitly in the RFP document, so that the service provider cannot later argue that it did not understand the purpose for which the services were being delivered (see the chapter on warranties and delivery commitments for more detailed information). To get the full benefit of the service provider's explicit knowledge of the purpose for which the customer is purchasing the services, the customer could consider including warranties that the services will be fit for purpose. Service providers will often seek to exclude such warranties, but there is no justification for a blanket exclusion if the customer has clearly stated the purpose and benefits in the RFP. An example of an outcome-based requirement might appear as follows:

Requirement number Requirement		**Benefit(s) to be delivered**
X-01	Inbound calls to the helpdesk answered promptly: • 97% within 3 rings • 99% within 5 rings	• Users have confidence in the helpdesk • Issues are resolved more quickly • Users' productive time is increased as they spend less time waiting for issues to be fixed

Another good reason to avoid being too prescriptive in terms of how a particular requirement is to be met is that it precludes the prospective suppliers from proposing their own solution to the problem. Henry Ford is credited with having declared that if he had asked his customers what they wanted, they would have asked for a faster horse. What they really wanted was faster transportation that does not get tired or leave manure in the street. This illustrates that describing the individual requirements and benefits at a higher level, rather than by reference to existing solutions, allows for the possibility that suppliers will propose something that the customer had not thought of, but which delivers all of the customer's desired outcomes more effectively.

In a similar vein, particularly with technology-centric services, it is easy to fall into another trap by assuming that a particular software platform or vendor's product is essential. Some vendors have encouraged this when it helps to support dominant positions in relation to areas of business – it does not take too much effort to think of pertinent examples of proprietary PC operating systems, or enterprise database products where this has been the case. Following the above logic, it is easy to see how this falls into the same trap of being too prescriptive and precluding other possible solutions. This also risks freezing the solution at a point in time, and reducing the possible benefits to be realised via technology change during the term of the contract. With outsourcing contracts often having a term of five years or so, and the pace of technological change being as swift as it is, this lock-in can be detrimental to the customer over such period. Some of the clearest examples of this can be found by looking at enterprise communications outsourcing arrangements over the past several years. The rapid growth (and in some cases similarly rapid decline) in the deployment of technologies such as the BlackBerry, iPhone, and Android phones have caught out unwary customers that were too prescriptive about the device families that the supplier should provide and support.

Openness and flexibility can take on a new importance in regulated procurement processes. Again, looking to regulated procurements within the European Union as an example, a customer that too narrowly specifies its requirements (by dictating that a particular process, methodology or software platform be mandated) could leave itself open to challenge in court on the basis that its criteria unfairly favour bidders with a particular commercial relationship with the relevant vendor. Where the procurement is regulated, the customer must ensure at the drafting stage that its requirements comply with such regulations.

3.3 You get what you measure – but might not get what you do not

From an operational perspective, the service level regime in an outsourcing contract is at the heart of the delivery of services. The RFP pack should set out those service levels that the customer expects to be met. While customers should provide a strong guide as to service credits and termination triggers that might be calculated within the RFP pack, other elements relating to the service level and credit regime can be left until the negotiation process. This is particularly true of the level of the monthly charges that will be at risk to service credits – with bidders being encouraged to offer a higher amount than the other bidders in the process. Setting a minimum expectation in line with market norms, and then asking for the potential suppliers to offer more than that as part of the scoring of their bid can be very effective.

The chapter on services and service levels explains more about the theory of how service levels should be set and credits calculated. For the purposes of the RFP document, it is worth considering that any aspect of a service that is measured tends to get special attention from a supplier – particularly if it has credit consequences attached to that measure. The inevitable consequence is that unmeasured areas tend to be ignored. It is therefore essential to ensure that the service levels represent a complete picture at the outset of the RFP process, with all key aspects of the service being identified and measured.

3.4 The draft contract

The RFP pack will also include a starting draft of the contract or at least a set of detailed key principles, and the bidders will be asked to review and submit a mark-up as part of their response.

Some see this as the customer's best chance to draft a contract that is skewed heavily in its favour. The logic for this being that throughout the rest of the process, the bidders will all seek to chip away at it with more supplier-friendly terms. While this temptation to impose every possible risk upon the service provider can be strong, in reality there is little to be gained by starting out with a heavily biased contract knowing that it contains provisions that will be challenged and in respect of which the customer will concede. This wastes time for the bidders in reviewing and responding to the draft, and makes the customer's position on other issues look weaker by reason of earlier concessions. Instead, starting with a more reasonably balanced contract where the customer can justify each provision as necessary will result in a better overall process (and avoid the service providers also adding unnecessary elements of risk premium into its pricing).

The draft contract should be as complete as possible. While the exact detail of the services descriptions, transition timetable and activities, transformation timetable and activities, and charges will depend upon each bidder's response, in almost every other area it is possible to provide detailed drafting. This should include all front-end terms and conditions, the service credit mechanism, the basics of invoicing and payment, governance, disputes, change procedures, acceptance procedures and the effects of delay.

3.5 Insert tab A into slot B

A good RFP pack will include a very clear roadmap for the entire process through to contract signature. It should, among other things, specify:

- the deadline to submit responses;
- the format(s) that the responses should be in, which may vary for each element within the required response – for example, the draft contract might need to be submitted as a marked-up document using Microsoft Word's track-changes function, whereas any pricing might be submitted in a spreadsheet worked out against a notional service demand forecast over the term;
- the date, time and location for meetings;
- the names/functions of the bidder personnel who must attend each meeting, to ensure that persons with the correct expertise are available – lawyers and commercial leads at contract meetings, technical staff at solution design meetings, etc;
- the date for down-selection decisions; and
- the criteria for scoring bids and making selection decisions.

Some additional guidance on the way that the bidders need to address their remarks regarding the draft contract or the key principles may save a lot of time during the selection process. The customer could, for example, consider stating that the bidder must indicate unambiguously if it agrees with the proposed positions. If the bidder disagrees with the proposed positions, it should make that clear and also set out in full what its proposed alternative would be. In order to void any delay in the process, it can also be helpful to mention that responses that are deliberately evasive or that state that the issues are "to be discussed" at some later stage (or similar) will be viewed negatively. Again, in order to speed up the process, a bidder should be requested to respond in a way that enables the customer to see exactly how the bidder would wish to propose that the contract would deal with the issue concerned, including suggested drafting where necessary, along with supporting rationale. The RFP instructions should also make it clear that the bidder's response in relation to the draft contract or key principles should be exhaustive and that, following submission of its response, further disagreement and/or alternative positions to those set out in its response will not be considered. The customer should reserve the right to modify and/or add to its requirements in the framework of further discussions and negotiations. The question may also arise as to which extent references to any approaches or positions adopted in any existing contract in place between the customer and/or its affiliates and the bidder should or should not be made. If the customer would like to avoid this, it could state in the RFP that it views this new and current contractual process as unique to the requirements of this project, and that, accordingly, positions agreed in relation to other arrangements or projects will be neither necessarily relevant nor a guide to what the customer may be willing to accept this time around.

This will set clear expectations for the bidders, and result in a smoother process for the customer, where it is easier to compare bids like-for-like. That said, all of this should clearly be made subject to the customer's ability to vary the requirements or any other aspect of the process at any time without liability to the bidders.

Again, this takes on a greater degree of importance where a public authority is engaging in a regulated process, as stepping outside the rules set down at the outset could provide disgruntled bidders with grounds to challenge the process.

3.6 Confidentiality, liability, costs

That mention of liabilities takes us to the final part of the process – the need to consider liability and other, more traditionally contractual, aspects of the arrangement.

In private-sector procurement processes, it is common for bidders to be asked to sign full non-disclosure agreements or confidentiality agreements before being sent the RFP pack. These agreements will cover the entire procurement process, including the existence of the process and all information shared during the process. As will be discussed below in section 5, the due-diligence elements of a procurement can result in the customer making a considerable amount of confidential information available to suppliers.

In the public sector, it is more common for some aspects of the procurement to be in the public domain. Often, the public authority will have advertised that the procurement is underway, and publically invited the submission of tenders. Even so, it is still usual for bidders to be asked to sign non-disclosure agreements covering the more detailed information that will be shared later in the process.

In different parts of the world, a customer's liability to a potential supplier for pre-contractual expectations that may have been created varies considerably. In some jurisdictions, the customer will bear no responsibility to a service provider for any pre-contractual discussions, even if the customer is later shown to have dealt with the service provider in apparent bad faith. In other jurisdictions, however, the customer and service provider might bear some responsibility for pre-contractual discussions if they later prove to have made untrue statements that induced the entry into the contract (eg, misrepresentation). In other cases, applicable law may provide for material remedies for any bad-faith dealings during the negotiation. Any procurement needs to consider these issues carefully. Where the procurement covers multiple jurisdictions, all of the rules applicable in each relevant jurisdiction need to be examined, with the process being run in accordance with the most stringent requirements across all relevant regimes. These requirements for fair pre-contractual dealings are yet another reason for the customer to set out the detail of how the process will be run at the outset, as that way the service provider cannot later claim to have had different expectations about its engagement in the process or chances of success.

Lastly, for clarity it should be expressly stated that the bidder is entirely responsible for all of its bid costs and other expenses incurred throughout the process, regardless of whether it is ultimately appointed as the chosen supplier or otherwise. This is particularly relevant in those jurisdictions where a customer may run the risk of being exposed to pre-contractual liability in the event that negotiations are terminated with one or all of the bidders during the negotiation process. This is also the reason why the authors often see that in those jurisdictions where pre-contractual liability risks are most present, the bidder is requested to confirm that the customer may at any time and for any reason cease discussions and negotiations with the bidder, and that the bidder shall not have the right to claim any compensation or reimbursement of costs in relation thereto or as a result thereof. Such confirmation can be obtained through a separate contract that will be signed (eg, the non-disclosure agreement as referred to above or by stating in the RFP that following submission of a proposal the bidder has irrevocably accepted those provisions of the RFP).

For consideration of issues associated with preferred-bidder status and any request that a letter of intent be executed or exclusivity granted, see sections 4.5 and 4.6 below.

4. From RFP to contract signature – the negotiation

4.1 Keep it competitive

As indicated above, the customer's best chance of securing a good deal from its appointed service provider is to retain a degree of competitive tension during the negotiation process. Designing a process to maintain that tension is likely to result in a materially better deal for the customer than any process that lacks such tension.

That tension must be genuine – the bidders all need to have a real expectation that the customer might select one of their competitors. If that belief is lacking, then any potential benefit of a competitive process will be lost. This tension can be lost in several ways. It may be that a bidder discovers who the other bidders are and realises that none of them pose a real threat. It may be that the key decision-makers within the customer consider one particular bidder to be a far safer bet than the others, and this information is leaked to that bidder (whether deliberately or inadvertently). In other cases, it may be that the other bidders pull out, leaving only one bidder.

In other circumstances, it may be simply impossible for any other bidder to be included in the process. For example, if the service is dependent upon a proprietary technology, and there is only one provider of such technology, then that eliminates the potential for competition at the outset. In other cases, the business team might come to the legal function too late in the process, having already 'selected' their supplier and perhaps having even told the relevant service provider as much. In these cases, there is no (or at least very little) scope for competitive tension.

The advantage of a competitive process is clearly that the bidders are each likely to feel under pressure to make a better offer (lower price, a commitment to higher service levels, a larger percentage of monthly fees at risk to service credits, etc). It also provides the customer with a useful extra weapon for its armoury during the negotiation. It avoids the customer having to appeal to market practice to justify why a bidder should accept a particular clause. Where another bidder has accepted such provision, then the customer can state that it need not look at what the wider market position is for the purposes of the current engagement – since other bidders are willing to accept the provision, the bidder that refuses to accept it is at a disadvantage.

Where it is simply impossible to retain competitive tension, which tends to be the case at the end of a process where a preferred bidder is appointed, then the customer must fall back on the usual array of arguments to justify its position. Considering which party is best placed to manage a particular risk, what operational and governance mechanisms can be used to mitigate against those risks, and what non-contractual remedies each party might have in such circumstances can all help to smooth over the last sticking points in the process.

4.2 Planning it out – timings and deadlines

One of the toughest questions to answer when starting a procurement process is: How long is it going to take? Inevitably, the business will want the procurement wrapped up as quickly as possible, but there is a real risk of underestimating both the work involved, and the time that it is likely to take. Securing the time and attention of the relevant key personnel at the customer organisation (whether decision-makers or subject-matter experts) may be difficult, especially where they have their day job to attend to on top of the negotiation. Carefully planning a sensible negotiation timetable, with down-selection points, and time for reviews, bidder response preparation, scoring and negotiation built-in will help to set reasonable expectations at the outset. It can also help to reinforce in the minds of potential bidders that they will be rejected from the process if their bid is not good enough at each stage.

Assuming that the RFP document is sent out to bidders at the beginning of a month (Month 1), then a reasonable timetable for negotiation might look like the Gantt chart on the next page.

Activity	Month 1	Month 2	Month 3	Month 4	Month 5	Month 6
12th Month 1 – all bids received (except at least 4 or 5 bidders).	◆					
12th–31st Month – Assessment of initial responses/scoring. If more than 4 or 5 bidders, this could include rejection of worst initial offers to narrow the field. Communication to non-selected bidders 31st month 1.	◆					
19th Month 1–14th Month 2 – Feedback (not negotiation) meetings/calls with 4 or 5 down-selected bidders. Customers should provide brief written feedback highlighting issues in the contract response prior to the call. Each bidder given two weeks from the date of its meeting/call to revise its contract mark up/bid pack.	◆	◆				
3rd – 28th Month 2 – Receipt of revised contract mark ups/bid packs from bidders following the feedback call (2 weeks after each call). Customer re-runs bid scoring.		◆				
29th Month – All revised dashboard scores for all 4 or 5 bidders circulated to all stakeholders within the customer (business, procurement, technical, operational, risk, legal) ahead of down-select meeting.		◆				
1st Month 3 – Initial formal down-selection. From the 4 or 5 bidders, 3 are selected for continued dialogue. Decision communicated to bidders.			◆			
3rd Month 3–16th Month 3 – Initial 1 (full) day negotiation sessions with 3 bidders. Revised contract drafts/commercial offers produced following each 1 day session.			◆			
19th–23rd Month 3 – Feedback to wider customer stakeholder team on quality of bidder responses so far. Down-select to 2 bidders for more material negotiation.			◆			
26th Month 3–4th Month 5 – Detailed negotiations as a 'two horse race' with remaining bidders (6 weeks).			◆	◆	◆	
4th–11th Month Month 5 – Bidders prepare BAFO submissions.					◆	
11th Month 5 – BAFO submissions received.					◆	
11th–18th Month 5 – BAFO evaluation.					◆	
18th Month 5 – Preferred bidder selected.					◆	
18th Month 5–1st Month 6 – Contract finalisation negotiations (2 weeks).					◆	◆
1st Month 6 – Contract signature.						◆

The above chart provides for the field to be narrowed from the initial bidder group to a single preferred supplier in four stages:

- If more than four or five bidders respond to the RFP, then it might be necessary to conduct a cull at the end of the initial review of bidder responses. In the above chart, that would happen at the end of Month 1.
- After initial feedback to the four or five remaining bidders, and a chance for each of them to resubmit their (hopefully improved) bids, there would be the first formal down-selection process. This would leave three bidders in the process. In the above chart, that takes place at the start of Month 3.
- The field is than narrowed from three bidders to two after initial one-day face-to-face sessions with each of the three bidders. This should be enough time to establish with each of the three how easy they will be to work with, how likely they are to yield additional concessions in the process, and how much they want the business. In the above chart, this takes place on the 23rd of Month 3.
- The last selection point is after the BAFO stage, following a six-week face-to-face negotiation run. This selection point, and the formality of a BAFO process, is critical. After this point, the remaining bidder is, whether officially named as such or not, the *de facto* preferred bidder. The competitive tension will have dissipated, and the customer needs to have wrung all of its desired concessions from the selected bidder by this point.

Having several bidders multiplies the work required in reviewing and scoring their responses. Outsourcing contracts tend to be long documents. Even for a relatively straightforward outsourced service, the contract without the service description might be 150 pages long, the service description and service level chart another 150, and the charges mechanism and supporting spreadsheets another 50 or so. Reviewing and scoring these documents, and then negotiating them, for multiple bidders is time consuming. The longer review periods at the start of the chart may look generous, but reviewing, evaluating and comparatively scoring more than five bidder responses in just over two working weeks will stretch most procurement teams.

Therefore, the above chart is designed to apply pressure to the bidders earlier in the timeline to improve their offer and stay in the process, with significant negotiation effort being saved to the two-horse race phase starting in Month 3. The six weeks allowed for that phase across two bidders effectively gives three weeks per bidder. That can be split up in various ways – a week with bidder A followed by a week with bidder B, or seeing each bidder for two days in each week, with the fifth working day reserved for drafting.

Time can be easily saved within such a process. Where possible, tasks can be run in parallel. The above chart includes an example of this, where the initial feedback conversations with bidders can start while the reviews of other bidders' submissions are ongoing. If the customer has received five bids on the 12th of Month 1, it might have fully reviewed the first of those within a few working days and be able to provide initial feedback to that bidder accordingly. That bidder can then be working on revising its bid in accordance with the feedback, while the customer is still reviewing and providing feedback to the other bidders.

4.3 Multiple-appointed suppliers

All of the above has assumed that the customer wishes ultimately to appoint a single supplier. In many cases, customers will wish to run a process to appoint multiple suppliers, with common scenarios for such multiple appointments being as follows:

- a complex array of services, where different suppliers have expertise in different fields. Consider, for example, the outsourcing of an entire enterprise IT function. That might involve the outsourcing of service lines including desktop, servers, mainframe, hosting, storage, security operations, networks, telecommunications, application development and application maintenance. It is conceivable that the customer might wish to appoint expert suppliers to cover each area, which could see one supplier appointed for desktop, another for back-end services such as servers, mainframes, hosting, storage and security, a third for networks and telecommunications, and a fourth for application development and maintenance; or
- a framework contract under which multiple discrete work packages will be offered, with a desire to retain competitive tension for each work package. In this scenario, the customer might appoint three of the bidders on substantially similar framework terms and then, as each of the work packages is let, run a mini-competition between the appointed suppliers to see which of them will win that work package.

Where the outsourcing is to result in a multi-bidder appointment, then the complexity increases, and the timelines to run the procurement process also increase, but the same basic principles apply.

For each additional final appointee, the initial field of bidders should ideally be greater by at least two to maximise the quality of options for the final choice. Thus, the initial field of four or five bidders recommended for a single supplier becomes eight or nine for three suppliers. That then means that a two-and-a-half week initial review period might take nearer to five weeks, and so on. That said, as the customer increases the number of likely appointed suppliers, the opportunities for parallel working increase. Therefore, it might be possible (depending on resources within the customer and its various advisers) to have different teams working with different bidders in parallel, thereby shortening what could otherwise be a very lengthy lead time.

4.4 BAFO and the preferred bidder

A key phase in any process is when each bidder is asked to submit its BAFO. Ideally, it should be an opportunity for the bidders that remain in the process to put forward the offer upon which they wish their bid to be reviewed. The threat that, after this stage, only one bidder will go forward to be the appointed service provider (or a small defined number if a multi-supplier project) ought to be the incentive to make sure such final concessions are as required.

As much as the intent of the BAFO process might be to achieve a final executable contract document, in reality there almost always remain several points to be finalised. Therefore, there is usually a need to allow for some additional closing of issues. However, the BAFO process should not take place too early. If there is a possibility that, instead of just a few final points, a larger number of key issues will remain outstanding at or after BAFO, then the time is not right for BAFO. Instead, the customer will generally be better served by delaying BAFO until just a handful of minor outstanding points remains, and by retaining the competitive tension of the two-horse race for longer.

After BAFO, the selected bidder will in all likelihood realise that it is in a relatively strong position. It therefore becomes more difficult for the customer to persuade the bidder to make additional material concessions thereafter. That is to be expected, and it is the reason for ensuring that as few issues as possible remain after BAFO. One very serious matter that the customer needs to protect against is the potential for the appointed preferred bidder to seek to reopen previously agreed points. The best defence against such request is for the post-BAFO process to be kept relatively short, and for the other bidder to be kept in the background if possible. That way, in the event that the preferred bidder starts to backslide on issues, the customer can reopen negotiations with the other bidder instead.

4.5 Letters of intent

Particularly upon being selected as preferred bidder, a service provider may seek to start work. The extent to which there will be pressure to do this will depend upon how aggressive a timetable the customer is pursuing in relation to transition and service commencement. The types of activity normally envisioned include knowledge transfer, design and set-up.

Before starting any pre-contractual activities, the service provider may seek coverage in the form of a letter of intent, specifying that, regardless of whether the customer ultimately enters into a full contract with the service provider, the customer will pay the service provider for work undertaken. This is not unreasonable, especially if the customer is expecting the service provider to expend material amounts of effort or to incur material costs.

Particular attention will need to be given to the scope, pricing, liability, term and termination clauses when drafting such a letter of intent, as these will be the most contentious areas when negotiations would need to be terminated and no final contract would be agreed upon.

Where the timing pressure that drives the need for the service provider to start work before the contract is finalised genuinely is coming from the customer – and this should be distinguished from a service provider simply claiming that it needs to start work early to meet a timetable – then it is not unreasonable for coverage in the form of a letter of intent to be provided. In such circumstances the customer should ensure, as a minimum, that:

- the letter of intent provides coverage to a defined cap (eg, $100,000);
- the cap is structured as a true cap rather than a fixed fee, costs will accrue in line with an agreed rate card, and the customer will pay a lower sum if the value of work is below the cap;
- the value of work will be set off against the charges under any contract eventually executed – otherwise the letter represents an increase in the costs of transition;

- ownership of all work product (and intellectual property in the same) produced under the letter vests in the customer; and
- the customer can terminate the letter at any time – with the proviso that it will pay to the cap for work done before termination.

The preferred bidder may seek to introduce some form of penalty or liquidated damages payment in the event that the full contract is not executed within a particular period. However, we have never encountered a circumstance where any proffered justification for such a move by a bidder withstood serious commercial scrutiny, and the customer should resist such a move.

4.6 Exclusivity

The preferred bidder may seek a period of exclusivity in relation to the negotiations, where the customer agrees not to discuss the deal with any other party (and particularly any of the other bidders) for a given period. Again, within the content of the multi-bidder process described above, this tends to be a request made after BAFO.

There is rarely any advantage to the customer in agreeing to such an arrangement. Very occasionally the supplier may request exclusivity in exchange for undertaking pre-contractual work at its own risk (ie, without the type of capped fee coverage described in section 4.5 above). This is often sold by a bidder as a demonstration of its commitment to the project by being prepared to undertake some of the early-stage work for free. If that is the case, the customer might query the extent to which it really is getting work 'for free', because it might simply be delayed payment of the bidder's fees if the quoted transition costs within the bid remain as they were.

On the whole, exclusivity periods benefit the bidder more than the customer. In addition, they can provide coverage for backsliding by the bidder, while precluding the customer's ability to reopen discussions with the other bidders. For that reason, if exclusivity is to be agreed to at all, it needs to be on the basis that any settled points in the negotiation would not be reopened by the bidder. This can be achieved contractually by appending to any letter of exclusivity a copy of the then-current travelling draft between the parties in which only those areas of the contract that are not settled are shown with track changes. The letter can then provide that the bidder will not raise any issues affecting those areas of the draft not showing track changes as a guard against backsliding. While not bullet proof (the bidder could simply introduce a new point within a track-change area instead), it clearly captures the intent of the parties to limit the subject matter of discussions during the exclusivity period to a narrow range of known issues.

4.7 Regulatory requirements

This chapter has touched several times upon questions associated with particular regulatory regimes that might affect a procurement process, using the European Union's regulated procurement process for public authorities as a prime example.

Clearly, where the customer is subject to such a regulatory burden, the process must comply with it. In such cases any timetable would differ from that set out in section 4.2 above in order to accommodate the particular requirements of the process. Sticking with the EU model as our example for the time being, where a regulated procurement is proceeding in accordance with the 'competitive dialogue' procedure, then any timetable will need to allow for a pre-qualification questionnaire phase and a standstill period before final contract award in accordance with the legal requirements applicable to that procedure.

4.8 Second generation – fitting into an exit timetable

Lastly, one of the greatest sources of pressure upon any procurement timetable might be a ticking clock toward termination of an existing supply arrangement. In that case, the process needs to be timed to ensure that a new supplier has been appointed not just prior to the end of the current contract term, but ideally so that the transition period in the new service provider's contract coincides with the latter part of the exit period under the old service provider's contract. The overlap should ideally be a period of several months to allow for all aspects of the transition to be completed (knowledge transfer, asset transfer, novation and assignment of contracts, and, where applicable, the transfer of employees from one supplier to the other). The ideal for multiple generations of outsourcing is illustrated below.

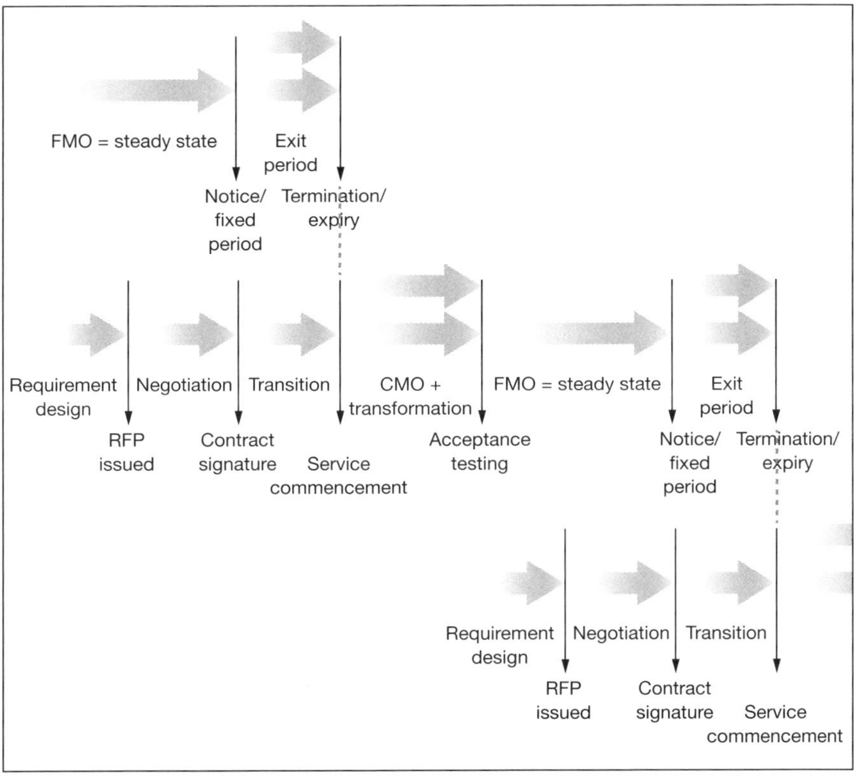

It is always a good idea to be realistic about the potential for a process to be delayed by unforeseen events. Where the termination of an existing contract sets a hard deadline for service commencement under a new agreement, adding some padding to the process is advisable.

5. Due diligence

Alongside any negotiation process, the customer and bidders will each need to conduct due diligence in relation to the proposed services. The information gathering undertaken by the bidders upon the customer is known as 'inbound due diligence', and the customer's checks upon the bidders is referred to as 'outbound due diligence'.

5.1 Inbound due diligence

As noted in section 1 above, the appointed service provider will be taking on an obligation to deliver a service to a particular standard during the term of the contract, and receiving an array of assets, contracts and staff to support that delivery. It may be taking a lease over premises; it may be required to refresh systems and hardware, renew contracts, train and develop staff and renovate premises during that period. Such a contract is therefore genuinely akin to a business and assets transaction in the corporate world.

In order to ensure that the customer's requirements can be met with the assets, contract, people etc that it will inherit if appointed, the service provider needs an opportunity to check these and verify their status and quality. Most importantly, where the service provider will be asked to meet certain service levels, it needs an opportunity to check (as best as it can) the historic performance or alternatively, where historic data is not available, the quality of the systems and people to make a reasonable assessment about their ability to deliver to the required levels.

This will usually involve access to a data room where relevant documents (contracts, records, etc) are stored, and visits to check sites and systems. It can also be helpful to conduct workshops with key personnel and subject-matter experts, who can explain any issues not evident from the records and visits.

The customer may have legitimate concerns about sharing certain data with bidders as part of the due diligence process. In addition to the contractual confidentiality protections that the non-disclosure agreements provide, it is common for customers to remove particularly sensitive data (eg, regarding prices and liability limits) from documents in the data room, and make this available only to the preferred bidder post-BAFO. This might then mean that the preferred bidder needs to be afforded an opportunity to revisit its pricing – to the extent that it is genuinely affected by the new data – after the unredacted documents are shared.

Any sharing of data with bidders during inbound due diligence needs to be subject to any confidentiality obligations that the customer owes to third parties. Particularly in respect of any contracts that will be shared in the data room, the confidentiality provisions that apply between that third-party contractor and the customer need to be checked to ensure that the relevant contract can be shared in the data room, always subject to the terms of the non-disclosure agreements with those bidders. It may be necessary to approach some third parties for consent to sharing of the contracts prior to their being made available to the bidder group.

5.2 Outbound due diligence

The customer will also wish to check that each bidder is able to deliver the services, and outbound due diligence will usually concentrate upon the three areas outlined below.

(a) *Site visits to the bidder's facilities*

These are to check both the quality of the facilities and people, and the security arrangements. The latter series of checks are particularly important where the customer is subject to legal data protection or privacy obligations. These commonly mandate that the customer satisfy itself as to the technical and organisation security arrangements in place at the facilities where data processing is carried out before such processing begins.

(b) *Reference conversations with the bidder's existing customers*

While the bidder will normally nominate its reference customers (and generally, therefore, pick its happiest customers to act as referees), customers nevertheless often glean important details about the ethos and approach of organisations from these conversations. Is the bidder sufficiently flexible? Are issues escalated and resolved quickly or swept under the carpet? Has the bidder tended to take a nickel-and-dime approach to costs via change control?

(c) *Credit/public information checks*

Lastly, the customer should undertake checks of public information sources both at the start of the process and immediately prior to any final down-select decision and contract signature. News of any high-profile incidents involving the bidder, or any concerns regarding its solvency, need to be weighed carefully.

6. Delivery

6.1 The contract

Once the preferred bidder has been selected, all final issues have been resolved and the contract has been signed, the only thing left to do is the minor matter of delivering the outsourced services. If the proof of a pudding is in the eating, the proof of a procurement process is in delivery.

Key throughout delivery is for the contract to be a living document that guides the process, and regulates the relationship between customer and service provider. Too often, commercial teams within customer organisations will suggest that the contract be 'put in a drawer and forgotten' as soon as it is signed. The danger in doing that is that, in practice, the parties will then follow processes and approaches different to those in the contract, and over time be deemed to have amended it (depending on the laws of the jurisdiction applicable to the contract). This is inevitably disadvantageous for the customer as all the hard-fought protections in the contract itself will have been wasted and erased.

Instead, the contract should be written with processes and procedures that the parties will actually follow. It should guide governance, change and (if necessary) disputes.

6.2 Transition

As noted above, transition tends to be about knowledge transfer, system set-up and people transfer. It is fairly rare for a contract to go badly off the rails in the transition phase. That said, as with transformation below, delay is the biggest risk. The customer should be monitoring progress throughout this period and flagging delays early.

As this is the first part of the engagement before the service provider takes on service delivery responsibility, it sets the tone for the entire remainder of the engagement. A no-nonsense (but not unnecessarily aggressive or punitive) approach by the customer is recommended. Where delays occur, as a minimum the customer should flag that a remedy has accrued. Even where the customer does not wish to pursue the remedy immediately, it should not waive it entirely. Instead, it should explicitly set the claim to one side on the basis that it is – in effect – being 'put on ice'. That way, if any other failures should occur, any 'banked' remedies for earlier breaches can then be reactivated.

6.3 Transformation

As with transition, the issues most likely to arise during transformation are delay related. It is far more likely that these may occur during transformation, as the activities tend to be more complex and specialised. Whereas any major supplier will have successfully undertaken transition many times, transformation projects are not so reproducible.

By the time any transformation acceptance dates are due, customer and service provider will likely have been working together for some time. The shape and nature of the relationship at that time will therefore inform likely reactions to failure – is this a trusted partner that has demonstrated a commitment to excellence in other areas and ought to be given the benefit of the doubt, or has the relationship been rocky from the start, and this is just another boulder? Giving the service provider an opportunity in the early period to earn trust and build up goodwill can then pay dividends in preserving the relationship later on.

6.4 BAU/steady state

Whatever the relationship between customer and supplier, whether friendly or fractious, regular governance meetings and acting in accordance with the provisions of the contract are key throughout. As noted above, failure to do so could equate to the customer losing rights and remedies.

Where things are going wrong, customers tend to be surprisingly nervous about using any dispute resolution procedure provided for in the contract. It might sound trite, but the reason that a disputes process is included within an outsourcing contract as a matter of course is for it to be used. It is almost always better for a dispute to be aired and escalated (and therefore, with any luck, resolved) than for it to fester and manifest itself in disgruntled users and low-level sniping.

Governance meetings tend to be set to a monthly cycle, and are therefore relatively easy to stick to. Most contracts will also provide for a range of longer period obligations: exit plans might be updated annually, a right to audit (other than for regulatory reasons or where fraud is suspected) might be limited to one per annum, and benchmarking or market-testing of prices might be on a longer than annual cycle. Customers should set a checkpoint at least once per annum to ensure that these longer period rights and obligations are being met.

Role of the client

Paul Allen
Gregory Manter

1. Outsourcing: success in the face of complexity

In contrast to more traditional customer-vendor service agreements, outsourcing arrangements are characterised by their tendency to be complex and at the same time critical to the customer's business. Broadly, outsourcing involves the transfer of a function (or elements of a function) to an outside service provider. This involves the service provider contractually assuming responsibility for the performance of what can be highly mission-critical and sensitive elements of the customer's organisation, including taking over:

- the employment of the staff making up the function;
- ownership of real and personal assets of the organisation;
- the management of third-party suppliers;
- responsibility for the achievement of service levels; and
- the storage and security of highly sensitive data, such as personal, financial and health data, and the customer's own confidential information.

This book dispels any doubt there may have been about the complexity of outsourcing. Yet, despite this complexity, organisations all over the world have turned to outsourcing as a tried and tested way of achieving certain strategic objectives and operational efficiencies. In our experience, customers that understand the critical role that they play in the build-up to and execution of an outsourcing strategy are best placed to ensure the successful achievement of their desired objectives.

So what is the role of the customer in an outsourcing? In a nutshell, the customer is responsible for ensuring the success of the outsourcing at least as much as, if not more than, the service provider. This may sound controversial at first; after all, does the customer not pay the service provider to fulfil the outsourcing contract and provide the requisite services? The answer is clearly yes, but while service providers will take on contractual risk under the outsourcing contract, and receive payment for both taking on that risk and delivering the outsourced services, ultimately it is the customer that will suffer the most if the outsourcing fails – and whatever contractual remedies it may then have are unlikely to compensate it fully for the impact on its business. Equally, while risk of service delivery passes to the service provider, there will invariably be at least some level of retained responsibilities for the customer to fulfil.

Viewed another way, outsourcing transactions are not true partnerships or joint ventures, where each party has a stake in the success or failure of the services (no matter how much outsourcing contracts are sometimes compared to marriages).

Rather, the service provider stands to gain in a single way – the revenue stream generated from fees paid by the customer. By contrast, it is the customer's end clients that will leave if they are not getting the service that they require because an IT system is down; it is the reputation of the customer that will be damaged if sensitive customer data is stolen due to lax security on the part of the service provider; it is the customer that will suffer regulatory fines and other penalties if it fails to meet its regulatory commitments due to the service provider's performance failures. The customer cannot, therefore, afford to see the outsourcing fail; it should treat the outsourcing activity, from the moment that the idea emerges within the organisation and throughout all the various stages of outsourcing (tendering, contract negotiation and execution, service delivery and any transition to a third-party supplier or back in-house) as an activity that it owns and must remain responsible for at all times. Adopting such an attitude towards the outsourcing will help the customer to ensure that it reaps the benefits of a successful outsourcing programme.

2. Hallmarks of a successful outsourcing

Before delving into the specifics of what the customer role entails, and what the customer should do to help to ensure the success of an outsourcing, it is useful to clarify what a successful outsourcing looks like and compare that with what amounts to an outsourcing failure.

Procurement specialists always mention two key elements of success – namely, the solution and the price. Procurement specialists want to ensure that they are contracting with the service provider for the right solution and that they will be paying the right price. But is the right solution at the right price enough to equal outsourcing success? What does 'right' mean anyway? In our experience, 10 elements mark an outsourcing as successful, although these hallmarks are neither definitive nor to be given equal weight when assessing the success of an outsourcing.

2.1 Customer's needs satisfied

First and foremost, the customer must receive from the service provider the specified services and deliverables that it requires to satisfy its particular needs. If this is not the case, then the fundamental requirement of achieving the right solution is not satisfied. It is therefore critical to the success of the outsourcing that the customer understands its requirements, is able to communicate those requirements to potential suppliers and can determine satisfactorily whether the proposed service providers are able to meet those requirements. The chapter on services and service levels provides in-depth, best-practice guidance on how to define these requirements and articulate them in the outsourcing contract.

2.2 Good value obtained

Obtaining good value is a key success criterion for any commercial transaction. In the context of an outsourcing, which typically lasts for periods of three or more years, the concept of good value needs to be considered not only at the point of contract signature, but throughout the life of the outsourcing relationship. Given that the economics of the deal will change over this period, determining whether the deal is good value is no simple task, especially as it involves a consideration both of the prices payable to the service provider and the total cost of ownership (including the retained costs of the customer). The chapter on charges and charging models explores various pricing models and other commercial issues relevant to ensuring that good value is achieved and maintained for the duration of the outsourcing.

2.3 Risks allocated reasonably

Achieving a reasonable allocation of risk that aligns with each party's control and scope of responsibility is important for any outsourcing arrangement. A misalignment in this regard can have numerous negative effects on other aspects of the outsourcing. For example, if the service provider is not carrying an adequate level of risk in relation to the performance of the services (eg, it has committed only to using 'reasonable endeavours' to perform the contracted services, even though such performance is fully within its control), it may be prepared to provide a less than adequate service knowing that it is less likely to be liable for any poor performance (ie, because 'reasonable endeavours', at least under English law, does not amount to an absolute obligation to perform). As a further example, if the service provider is asked to carry risks that are not within its control, one response of the service provider may be to inflate the price payable for the outsourcing so as to cover the cost of mitigating that risk. Where prices are inflated in this way, it is likely to lead to a deal that is not good value for the customer. Apportioning legal and commercial risks is covered in detail in the chapters on key provisions and issues.

2.4 Impediments removed

It goes without saying that removal of any substantive impediments is critical to the overall success of an outsourcing programme. Sadly, however, situations occur where a customer may have invested substantial resources in an outsourcing programme only to see it fail before the contract is signed because such impediments have not been properly identified and removed.

Achieving this objective requires identifying impediments that are not always obvious to those unaccustomed to outsourcing. Likely impediments include those internal to the customer (eg, developing a suitable base case, obtaining stakeholder buy-in, finding the necessary resources to run the procurement), regulatory constraints (including those relating to employee transfers), and external constraints (eg, legacy providers, third-party contracts). Systematic identification and removal of these impediments will help to ensure that the outsourcing contract gets signed, and that no major surprise roadblocks surface along the way. The chapter on due diligence and transition is particularly relevant to this activity so far as it relates to the transition of the outsourced function from the customer to the service provider.

2.5 Procurement plans followed

"Anyone can do procurement!" is a flippant statement that we sometimes hear, usually from people who have never been involved in procurement. Truth be told, procurement is of fundamental importance to the success of any organisation, particularly those undertaking complex contracting activities such as an outsourcing.

Procurement specialists are best placed to know how to put in place a plan that will support the customer's ability to achieve its stated objectives. Once that plan has been designed, following the plan from start to finish will help to ensure the success of the outsourcing programme. If it is not followed, this could have an impact on the ability of the customer to achieve the business case or objectives underlying the outsourcing. For instance, if the objective is to achieve a certain level of cost savings in a particular financial year, but the outsourcing contract is signed six months late, the required cost savings are unlikely to be achieved. As another example, deviating from a well-designed plan can impede the leverage of the customer in the negotiation to achieve the customer's needs and overall good value (see case study 4 below). Time can become a weakness, unless the customer is able to control the competitive process and support that process with the proper internal and advisory resources.

2.6 Stakeholder buy-in obtained

Acceptance of the outsourcing by all relevant stakeholders (often referred to as 'buy-in', or 'taking ownership' or 'championing' of the project) requires significant planning, time and effort, and in some cases may even require a full change management programme. This critical element can have the most pervasive effect on the other elements, starting with the initial due diligence through to eventual governance of the steady-state solution. If stakeholders are not engaged throughout the outsourcing activity in a way that results in their concerns and needs being listened to and appropriately accommodated, it can lead to disastrous impacts for the outsourcing (see case study 2 below).

2.7 Deal is win-win

Has a deal been signed that is of benefit to both parties, or has the service provider lost out (eg, in the sense of having its margins erased by an aggressive squeeze on its pricing)? If the service provider has lost out, then far from being a win for the customer, the deal can have significant detrimental impacts on the outsourcing project. For instance, the service provider may decide to run its B or C teams instead of its A team if it stands to make only very narrow margins (or lose money) otherwise (eg, if its internal costs of its A team personnel are higher). Equally, the contract may become fractious, as the service provider is driven to try to improve its recovery levels by being more aggressive on the interpretation of its scope of services and what can/cannot be charged for in addition to the base changes (sometimes referred to as 'death by change control'). Alternatively, the service provider may, in extreme cases, be prepared to walk away from the deal and suffer the consequences because the cost of doing so is lower than the cost of fulfilling its promises. A well-advised customer will accordingly focus on balancing between permitting the service provider to achieve a reasonable profit margin for successful performance without granting a windfall (either up front or due to post-signing changes), while still preserving an earning structure where the service provider has the right incentives to perform with excellence, with consequences for failures that are not so onerous as to blow up the deal.

2.8 Contract future proofed

Will the arrangement stand the test of time, allowing for changes to the outsourced services, service levels, price, delivery model, contract terms and so on to account for changes that are affecting the customer or the service provider, including changes in law, in the customer's strategy, in the marketplace, and improvements in technology? In this regard, it is possible for the customer and the service provider to enter into an outsourcing contract that stands the test of time and requires changes only around the edges of its terms over multiple generations of outsourcing, but doing so requires a highly skilled team of professionals from the outset who have seen what changes occur in practice and know how to shape the contract in a way that allows for those changes in a sensible fashion.

2.9 Governance framework established

An outsourcing programme has many moving parts, often involving interactions between operational, executive and strategic levels of both the customer and the service provider, possibly over multiple locations or geographies, and involving tens, hundreds or even thousands of people, not to mention personal and real assets, IT systems, HR issues – the list goes on. Making all of these moving parts work together is not the outcome of signing a contract; it is the outcome of continuous management and good governance throughout the life of the outsourcing programme. To achieve this, the outsourcing contract should contain the intended governance framework of the customer and service provider; a framework that addresses the operational, executive and strategic interactions that must take place to manage the ongoing issues and risks, and ensure adherence to agreed plans, both as set out in the contract and as agreed between the parties from time-to-time.

2.10 Business case satisfied

The customer's business case is the ultimate yardstick by which the success of any outsourcing should be measured (at least from the customer's perspective, but also to a large extent from the service provider's perspective). This makes the initial development of the business case essential; after all, if the customer does not know where it wants to go, how can it get there?

Knowing where you want to go is one thing, getting there is of course a whole different matter. The customer and the service provider have a role to play in ensuring that the client reaches its intended destination, but as stated already, as the customer is likely to suffer (possibly the most) from a failed procurement, it is the customer that has ultimate responsibility for ensuring that its business case is achieved.

So how does the customer get there?

3. Case studies: what happens if the customer does not fulfil its role properly?

While it is possible to define the criteria of a successful outsourcing, it is well known that outsourcings fail from time-to-time. This could be put down to the complex nature of the outsourcing, but then that too is well understood.

One of the key overarching reasons outsourcings fail is because the customer does not play the role that it is required to play to deliver a successful outsourcing. Without wishing to engage in scaremongering, set out below is a series of short case studies. These case studies provide examples of what can go wrong in an outsourcing and are then used to demonstrate both why it is of critical importance to the outsourcing for the customer to take ownership of the programme, and what specifically the customer should do to avoid disaster and achieve success. While these case studies have been drawn from real life experiences, the case studies themselves are fictitious.

3.1 Case study 1 – insufficient due diligence

(a) *Scenario*

Outsourcing often involves the service provider requiring a licence to use certain software that has previously been licensed by a third-party software vendor to the customer under a software licence agreement. This is particularly true in the context of an IT outsourcing involving application (ie, software) maintenance or application development services. In such a case, where the service provider itself is responsible for maintaining and developing the software (rather than simply passing the job to the software vendor), it will be able to do so only if it has access to the source code for that software and has the necessary rights to copy and modify that software as needed to perform the relevant services. Except where the service provider is able to rely on its own licence from the software vendor, the service provider will need an assurance (in the form of a licence) from the customer that the software licence agreement allows the supplier to access (at least), use, copy and modify the software's source code. Without this assurance, the service provider would be unwilling to perform the outsourced services as to do so would put it in breach of the relevant software vendor's IP rights (ie, the copyright in the software).

In our first case study, a well-known retailer intended to outsource its HR function. To do so, the organisation knew that the relevant supplier would need to have the necessary rights to access, use, copy and modify a software application that had been licensed to it by a third-party software vendor.

Negotiations with the service provider were coming to a close and the deal was about to be signed when, at the 11th hour, the customer's in-house team was tasked with doing a due diligence on the relevant software licence. Only at that (very late) time did the team identify that the relevant software licence forbade the customer from giving any third party rights to access, use, copy or modify the software's source code. Without the ability to do so, the outsourcing could not go ahead.

As the saying goes, "everything is negotiable". In this case, the customer had to renegotiate its deal with the software licence vendor so as to ensure that its licence terms were suited to the intended outsourcing arrangements. Clearly, the amounts that it had to pay consequently could have been significantly worsened by reason of the weak bargaining position that it then found itself in.

(b) *Lessons learned*

Identifying impediments to an outsourcing at the earliest opportunity will give the customer a better chance of managing or removing those impediments successfully. While in our case study the customer succeeded in renegotiating the terms of the software licence, it came at a higher cost than would probably have been the case had the necessary terms been sought and agreed to at the time that the original contract was entered into, or at least not in the context of the by then well-known outsourcing programme. In the end, Hallmark 4 (impediment removed) was achieved, but it was a very close (and expensive) shave and had an impact on Hallmark 2 (good value obtained) in that the total cost of the deal increased.

3.2 Case study 2 – stakeholder engagement is critical

(a) Scenario

A global organisation was embarking on a global outsourcing in respect of its accounts function. The customer had a detailed outsourcing contract prepared and, as part of a competitive procurement process, issued it to potential service providers. The potential service providers were then asked to mark up the outsourcing contract, share their versions and attend face-to-face contract negotiations.

Negotiations had been going on for a month when rumours reached the project team that certain offices of the customer's global organisation were no longer willing to take part in the programme. First it was the Beijing office, then the Sydney office and then other major offices around the globe.

For one reason or another, the offices were not supportive of the programme and were therefore dropping out. By doing so, they undermined the programme's business case, so much so that the programme was cancelled. This was after the customer (and the potential service providers) had expended significant human and financial resources on the programme.

(b) Lessons learned

Stakeholders can and will sink an outsourcing programme if they are not supportive of it, which is why it is essential to achieve Hallmark 3 (risks allocated reasonably). Stakeholder engagement cannot be a follow-on thought. Instead, it must be considered at the outset of, and embedded in, the outsourcing programme.

3.3 Case study 3 – get the contract right

(a) Scenario

The customer, using only its internal legal team, concluded a deal with the service provider for an outsourced IT implementation and managed service for a payments solution. Some months after the conclusion of the contract between the customer and service provider, the customer sought external legal advice on what could be done about the service provider's non-performance. It transpired that:

- the customer had agreed to pay a multi-million dollar fee for the design and implementation of the solution;

- the customer had agreed that half of the fee would be paid up front;
- the description of the solution was vague and incomplete in many respects, meaning that Hallmark 1 (customer's needs satisfied) had not been met;
- while the contract had a project plan attached, the milestones and milestone dates for the project plan were missing – the plan was effectively a blank placeholder; again, a failure in respect of Hallmark 1;
- at the time of seeking advice, the upfront fee had been paid, but no solution had been delivered – the very opposite of Hallmark 2 (good value);
- as no timeframe had been prescribed for delivery of the solution, there was no breach, let alone a material breach, of the contract and therefore no right of termination existed – in effect the risk of delivery sat with the customer, even though the service provider had full control in this regard – a clear failure in respect of Hallmark 3 (risks allocated reasonably).

The contract failed to address three of the most critical hallmarks of success for an outsourcing deal. In the end, the customer lost the upfront fee and had nothing to show for it.

(b) Lessons learned

There is a common misconception amongst non-lawyers that contracts, once signed, sit in a drawer never to be seen again. While that may be true in the vast majority of simple commercial transactions, it is rarely the case in the context of an outsourcing. This misconception can lead to a lack of respect for the contract, so much so that little to no attention is given to the content – let alone the accuracy of its terms. In a worst-case scenario, this can have disastrous consequences as the above facts show. Such situations can be avoided by ensuring that a lawyer with experience in such transactions properly documents the deal, and that both parties (including the customer) then take care to perform their obligations thereafter.

3.4 Case study 4 – stick to the plan

(a) Scenario

In a competitive procurement, the customer had down-selected four potential service providers for parallel negotiations. By taking this approach, due to the competitive tension created among the bidders, the customer was likely to reach a better overall outcome than it would if negotiating with only one or two service providers. Ultimately, the customer intended to choose more than one service provider (ie, on a multi-vendor basis), with each service provider to be given an opportunity to bid for certain outsourced projects over the term of their contracts.

The customer had significant negotiating power, being one of the largest and best-known brands for its particular services in its territory. This significant negotiating power was boosted by the customer's plan to conclude negotiations and execute contracts with the service providers before they commenced any work for the customer. Such a plan meant that negotiations could continue until the customer was satisfied with the overall deal. All of this was in line with best practice when it comes to competitive procurement practices.

However, there came a point during the procurement process where the customer required the potential service providers to start providing services, even though the contracts had not been finalised. Rather than putting in place an interim contract, or stalling the commencement of the services until the strategic contract had been finalised, the customer went ahead and started to receive services from two of the service providers. Consequently:

- the service providers' commitment to the negotiation process fell away almost instantly (as the ones asked to do the work became convinced that they had, in effect, won the bidding process, and the others simply lost interest);
- negotiations became protracted and the customer found itself unable to obtain movement on outstanding elements of the contracts, particularly in relation to commercial terms;
- overall procurement timelines were not achieved; and
- the customer was receiving services and deliverables without any written contractual protection, leaving it exposed to significant legal and commercial risk.

While contract terms were ultimately signed, those terms were not consistent with the outcome to be expected of a competitive procurement.

(b) Lessons learned

No one has a crystal ball and so it is often the case that outsourcing procurement plans need to be amended to take account of unforeseen events or circumstances. Making such amendments is often unavoidable. However, in the context of a competitive procurement, where a change in plans is likely to reduce or remove the competitive tension among the potential service providers, this can undermine the expected value to be received from the competitive process.

In this particular case, not only was the customer receiving services without a written contract in place, the balance of power in the negotiation completely shifted to the potential service providers as there was no longer any strong chance of them losing the deal because of not agreeing to what would otherwise have been accepted as reasonable terms.

The change in circumstances need not be as severe as the one given in this example. Repeated delays or failures to follow the procurement plan, unfair treatment of potential service providers, a lack of transparency and poor communication are some other examples of when failure to adhere to best practice in the context of a competitive procurement can result in the value of the process being undermined.

4. Follow best practice to achieve success

If the customer wants to avoid scenarios like those described above, and achieve a successful outsourcing, it should follow the guidelines set out below.

4.1 Begin with the end in mind – establish and fund the business case

Arguably, unless through sheer luck, a customer will not achieve the hallmarks described in section 2 above if it does not first know its business case, and of course the business case stands no chance of success if it has not been funded.

As to what the business case of the customer should be, the permutations are endless. 'Your mess for less' is a common type of business case. In this situation, the customer simply 'lifts and shifts' (transfers) its function to the service provider on a promise from the latter to provide the same services and service levels at a lower overall cost. 'Transformation' is another common type of business case, whereby the customer expects some form of new and/or improved services following a period of transformation activities (eg, implementation of new IT systems). And there are many others. What type of business case a customer is likely to adopt will of course depend on the circumstances, and will also then affect the type of input and commitments that the customer will need to provide in order to make the project a success.

In Europe, the United States, Australia and other more mature markets, businesses are going through third, fourth and fifth-generation outsourcing activities. They started their journey into outsourcing a decade or two ago, after the commercial advent of the Internet had made remote delivery of IT services a real possibility. This opened the door for cost reductions through the use of highly educated work forces in low-cost jurisdictions such as India. The business cases adopted by these businesses will be very different from those of business in less mature markets.

In the developing markets of the Middle East region, by contrast, the trend towards outsourcing is one that has emerged far more recently. For various reasons, businesses in the Middle East have started to embrace outsourcing in its various guises. However, the reasons for outsourcing among Middle East customers are often very different from, and subject to a range of considerations that contrast with, those of customers in other parts of the world. Private and public sector organisations in the Middle East are often turning to outsourcing for specialised skills that are scarce or non-existent locally but can be shipped in by international outsourcing organisations. It is these specialised skill sets that might help a telecommunications operator to achieve a convergence strategy, a bank to implement modern banking systems and platforms, or government sector entities to achieve nation-enhancing objectives through egovernment programmes, new health service offerings and state-of-the art education initiatives. Leveraging foreign talent and skills into any emerging market is a known business challenge, and the Middle East is no exception. Outsourcing offers one proven way of meeting that challenge.

Whatever the business case is, it should be very clearly defined and supported by metrics that can be measured and reported from the outset of the outsourcing until its conclusion. Customers should ensure that service providers are required to provide the data, information, reports and other inputs necessary for this purpose.

4.2 Don't be a fool – know your risks and how you wish to deal with them

Potential benefits always come with potential risks. The risks inherent to outsourcing must be systematically dealt with throughout the outsourcing programme, otherwise the programme is set for failure. The good news here is that there is a global community of outsourcing experts who specialise in advising customers (and indeed also service providers) on the risks associated with outsourcing and how they should be managed. That said, while experts can advise, it is the customer that must decide and give instructions on how any given risk is to be managed. This is because it is ultimately the customer that is best placed to understand its own appetite for risk and its willingness to assume or transfer risks in return for an increase or reduction in some other associated benefit.

Each of the case studies in section 3 above provides an example of a situation where the customer has failed to appreciate a risk, ignored a risk, or chosen to take a risk in the hope of achieving a benefit. As will be seen in future chapters, the range of risks that arise in the context of outsourcing, the potential severity of those risks and the way in which those risks may be managed underscores the need for the customer to know the risks and how it wishes to deal with them.

4.3 Do your homework – plan and prepare thoroughly, including due diligence

As legal advisers to customers and service providers alike, we have seen it all when it comes to the level of preparation – from a 'let's wing it' to a 'this must be perfect' approach. Somewhere in between is probably best: a 'don't let perfection stand in the way of good' approach. So what sort of planning and preparation is required? Examples include:

- requirement collection and definition, through which the customer will define the detailed requirements for the outsourcing and that will at least inform, if not form the basis of, the ultimate services description and service level agreement;
- project planning, from high-level plans at the business case phase through to low-level plans produced regularly during the procurement;
- market evaluation, including through requests for information from the supplier community, site visits of potential suppliers and seeking inputs from service provider referees (ie, their previous clients);
- benchmarking, especially in relation to the prices and service levels that are available for the types of service being sought;
- data collection, to support the customer's requirements during the procurement. By way of example, in a 'lift and shift' situation, service providers will often seek data that confirms that the customer can achieve the service levels that are being requested. If the customer is able to provide data in support of such service levels, this can short-circuit what can become protracted discussions around the service level schedule. If that data is not available, a service provider may seek additional costs to cover any perceived investment to achieve the service level improvement, at which point the customer will need to make a decision on the best way forward (eg, as to whether it really needs the services to be performed at the enhanced level being requested);
- risk registers, to identify and manage risks throughout the procurement and thereafter in relation to all elements of the outsourcing programme; and

- contract design and preparation, bearing in mind that there is no 'one size fits all' approach when it comes to outsourcing, and therefore it will be necessary for legal advisers to consult closely with other customer stakeholders to ensure that the contract is fit for purpose.

4.4 Hire the A team – establish the right team and appoint the right resources

The best-run outsourcing programmes are those that are supported by a team made up of the right roles and right people for those roles. The customer needs to make sure that it has such people in place both for the negotiation/procurement process, and the ongoing management of the services thereafter (see section 4.5 below).

A variety of skill sets and roles will be required. There will need to be an identified leader for the negotiation process, who ideally should not have to juggle it with his day job. He will need in turn to be supported by appropriate specialists: legal (both in-house and, in all probability, external too), technical (eg, as to the details of the customer's IT environment), financial (eg, regarding the customer's current cost base, and to analyse the service provider's proposed pricing), sourcing/procurement (to help to manage the negotiation process, gather data, etc), HR (to manage the potential people impacts), and so on.

4.5 Don't let go of the reins – project manage from start to finish

Whether or not the customer runs a competitive process, project management and internal alignment during negotiation will serve as a point of leverage and counter attempts by the service provider to 'game the process'. After signing, the same is true – in many ways, that is when the negotiations really begin. The customer has much less leverage (the contract has been awarded, after all) and will need to derive leverage from the hard-fought protections won during negotiations (eg, service level agreements, schedule deadlines, precise invoicing, etc).

The customer will accordingly need to recognise the burden of contract management and ensure that its retained organisation has both the personnel and expertise to ensure that the service provider's performance can be properly monitored and managed. One particular mistake to avoid is the assumption that people previously involved in the in-house delivery of the service will automatically be best placed to manage the service provider once the services have been outsourced. Such an approach is fraught with risk; not only is vendor/supplier management a specialist skill, but also those involved in the historic delivery of the services will often have firm views as to how these services should be delivered, which may then be at odds with the intended approach of the chosen service provider, leading in turn to potential conflict and micro-management by the customer.

4.6 Win them over – ensure engagement and buy-in among all stakeholders

Stakeholder engagement is tricky because no two groups of stakeholders are alike. The employees making up the internal function of the customer who are about to have their jobs transferred to a service provider, the unions that represent those employees, the users of the end services, the service provider itself, not to mention the senior executive and board of the customer, all need to buy into the outsourcing.

To underscore the challenges faced in stakeholder engagement, consider the fact that in some parts of the world/society 'outsourcing' is a dirty word, especially when it involves offshoring of jobs to a foreign country, or even to a company owned by 'foreigners'. As an example, in many countries within the Middle East, quotas have been established for the employment of nationals, with outsourcing sometimes being perceived as incongruous with the achievement of these quotas. Cultural, societal and other demographic differences will all potentially play a part in determining the best stakeholder engagement approach to follow.

Given that the various stakeholders will have different interests and needs, identifying understanding and achieving sufficient alignment among those interests and needs requires a sophisticated and situation-specific mix of public relations, consultation (including via forums such as 'town halls'), problem solving, legal advice and good judgement. Failing to get that mix right could mean that the outsourcing does not go ahead or, worse still, goes ahead but results in customers or other external stakeholders not supporting the customer because it has 'outsourced' its people.

4.7 Keep it simple – avoid overcomplicating matters

This is a rule to follow from the start to the end of the outsourcing programme because it will really help to achieve each and every one of the hallmarks. While outsourcing is complex, and in many cases business-critical, over-complication must be actively avoided, particularly in the terms of the operational, technical and commercial schedules of the outsourcing contract. This is a crucial responsibility of the customer, both in setting up the outsourcing process and thereafter negotiating the associated contract.

Outlined below are two classic examples of over-complication and the negative impact that they can have.

Service level agreements that require an engineering degree to decipher: It is absolutely critical for the provisions of a contract to describe the service level/service credit regime clearly and comprehensively. However, that description should be one that can be easily understood by anyone picking up the contract and trying to implement it after it has been signed. If the service level arrangements are too intricate, this will not be the case and can lead to ambiguity and, consequently, disputes. The customer must accordingly resist the urge to ask for overly complex or numerous service levels on the basis that they are 'nice to have' rather than genuinely relevant to the business.

Over-specification of components of IT systems/platforms in respect of which outsourced services will be provided: IT systems are dynamic, with the configuration of the system in a constant state of flux. Every time a patch is applied, or a change implemented, the configuration of the IT system will be modified. Over-specifying the IT solution can act as a straightjacket for the parties and, worse still (especially for the customer), endless rounds of contractual change control. It may be better to refer to the IT system by reference to its functional purpose, rather than trying to hard-wire every element of it into the contract.

Simple solutions do not mean easy solutions, but they should ultimately mean less headache, management time and rectification time during the life of the outsourcing.

4.8 Accept responsibilities

Some customers seem to be of the view that an outsourcing agreement should be a oneway flow of liabilities and responsibilities of the service provider, as owed to the customer. While it is certainly true that the service provider will have overall responsibility for delivery of the outsourced services, there will almost always be retained responsibilities of the customer and dependencies that the service provider will have upon them.

The service provider will (understandably) be keen to ensure that the customer recognises this fact, and reflects this in the contract. Rather than view this as illegitimate and seek to attach any list of responsibilities offered up by the service provider, a well advised customer would instead review the list in detail, on the basis that it is arguably more helpful to have a long and detailed list of customer responsibilities, if indeed they are the things that will need to be done if the outsourcing project is to be a success (which is, after all, what the contract is intended to facilitate). It is also arguably better for the customer to have such clarity, rather than a shorter (but far less certain) contract obligation to simply provide 'reasonable assistance' to the service provider.

4.9 Dot the Is and cross the Ts – get the contract right

Case study 3 described above provides all the evidence needed to emphasise the importance of getting the contract right. What it does not do is deal in any depth with what this actually means. The remainder of this book will hopefully provide the necessary guidance in this regard.

4.10 Always be closing – change after contract signature is not original sin

It is highly unlikely that an outsourcing deal, once concluded, will not be subject to change. Just as change is a fact of life, so it is in the context of outsourcing. And yet, there are times when a customer will agonise over closing a deal because of the possibility that a change in their organisation is on the horizon (or perhaps even only rumoured) and that the change will affect the terms of the outsourcing. This is completely understandable. The consequence, however, is that as time drags on the chance of the deal unravelling increases because, just as the customer might be getting cold feet, so too might the service provider (in its case, over the level of discount offered, or the highly favourable terms of the benchmarking provisions, or the uncapped liability for some form of loss, etc).

A well-drafted outsourcing contract will be developed with change in mind. It will not only allow for change, through a boilerplate clause covering variation, it will also set out a process by which the parties can propose, consider, agree and implement changes, including in terms of how prices will be affected, what happens if agreement cannot be reached, when certain changes must be implemented without agreement and so on. Properly implemented, this will allow increases or decreases in prices that are proportionate with the changes being made.

4.11 Govern well – support through good governance and contract management

Signing an outsourcing contract is just the beginning. After the contract has been signed, the customer and the service provider must remain committed to the success of the programme, with the governance arrangements playing a critical role in ensuring that this is the case. In this regard, the customer should, among other things:

- be fully aware of all key commitments made by the service provider, especially in terms of important dates, milestones, service levels, pricing and so on, but also mindful of its own responsibilities and any dependencies that the service provider may have upon the customer;
- require regular detailed reporting on the service provider's performance, particularly in relation to the achievement of milestones and service levels and details in respect of any relevant failure;
- monitor the service provider's performance against its commitments, and identify, record and communicate to the service provider its failures and any consequences flowing from those failures and whether the customer intends to reserve or enforce its rights in respect of those consequences (while also hopefully celebrating with the service provider any successes – milestones successfully met, targets achieved etc);
- ensure that all governance arrangements are followed, including holding of governance meetings, taking and sharing of minutes, and completion of actions arising from those meetings; and
- use the governance meetings as an opportunity not only to look at current performance, but also to discuss possible improvements, deal with risks and foster good relationships among the parties.

By applying good governance and contract management practices, the customer will have a much better chance of ensuring that the outsourcing stays on track and that any problems which arise along the way are dealt with at an operational or executive level, rather than being escalated to more senior levels or to external legal advisers.

5. Outsourcing success

Success, in the context of outsourcing, is not black and white, and hinges significantly on the customer having a full awareness of what direction it wishes to travel in, the risks that it is likely to encounter along the way, and how those risks can be dealt with in a way that ensures that it arrives at its destination as intended.

Practical perils and pitfalls – or why do projects fail?

Stéphane Lemarchand
Scott Thiel

1. Introduction

Like any relationship, the success of an outsourcing project depends upon both parties. While the critical role of the customer in this marriage is discussed in more detail in the chapter on the role of the client, key customer-side project risks will also be identified in this chapter to balance the more comprehensively considered service provider risks. Project success also needs to be analysed with regard to the three primary phases that make up the total project lifecycles: pre-go live, service delivery, and exit and service migration.

The contract is too often seen as little more than a necessary evil, driven by things such as mandatory regulatory requirements, in-house procurement rules and contract authorisation procedures. The priority sometimes appears to be to complete the contract negotiations as quickly and efficiently as possible, triumphantly sign it as a symbol of a job well done, and then promptly put it in a drawer to gather dust. Commonly, it will re-emerge only to try and solve a problem or provide legal remedies when an incident has arisen. As this chapter explores, the formation of an effective and comprehensive contract, its judicious use to regulate, monitor and manage the delivery of services, and the inclusion of pre-agreed exit obligations within it should in fact provide the foundation for a successful project for both parties.

A well-run contracting process will uncover erroneous assumptions, reveal and help to resolve areas of non-agreement, provide certainty as to who is doing what and, ultimately, avoid nasty surprises. Although a winning day in court may be cathartic for some of the stakeholders, the real value of the contracting process is its ability to assist in preventing project failure rather than provide grounds for legal recourse when all has gone wrong.

Likewise, a well-governed customer and service provider relationship during the service term is essential to help to deal with the re-prioritisation or focusing of service delivery imperatives, issue identification, root cause analysis of those issues and rectification options. Many legal, commercial and governance levers can be adopted to mitigate these business-as-usual operational risks, and a well-drafted contract should help to facilitate this.

Lastly, and as with any kind of divorce proceedings, the exit phase is best regulated by a pre-agreed exit plan with obligations and commercial terms established on a pre-nuptial basis. In most business-critical service outsourcings, life must go on regardless. So the need for a clear transition plan to the new order is best established in advance, and should be clearly provided for in the contract.

This chapter accordingly considers the key issues in each of these three phases that contribute to, or even cause, the failure of outsourcing projects.

2. Phase 1 – the procurement phase and pre-service delivery activities

This is the rock upon which it could all be built, or the time to decide that it is the shifting sand upon which it should not.

This phase comprises the procurement and bid process, contract negotiation, contract signing and service establishment transition activities (the latter being discussed in more detail in the chapter on due diligence and transition). Perhaps the greatest practical risk to any outsourcing project is doing the wrong deal – that is, one that does not meet the objectives of either or both parties. Pre-contract is the best time for one or both parties not only to realise this fact, but also be prepared to walk away once that conclusion makes itself self-evident. Paradoxically, this is also the phase that is generally driven by teams of people within both organisations whose interests are rarely aligned with the possibility of a 'no deal' outcome, irrespective of the flashing red lights demanding caution or cessation.

Within the would-be service provider organisation, the bid phase is generally driven by the business development and sales function. Aggressive revenue expansion targets, human nature, job security, global financial crisis, increased competition, margin squeeze, commission-based remuneration and bonus arrangements drive a win-everything, and at-any-cost, approach to replies to requests for proposal and pre-contract negotiations. Furthermore, as this is by definition a speculative phase for any potential supplier, there is limited appetite for engaging too many internal or external financial overheads such as lawyers, compliance personnel, risk management teams or service delivery functions – plenty of time to get their sign-off once the deal (and the bonus) is in the bag. This is in our view a mistake that will be liable to cause problems downstream. Too often, therefore, the earth, moon and stars are promised as part of a deal, but with limited prospect of them being delivered.

Customer-side behaviour can be similarly hamstrung during the procurement phase. Even if evaluation criteria are carefully considered and documented, economic drivers have a habit of superseding nuances such as technical capabilities, and legal and risk transfer positions. By way of example, we often find that the 'worst' service provider response in terms of the proposed contract terms seems to emerge as the preferred bidder. Cash is king within procurement and the relevant senior stakeholders, and so a bid that appears to be cheaper will often be preferred, even if the contractual covenants means that cost increases and disagreement as to scope may be more prevalent in future.

If customers are honest with themselves, they may recognise that they sometimes fall into the trap of pressing a service provider to concede as much as they can get, rather than what they should get. Creating a one-sided contract in favour of the customer is not wholly a recipe for a successful outsourcing programme. The reality of this aggressive commercial landscape drives a number of risky behaviours that can seriously jeopardise the success, or result in the failure, of the project. Irrespective of legal rights, claims and damages awards, a failed project is a lose-lose scenario.

2.1 The wrong deal – service delivery deficiency

Ambitions to create revenue drive potential service providers to target opportunities that may not be within their core competencies. The bid teams can be prepared to make assumptions about their service delivery capabilities rather than confronting the possibility that this may be the wrong deal to try and do. This also commonly occurs in complex multi-service line projects where a service provider may have some of the requisite expertise, but not for all elements of the required solution. Complex IT outsourcings will require a service provider to work with, or interface to, existing customer infrastructure, applications and networks. Large corporate customers make this challenge worse by having bespoke or highly customised IT and information system environments. Does the would-be service provider really have the skills, licences and resources needed to support such systems and requirements?

This is a significant project risk. How can a service provider be sure that it can deliver on services that are not core to its existing offering? How can it properly price for these services? How will it acquire the necessary skill sets? This problem is exacerbated by a tendency by the sales force to think that such non-core projects represent an opportunity to develop new business lines and create new revenue streams on the back of such a flagship and highly referable engagements.

HR constraints create a related issue. Lean operating models mean that service providers will not have teams of spare resources sitting around just waiting for this latest new opportunity. So, where will the extra 10/100/1,000 resources come from to support this transaction? Are such people available and in the required numbers? Are they available in the mandated geographic delivery centres? Has the cost of such acquisitions been properly worked into the commercial model? Have they got the required specialist skills? If not, then the project is at significant risk of delivery failure or financial distress.

Developing markets such as Asia, South America and Africa represent some of the biggest growth opportunities for many multinational service providers. However, the experience of many service providers, including those already located or headquartered in such regions, has been historically focused on supporting the more mature western markets in places such as the United States and Europe. Cultural, linguistic and regulatory issues can entirely change the shape of outsourced service delivery models. China, for example, is increasingly requiring the use of onshore delivery models, locally established research and development facilities, and the disclosure of third-party source code and other technologies used to support customers in designated market sectors. Thus, banks operating in China are now likely to be requested to deposit the source code of all information systems of their outsourcing partner with the relevant Chinese authorities. That will inevitably be a very difficult conversation. Both parties need to understand these types of regulatory requirement and ensure that the issues are considered as part of this 'deal or no deal' phase.

Another factor that heightens the 'wrong deal' risk is the tendency to exclude the service delivery teams from the procurement phase. As these are the people who will have to deliver the services once the contract is signed, they are clearly the ones best placed to identify and call out any concerns regarding skill shortages, resource constraints and technical delivery deficiencies. How is the delivery team going to feel when it analyses an undeliverable service specification after the ink has dried on the contract signatures? Clearly, that is the wrong time to find out that there is a problem. Too often, however, the service delivery teams are omitted from the procurement phase and end up inheriting someone else's mess.

As discussed in the chapter on due diligence and transition, the customer has a risk mitigation role to play by undertaking adequate due diligence on the vendor's ability to deliver the required service. The fact that one potential supplier has the cheapest and therefore most attractive bid could mean either that it is the absolute expert, does this day in, day out and has a highly efficient service delivery model, or that it does not know how to price it properly because it does not know what this type of solution involves.

Where gaps in delivery capabilities are identified, then the parties should either walk away or actively take steps to address the issues. This can be done via a clear and achievable skill set or technical capability acquisition plan by the service provider, or via sub-contracting or consortia delivery models. However, any such solution ideally requires to be worked through in detail pre-contract. High-profile and large-scale projects have failed where assumptions were made about a proposed sub-contractor, its capabilities, pricing terms and flow-down of contract terms. The terms of engagement of any sub-contractor or joint bidder should be agreed and contracted simultaneously with the prime contract.

2.3 The wrong deal – low-balling the bid price

As the third limb of the 'holy trinity' of any outsourcing contract (ie, the charges, alongside the other key elements of the services description and the service levels), it is somewhat inevitable that the economic drivers of both parties are pitted against each other. In short, the service provider wants more revenue and at a higher-profit margin, whereas the customer wants to save as much money as possible when compared with current in-house or existing outsourced service offering. In practice, service providers unsurprisingly expect and are required to earn a profit. A failure to appreciate this economic imperative will create a brittle deal that is more prone to collapse. Furthermore, it is probable that the cheapest solution will not produce the best result for a customer. Think about it for just a moment: How would you behave if every $1 that you spent working for someone only netted you 90 cents return?

The procurement process has, in many respects, unfortunately become something of a zero-sum game in this area. Reverse auctions, regulated public procurement rules, c-suite fiscal demands, increasing audit scrutiny and general financial austerity have driven a culture of 'cheapest wins the day and the deal'. And while cheapest can work quite well for spend-on simple off-the-shelf commodities, it is unlikely to be so for complex outsourced services. If you want an all-inclusive holiday, then you can get one for next to nothing, but is that the holiday that you want?

Service providers have inevitably responded to this 'price wins' procurement approach. As discussed in many of the other chapters in this book, and in particular the chapter on services and service levels, there will be gaps in any contract that service providers can and will exploit to remedy any financial pain that they have got themselves into after low-balling a bid to win the engagement. This will include the use of change control and other contractual remedies. Take a simple service description of "make a cup of tea". Now imagine the service provider that exclaims: "Oh, you wanted milk and a biscuit with that cup of tea, did you? Well, that will cost you... a lot. After all, milk and sugar cost money!" We once worked on a project where a watertight contract and overly tight commercial model were causing significant financial pain to the service provider. That service provider duly filed over 1,000 change requests in two years – by some measure this arguably involved more effort than the service provider invested in delivering the service! Equally, however, there are occasions when the customer may have failed to invest sufficient time in assessing the real requirements of its business users, such that a beautifully presented service specification bears little resemblance to what the business actually wants.

A one-off deal conducted without regard for any future relationship also represents a project risk to both parties. First-time deals are often done on an investment basis, to get the foot in the door, so to speak. This may be fine if it is part of a regional or global strategy, and the particular customer represents a significant growth opportunity either locally or otherwise. However, what if this is the only deal that is ever done between these parties? As above, an unprofitable one-off deal will undermine the relationship and drive defensive behaviours based on minimising the losses or extracting some returns.

There is of course a flip side to this debate, which thus far has largely considered the fixed or capped fee model, which many of us have had to become accustomed to post-2007/2008 global financial crisis. What about old-fashioned time and materials-based charging? This has been discussed in other chapters, but it is mentioned again in the context of being an option to assist to resolve the problems with low-ball bidding.

2.3 The real value of a proper contracting process

The contract is of vital importance as we have discussed throughout this book. If the parties fail to document the deal comprehensively and accurately, then the risk of project failure is considerably increased. Detailed negotiation and documentation of both parties' obligations invariably unearths erroneous assumptions and misunderstandings between the parties.

A comprehensive specification of the services is critical. The best front-end set of legal terms and conditions is of very limited use if it points to inadequately defined service delivery obligations. How can a service provider possibly meet the expectation of the business users if it has not been adequately informed about what is required? The commencement of a material outsourcing function is a difficult time, most people are naturally resistant to change and there is a tendency for the service users to seek out opportunities to deride the replacement external solution. This commonly leads to complaints where on the one hand a service recipient is saying, "John used to do A, B and C for me, he is now gone and the new supplier says it is not its job". And if the contract includes no responsibility to A, B and C, then there is no legal recourse for the disgruntled service recipient. This presents an opportunity for the service provider to build some profit back into a deal, particularly if it was under-priced for the reasons discussed above. The new partnership can very quickly become strained.

First-generation outsourcings are particularly prone to this risk because it is common that a would-be customer has little true appreciation for the details of its current in-house solution, or hard data relating to how it was performed in practice. Large organisations have typically grown organically and reactively to the needs of the business. Existing staff operate to meet bespoke requirements of the internal business based on personal relationships and experience. It takes considerable effort to capture and document all of these activities. Furthermore, the people who actually know what the current service involves are also still trying to do their day job. They need to be given the time, opportunity and support to capture and document the service particulars. Another common problem is that such personnel may be disenfranchised about the consequences for their own job in the new outsourced model. You are asking them to document their current role, which is about to be removed from the business. In many cases – for example, in an offshore service delivery model, this will likely result in job losses.

A related issue is service levels. As discussed in the chapter on services and service levels, any good outsourcing contract will look to capture detailed service performance standards and service levels. However, internally delivered services rarely operate on such a rigid service level and service reporting basis, and there may be little or no existing business information about the standards to which the service is currently being delivered. The typical sweep-up service commitment to ensure that the service operates at no lower a standard than pre-outsourcing is of no benefit if a customer cannot objectively evidence historic performance levels. If a customer abdicates this responsibility and simply pressures a service provider to commit to challenging (and, ultimately, unachievable) service levels, there is a significant risk that what is – objectively – a perfectly respectable level of performance by the service provider can become characterised as 'failure'.

Another key issue is the capture and documentation of the customer-side obligations. One very large print and mail outsourcing project that we were assisting with involved months of negotiations, hundreds of pages of specification of pick-up and delivery schedules across multiple sites. On Day 1 of the service, not a thing was picked up or delivered, and contracts were immediately under scrutiny and calls for breach and damages were being made. The reality was that delivery of the services was impossible because everyone had forgotten that the customer needed to issue security passes to the service provider personnel in order to gain access to the secure environments that were necessary to deliver this service! It is critical that the customer appreciates the need to analyse and document its role in the partnership and then invests the time and effort to achieve it. This process, if properly done, will identify misunderstandings about who is doing what and when. While such misunderstandings can threaten the underlying financial business, or even the viability of the project, it is far better to find this out during the contract negotiation process than once the service should be underway.

2.4 The wrong deal – other issues and recommendations

The global financial crisis has made us all acutely aware of the capacity for failure and/or insolvency on both sides of the outsourcing services equation, irrespective of the relative size or reputation of either party. In negotiations we used to say, "our client is a global financial services provider, so you don't need contractual rights associated with insolvency or compulsory merger". Times have changed.

Cultural alignment is also critical to the success of any major outsourcing. To work, any such arrangement must be a true partnership. If the respective organisations are not in sync, then they will always struggle to enjoy a symbiotic and successful project. Some of the best and most productive outsourcings involve service delivery personnel who become so entrenched within the customer organisation that they begin to lose their employment identity and see themselves as an integrated part of the customer organisation. While this can create *de facto* employment-related issues, it is a sign of a true partnership in operation.

2.5 Phase 2 – service delivery phase/business as usual

The service delivery phase is under way, service 'go live' has been and gone without undue turmoil. Management is happy with the deal team and the service provider has replaced its negotiation team with the service delivery team. What could possibly go wrong now? The answer is: quite a lot!

An interesting trend is for service providers to request 'honeymoon periods' during service ramp-up. This commonly comprises a period (perhaps three to six months) of exemption from meeting service levels and being liable for service credits. In one sense this sounds fair, as a new service provider is still learning the ropes and what it needs to deliver. As noted earlier in this chapter, the process of migrating to a new service provider, particularly in a first-generation outsourcing, is highly emotive to the internal business users and service recipients. If ever there was a need to convince the internal business beneficiaries that this is a good idea, it is this early service delivery phase. Accepting that the service performance is able to be less than specified or required during this period is a recipe for internal reputational disaster.

The contract, after weeks or months of negotiation, has now been signed and then filed and/or lost by the legal or procurement teams. It was intended to be a living and breathing representation of how the parties will manage the delivery of the services throughout its term. The days of debating the words associated with contract governance, change control, key personnel, service level performance reporting, dispute resolution and root cause analysis have long since passed. However, all of these operational schedules and obligations are core to both parties. Who is monitoring and reporting on that complex service level and service credit regime to ensure that it is motivating and driving the vendor performance in the way that it was designed to do? Who is capable of calculating or verifying the monthly service credit? The absence of proper monitoring and enforcement will render these important schedules nugatory. If the service is changing over time, as so often it does, who is keeping a log of contract amendments so that the current service commitment remains effectively documented? If there is no consolidated version of all such changes, then reliance on contractual remedies in case of a problem will be significantly undermined. What happens if the person or persons who designed the service delivery solution leave this project to design the next one?

Another practical problem is the failure to establish and appropriately resource a skilled in-house vendor management team within the customer organisation. Particularly in a first-generation outsourcing, many of the best, brightest and most capable may have left or jumped the fence to join the new service provider. Cost cutting and headcount reduction drive this deficiency. The customer must accordingly focus on its retained organisation, and ensure that it has both the headcount and the skill set to manage the outsource relationship. It is a mistake, for example, to assume that someone previously engaged in delivering the service in-house will automatically be best suited to managing it, in future. The two roles and skill sets are very different.

'Agreements to agree' create a serious delivery problem for both parties. All too often, this basket of uncertainty also becomes host to any set of obligations too difficult to work out now. The reality is that such arrangements establish fertile ground for practical and commercial dispute between the parties. As such arrangements are effectively unenforceable at law, they typically suit suppliers from a purely enforcement and therefore commercial perspective. However, they habitually undermine the vendor and client relationship. If it is an important part of the service, then it should be considered, defined and documented in advance.

3. Phase 3 – exit and transition

This section is relatively short given the detail provided in the chapter on renegotiations, retenders and exit assistance. However, exit – in terms of both insourcing or transfer to a new service provider – can be a key area of risk for the long-term viability and success of an outsourced service. While the legal provisions establishing the principle of an exit plan are commonly included pre-contract, who is to do what, who is to pay for it, and how much that will cost often remains undetailed. From a customer perspective, such a situation presents the same issues as noted in section 1 above. However, the supplier is now disgruntled (and is, therefore, about to lose this customer account), its obligations are often not properly set out and its payment terms are commonly not established. Terms often provide that the parties will agree on the exit plan within six months of the service commencement date. It is rarely the case, however, and an 'agreement to agree' provides neither party with any practical or legal certainty.

This presents a great opportunity for the supplier to have a last shot at extracting value or profiteering from the deal. Even worse, it could effectively deny the customer the practical or commercially astute opportunity to migrate to an alternative service provider because knowledge transfer, IP rights, licences and handover of documentation were not agreed in advance. Put bluntly, is it any wonder that a new supplier will not do a good job of transferring knowledge to a competitor if this was not agreed in advance? And given this, is it any wonder that it defers discussions on exit terms to the period post-contracting?

While it may seem unpleasant to start any partnership with the possibility of divorce in mind, such event is a key project risk for a customer; the concept of a prenuptial agreement exists for a reason in many contexts, and importantly so in major outsourcings. The inability to migrate away from a particular supplier on pre-agreed and commercially reasonable terms is also a key project risk.

Multi-jurisdictional deals

Kit Burden
Joris Willems

1. Introduction

Organisations increasingly operate on a global basis. A large manufacturing company, for example, may have headquarters in one country (eg, United Kingdom), manufacturing plants in several different jurisdictions (eg, France, Hong Kong, India, Brazil) and sales and marketing functions in many others. If, therefore, that company were to outsource elements of its back-office or IT functions common to all its operating parts, its service provider would need to be able to deliver the outsourced services on a multi-jurisdictional basis.

This need not necessarily be the case; we have seen, for example, corporate groups that operate on a more federated basis, where different operating parts (whether on a service line or geographic basis) make their own decisions as to their service provision and support, such that a decision by one part to outsource aspects of its operations need not entail all of the other parts following suit. However, there are obvious potential advantages to them doing so, not least those outlined below.

1.1 Cost

Bringing more parts of the corporate 'empire' into scope will inevitably increase the overall size and value of the deal, which should in turn enable the service provider to be keener on its pricing, and so deliver higher overall savings to the customer.

1.2 Control

Customers can sometimes face significant challenges in exercising strategic control over their own functions and costs across multiple countries and different parts of their business if different decisions are made by different buyers and involve multiple service providers. Devolving down to a single service provider can accordingly provide a far clearer path towards exercising practical control of the outsourced functions.

1.3 Consistency

Without a single service provider, there is a risk that different suppliers will adopt different approaches to what may be the same basic requirement of the customer, leading to additional integration challenge and potentially also additional cost for the customer.

Assuming then that the customer has decided to consider outsourcing on a multi-jurisdictional basis, what are the key procurement and contractual challenges that it may face?

2. Structuring the contract

There is no single way to contract a global outsourcing project, although one is certainly more prevalent than others.

Approach 1 may be simply to have a single contract between the lead customer and service provider entities (eg, the parent entities for their respective groups), which purports to require the provision of the relevant outsourced services for all of the customer's operations in all of the various countries in which it operates. The customer will ordinarily be functioning in such other jurisdictions by way of separate legally constituted subsidiaries and, accordingly, the contract will require that the lead customer party contracts as agent for and on behalf of such affiliates (or, where the law governing the contract allows for this, so as to have them as expressly identified beneficiaries of the terms of the contract, even though they are not signatories to it). The service provider may likewise need to involve subsidiary entities in the provision of the services in some of the in-scope countries, and will effectively be subcontracting elements of the services to such subsidiaries. In each case, the signing entities will ordinarily commit to procure the performance/ compliance with the contract's terms by their respective affiliates and subsidiaries.

While this appears straightforward, it hides a number of challenges and complexities. For example, the parties may intend to implement a standard set of services and service levels for all geographies, but the reality is often that the customer's operations are slightly different from country to country, and nuances need to be catered for in the way in which the services are to be provided. While it is possible to set these out in a single contract by listing country-specific amendments to the standard service descriptions, it can make the contract both lengthy and ungainly. Further changes are necessitated by the application of local law or need to be accommodated regardless of the choice of law for the contract itself (see section 3 below). Imagine, for example, a customer entering into a single global outsourcing contract with an entity headquartered in the United States and which therefore chose to apply the laws of the State of New York; while that choice of law would be valid and enforceable with regard to services provided to that entity's European-based affiliates, it would be prudent/necessary for the contract also to consider how the parties' responsibilities should be reflected in the contract in respect of non-derogable local laws dealing with such things as the EU Acquired Rights Directive (eg, regarding the transfer of the contracts of employment of personnel who were wholly engaged in the provision of the outsourced services) or in relation to the obligations imposed by the EU Data Protection Directive in respect of personal data derived from EU-based data subjects. Even though the choice of law clause in the contract would then govern the majority of the obligations in the contract, local law would still affect the services. In limited circumstances, it may be possible to contract out of such obligations, but in others it will not. Here, the focus will instead be on how contracting parties in the relevant country would usually reflect such obligations in terms of the division of responsibilities between them. For example, for the EU Acquired Rights Directive, the contract might typically require the original employer to offer up an indemnity in the contract for the impact of pre-transfer employment claims.

The parties could address these issues by having separate outsourcing contract documents created for each individual country/customer contracting entity. However, this would be unduly time consuming and might introduce the risk of the parties being tempted into negotiating different terms into each one, so reducing the degree of commonality between the various contracts.

A middle ground often chosen is to have a single contract between the lead customer and service provider entities (eg, the parent entities for their respective groups) that sets out the general framework with country-specific local agreements entered into between local entities (including branches or subsidiaries). Additional flexibility could be created by opting for statement of works for each project or work order, which allows for a further level of choice/adjustment through multiple different service types to be ordered separately in each country (with local additions or variations, as necessary and agreed between the parties).

The following diagrams illustrate the three models described above.

Diagram 1 – General framework

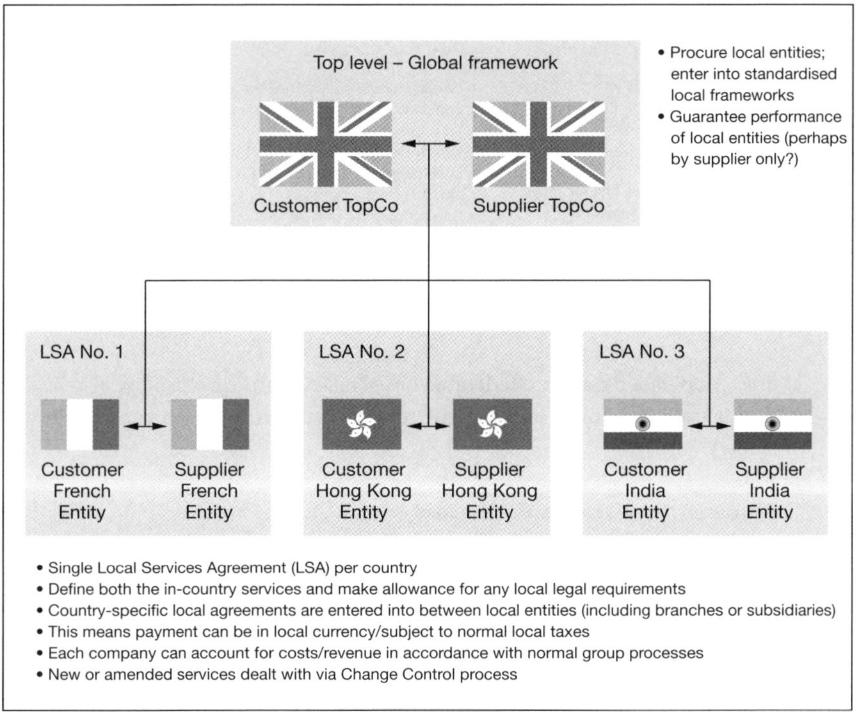

Whichever option is chosen, governance will be key. The parties will need to agree on the level of oversight and decision making that can take place at the local level, and how much will instead be left with (or escalated to) the global level. There is no single right or wrong answer to this question, and much will depend on the culture and set-up of the customer group (eg, does it have a strong parent entity, or

Diagram 2 – Additional framework flexibility

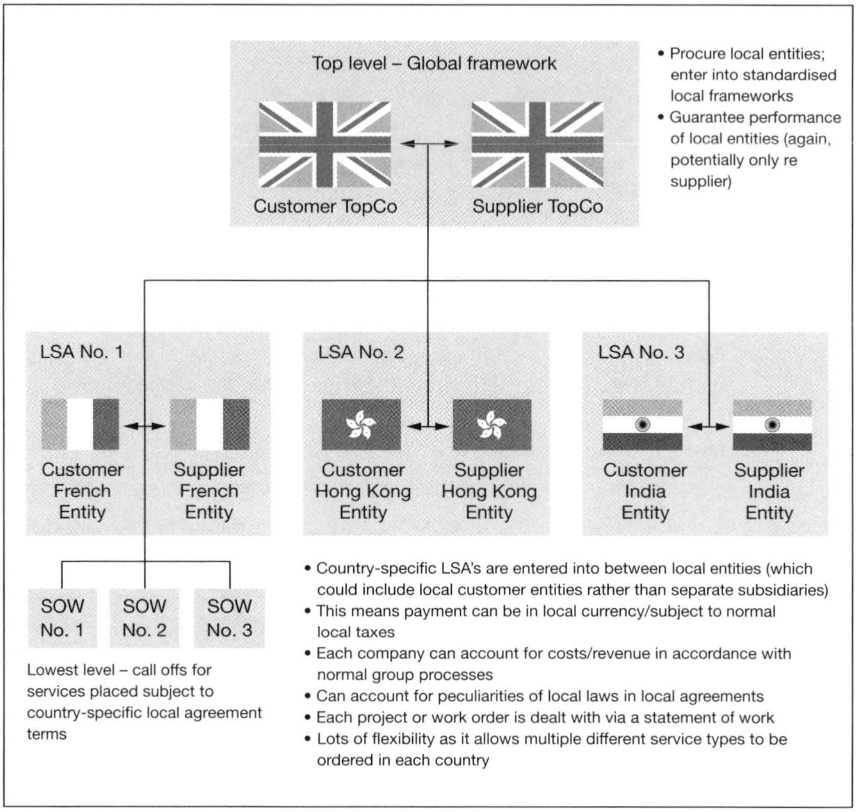

does it operate on a more federated basis?). Decisions on this may also be affected by the degree of regulatory oversight that the customer is subject to (see section 4.8 below).

3. Choice of law and jurisdiction

When choosing the applicable law and jurisdiction, a couple of points should be taken into consideration. The generally accepted concept of freedom of contract allows for parties to choose, in principle, any applicable law and jurisdiction that they want. However, for applicable law that is not always exactly the case. In many jurisdictions, the law requires that some sort of actual connection exists between the chosen law and the parties and/or the subject matter of the contract. If we use the same example as in section 1 above (a UK-headquartered large manufacturing company with manufacturing plants in several different jurisdictions, and sales and marketing functions in many others – but not the Netherlands), whereby the company has entered into a single global contract with a US service provider with no subsidiaries in the Netherlands and the choice of law is Dutch law and the agreed competent court is the Amsterdam court, that court might rule that although it has

Diagram 3 – Single global contract

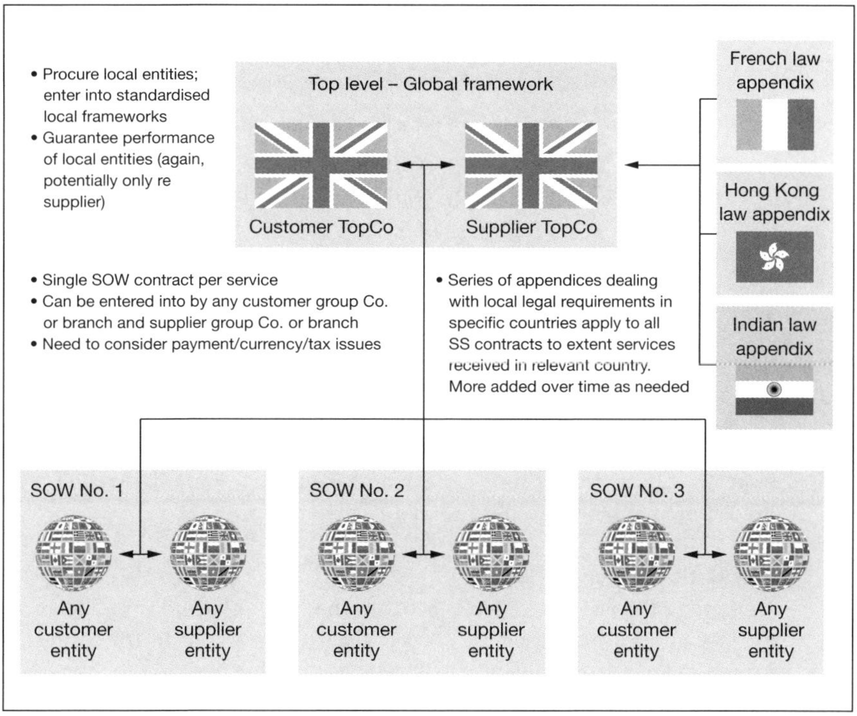

competence to hear the dispute (that choice will be respected), Dutch law cannot be applicable even though it is the chosen applicable law under the contract as there is no actual relation whatsoever between the parties, the scope of the contract and the Netherlands (other than the choice of law and jurisdiction). Another point for attention is that it is preferable to have one law governing the entire contract because if the applicable law differs from country to country, this will unintentionally alter the plain meaning of words and implied terms. In short, there could be unforeseen consequences due to the different meanings in the local laws. No jurisdiction is exactly the same, as what might mean something in jurisdiction A might mean something completely different in jurisdiction B.

The parties could address these issues by paying proper attention to the applicable law and jurisdiction provisions, choose an applicable law and jurisdiction relevant to the contract and ensure that the contract is structured in such a way that it also considers how the parties' responsibilities should be reflected in respect of non-derogable local laws. If the parties get it right, then these clauses can facilitate the proper management of the relationship, the cost-effective resolution of minor disputes in a way that minimises the risk of bad feeling, and provides clarity as to the process to be followed should a more serious dispute arise. If the parties get it wrong, the consequences can be time consuming and costly.

4. Specific issues

Other specific issues prevalent in multi-jurisdictional deals require careful consideration. We will discuss the most common ones below.

4.1 Service levels

Multi-jurisdictional deals should take into account that few services are truly global in application. While a number of generic service levels can be delivered to a common standard, there may be valid reasons for deviations from the norm (eg, in terms of level of performance to be achieved, or regarding the addition or deletion of specific service levels). Also, not all service providers can deliver all services to the same service levels in all locations (eg, due to reliance on local staff and/or sub-contractors and limitations imposed by local market conditions and/or infrastructure, or due to local differences in the legal and regulatory environment). This is not necessarily problematic to the customer as in all likelihood not all services being offered will be required in all locations to the same overall standard. It is therefore important to differentiate what service levels are necessary in each respective location and to what extent, taking into account that the relationship needs to remain manageable and that balance is key.

4.2 Calculation of service levels

A differentiation of service levels between the various locations should also be taken into account in calculating the service levels. For example, in the context of a 24/7 requirement, a requirement for 99.99% availability over a 12-month period will allow for only about 30 minutes or so of down time over the whole year, while a reduction of 0.49 percentage points to 99.5% will equate to 43 hours or so of down time over the same period. This can be addressed to applying different values to service levels in different locations to ensure that the objective of the service levels in the first place is achieved: the cost of failing to reach the service levels (and the probability of being caught) must outweigh the saving of not making the investment and, equally, the cost of failing on different aspects of the services must not outweigh the profitability of the contract for the service provider. The parties will also need to be clear on how the service levels will be measured on a global basis; for example, will they be measured on a country-by-country basis, aggregated up on a global basis, or a combination of both? To put this in context, a 90% service level measured across 20 countries could then allow a pretty poor level of performance in one or two of those countries, while still allowing the overall global service level to be met (which may in turn leave the users in the affected countries without any form of recompense, and in a somewhat disgruntled state of mind).

4.3 Aggregation of discounts

Parties should also take sufficient notice of how aggregation of discounts are applied, as both local subsidiaries of the customer and of the service provider can benefit or suffer from global volume discounts to a significant degree. If, for example, a local subsidiary signs on to the deal later in the contract year, and by that time additional discount tranches are reached, that entity might benefit from it, while the local subsidiary of the service provider faces the additional costs of that discount. This may be inevitable, but as long as parties have thought it through, it can prevent disappointments and discussions down the road (eg, if the 'top co' utilities of both the customer and the service provider consent to smooth out financial inequalities between their respective affiliates).

4.4 Approach to limits of liability

Liability can be limited in various ways, mainly by restricting the type and capping the amount of damages to be paid. There is often also a differentiation between liability events (regular liability versus indemnifications, etc). This will have to be specifically agreed in the contract. Attention should then be given to the calculation of liability caps in multi-jurisdictional deals; can a liability event in one location use up the entire liability cap for the outsourcing project as a whole, for example? This is often addressed by having various levels of caps, per incident and overall (eg, for consent of action arising in a contract year). It should also be agreed who can claim damages (and from whom) – the local subsidiaries or only at the top level? Often 'buckets' are applied whereby damages can be claimed only from a certain threshold. Using such methodologies will enable the customer to recover damages within the agreed framework and the service provider to mitigate its risk exposure throughout the organisation involved with the project. In short, is a matter of agreed risk allocation.

4.5 Linked termination

In multi-jurisdictional projects, parties need to consider the relationship between the various local contracts and services upon termination. For example, if the framework agreement terminates does this automatically terminate the local agreements or statement of work? Equally, if a local agreement or statement of work is terminated, how does this affect the other agreements (both at local and overall level)? These topics need to be carefully drafted as part of the termination provisions. Typically, a customer may argue for the right (but not the obligation) to terminate the contract relating to the wider outsourcing arrangement or project if there is a major failing/default, even if that arises in connection with just one or two countries. For their part, service providers will typically argue for termination to be addressed on a country-by-country basis.

4.6 Customer politics

Parties should also keep in mind customer politics. Is the customer organisation a benevolent dictatorship or a federation of equals? This is not an insignificant issue, as it is important to ensure that internal customer politics do not stand in the way of the overall objective of the project as agreed at the top level. Without sufficient local buy-in, it might just not work out (eg, if the 'top co' parties expand a lot of their effort agreeing on a deal and contract that relatively independent local entities then refuse to adopt or implement, or seek to or extensively re-negotiate). This should be taken into account by the parties and can be addressed through engaging the local organisations at the right time in the process.

4.7 Central governance

The key is for the parties to obtain the right balance between the sharing of information on the one hand and leaving the service provider to get on with providing the services on the other. By agreeing the processes up front the project can run itself – objective mechanisms getting the parties through difficult moments by taking the heat out of potential disputes, giving early warning of potential issues and allowing their quick resolution before they become material. For multi-jurisdictional projects, a proper governance structure should be in place not only at the local level but also at the central level, to ensure that local hiccups in one location do not affect the overall relationship for the outsourcing project as a whole, even though this can be affected by the intra-group dynamics of the customer's corporate group, as per the notes in section 2, above.

4.8 Approach of regulators

Depending on its sector of operation, the customer may find that its regulators also have a view on the provisions and structuring of multi-jurisdictional outsourcing contracts. They may, for example, wish to ensure that any disputes specific to their regulated entity are handled in their own country, rather than in the courts of another county where they may find it harder to intervene. The parties may accordingly need to allow for alternative dispute resolution approaches – for instance, by allowing disputes that are specific to one territory to be dealt with locally, if not in the courts in that country then potentially by an arbitration process that can be based there.

Service integration and management/multi-vendor projects

Callum Sinclair

1. Introduction

Any discussion of this topic should kick off with a clarification of what we mean by 'service integration and management/multi-vendor projects', also referred to as 'multi-sourcing'.

'Multi-sourced operating models' are service delivery models used by customers where services are provided by a spectrum of different vendors and internal departments. Operating in such an environment can present challenges if not properly managed, if different teams (both vendor and in-house) act autonomously and without coordination across the customer enterprise. To address such difficulties, customers often establish a discrete service integration and management (SIAM) function to enable them to take advantage of the flexibility and innovation of multi-sourcing and standard services, while delivering integrated services to the customer's business. The diagram below sets forth the typical role of the SIAM function in a customer organisation.

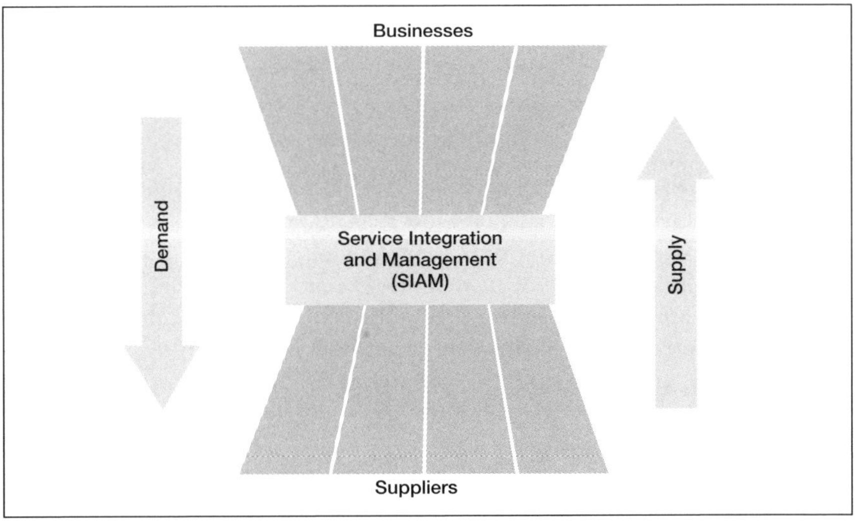

Customers have been operating in multi-vendor environments for decades, and increasingly in recent years using a SIAM function (with varying degrees of success) to govern their vendors. Service providers in turn are accustomed to providing hardware, software and services into those environments and working with other vendors and customer in-house teams under a SIAM approach. So what is new, not only with the use of a multi-source model, but also with how customers use and model their SIAM function?

Some commentators view moves towards multi-sourcing as part of a cyclical ebb and flow between 'big prime' single-source and multi-source models, perhaps reflective of a not untypical degree of dissatisfaction on the part of customer end users and/or senior management with incumbent arrangements. However, the following developments suggest that the increasing adoption of multi-sourced models by customers reflects an enduring evolution in the sourcing landscape:

- the rise of more flexible and customised cloud computing/'as a service' delivery platforms, rather than a one-size-fits-all service delivery provider;
- a shift from more elementary systems and software integration towards more complex services integration;
- an increased focus on outsourcing as an enabler of business performance and implementation of strategy, rather than bundling to maximise discounts and cost savings; and
- policy developments that encourage a move towards 'best of breed' tower-based solutions in functional areas such as telecommunications (LAN/WLAN/wireless), infrastructure (often comprising datacentre and hosting), applications development and management/support, help desk/service desk, etc.

This chapter explores these themes and how they are helping to drive the move toward multi-sourcing and more advanced SIAM models. It also considers the substantial challenges that multi-source arrangements present, which, if not tackled effectively, can rapidly offset any business benefits to be gained by the adoption of such models.

2. Why multi-source?

The principal rationales for adopting a multi-source model include:

- driving accountability across the customer's vendor base by managing and comparing performance across vendors;
- pushing standardisation of processes, tools and technologies;
- seeking to implement a 'best of breed' approach for the sourcing of services associated with particular streams/towers;
- aligning a multitude of contracts (including pricing, performance mechanisms and incentive structures) to the broader customer business objectives and goals; and
- reducing operational risk by avoiding reliance upon a single supplier.

Often, the failure of a current 'big prime' model to deliver to business expectations can be behind a desire to adopt a different way of working. While this may be a perfectly valid reason to move towards multi-source operating models, it is important to analyse the reasons for failure of the original model: the same underlying customer-side causes could result in failure – possibly even more serious failure – of a multi-source model.

The following table accordingly sets out some advantages and disadvantages of a multi-sourcing model versus a 'big prime' model:

Pros	**Cons**
• Allows selection of specialist ('best of breed') service providers with expertise in providing specific targeted services. • Greater likelihood of delivering service improvement and innovation. • Improves access to opportunities for small-to-medium enterprises (SMEs), which is an important policy objective in some countries.	• Lose protection of a prime contractor responsible for overall delivery of end-to-end service ('one throat to choke'). • More risk of gaps in individual contract service scopes leading to lack of clarity about supplier responsible. • Corresponding greater likelihood of disputes, and risk of the customer bearing responsibility as a default.
• Higher chance of better, more accurate pricing of discrete service lines/towers by specialist suppliers. • 'In-life' continuous competition between tower providers for new projects or opportunities can lead to micro-economies of scale. • Avoidance of the risk of a prime supplier applying margin on margin.	• Procurement and legal costs will be higher, particularly on first multi-source. • Ongoing management costs will also be higher than in a single-source scenario. • Economies of scale may be lost as the size of the overall customer account for any one vendor will be less. • There may also be additional costs attached to supplier interface/integration requirements.
• Reduction in operational risk from a lesser reliance on any single supplier (though this reduction could be offset by loose management of multi-vendor processes by the customer or outsourced SIAM provider).	• Increase in service integration risk – any failure to identify gaps and interdependencies is likely to default to become a responsibility of the customer organisation. • Duplication could lead to customer paying twice. • Change control across the contract suite becomes more complex and risky to manage.

continued on next page

Pros	Cons
• More flexibility to re-shuffle the pack where one vendor or aspect of service is underperforming. • Greater ability to compare supplier performance in generic skills areas and in behavioural approach and attitude, and to cross-fertilise. • Lower risk of vendor lock-in.	• Issues may arise from competitors or even different corporate cultures being asked to collaborate (eg, cross-licensing, sharing of confidential information/data, audit). • There may also be risks with potentially competing technology platforms or technology/knowledge dependency.
• Greater visibility and control of the supply chain. • In turn, tower suppliers will have closer direct involvement with the customer business and relationship with the customer.	• More customer-side resource will be required to manage multiple suppliers and contracts. • The customer may not have the resource or skill set to retain SIAM function in-house, and may have to outsource this business-critical role at additional cost. • The market for external SIAM providers is still relatively immature even in advanced economies.
• In EU countries subject to the Acquired Rights Directive, service fragmentation could mean no automatic transfer of incumbent prime/customer staff. • This may protect the customer and incoming providers from any negative cost and other consequences of applying the directive.	• Considerations relating to the directive may be more complex, and the lack of automatic staff transfer could also operate as a disadvantage for incoming suppliers looking to access knowledge and skill set of existing personnel.

In short, the business case for moving to a multi-sourced model is based on taking advantage of as many of the factors in the left column as possible and seeking to mitigate risk associated with those in the right column.

3. Multi-source models

Customers have adopted a wide range of multi-source models, but the most common are described below.

Model 1 – Direct multi-vendor with retained SIAM

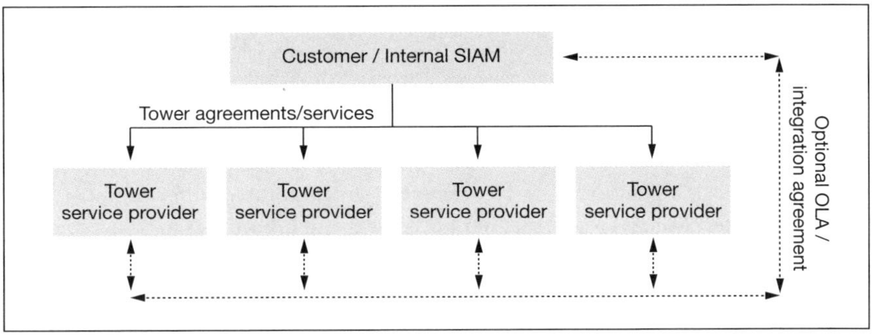

Model 2 – Direct multi-vendor with outsourced SIAM

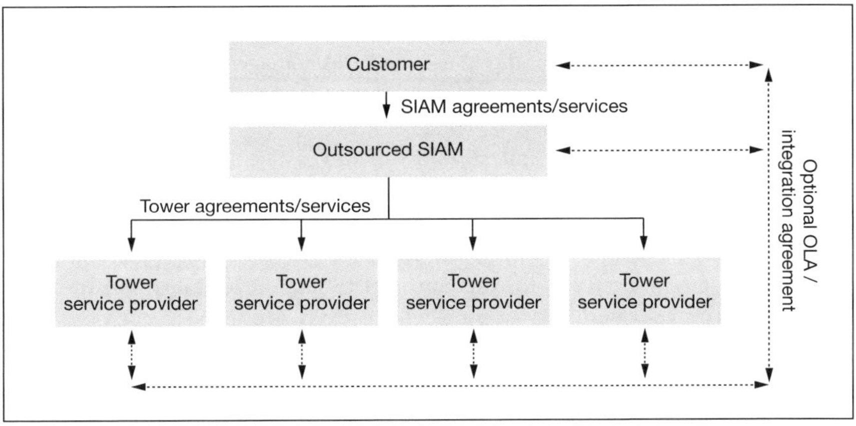

Not included, for these purposes, is a prime contractor that relies on multiple subcontractors to deliver the total service solution to the customer, though such a model involves multiple vendors and bears some similarities to Model 2 above.

Customers can also adopt joint venture and partnering models. These come in many shapes and forms, but most tend be complex to establish, run, exit and unwind so there generally needs to be a compelling reason to adopt them (eg, tax advantages).

However, this part of this chapter deals primarily with the most common of the multi-sourcing models represented by Model 1 and Model 2 above.

Which of these multi-source models – outsourced or retained SIAM – is most suitable will tend to be governed by the capacity and experience of an organisation's retained IT function. Given the (usually mission-critical) nature of the information and communications technology (ICT) services concerned, it is often less risky for a customer to retain control by maintaining an in-house SIAM function, assuming that it has the skilled resources in sufficient numbers to do so. However, this is rarely the case as the customer may have outsourced such resources in previous-generation outsourcing, or have a retained function whose primary focus has always been to maintain discrete systems as opposed to development or integration of services. In those circumstances, the customer will need to consider outsourcing the SIAM function too.

4. Explaining the SIAM function

The SIAM function, whether outsourced or otherwise, is responsible in most cases for technical, operational and commercial integration of the relevant services, and specifies the service management processes and procedures to be deployed across the customer enterprise and ensures that they are followed. It generally acts as an overall technical design authority for the customer organisation and delivers end-to-end service reporting: a 'single version of the truth' of the state of ICT across the organisation, or at least of the services in scope.

Beyond this, the extent of the role of the SIAM can vary, sometimes including involvement in tower provider contract negotiations, a level of control and/or delegated authority over evaluation and selection of suppliers, and a responsibility for service forecasting and end-user demand management. Clearly, with outsourced SIAM, the timing of the appointment of the SIAM provider will also be a factor in the role that it is able to play.

Certain functions and controls should always be retained by the customer organisation, such as the setting of business objectives, and the establishment of common standards and policies to be adhered to by all suppliers. That said, it is not unusual for customers to seek consultancy input from their appointed SIAM in these areas. It is also critical for the customer to retain the ability and the capability to oversee an outsourced SIAM provider effectively so as to be able to hold it to account.

Whatever the role of SIAM (and again whether it is performed in-house or by a third-party supplier), it is essential that it be independent – that is, independent from other parts of the customer organisation, senior management and other tower suppliers. Independence can be tricky to achieve, particularly with an in-house team accustomed to working in a different way with its colleagues or where individuals are wearing two hats. Similarly, for reasons that we will come to shortly, SIAM can be bundled with one of the towers, making genuine independence – both the perception and the reality of it – difficult to achieve. However, without genuine independence, the SIAM function will lack the necessary buy-in from stakeholders (end users and senior management) in order to perform its duties effectively and will be compromised from the outset.

It is also important for the SIAM provider to be appropriately empowered to carry out its functions. Where policies and procedures have been set by the customer organisation, the SIAM provider must have the necessary delegated authority to enforce them, and maintain a zero-tolerance approach to any failure to adhere to them. Adopting a zero-tolerance approach to any non-adherence to SIAM processes protects the integrity of an organisation's operating environment. It is only with this empowerment and zero-tolerance standard that SIAM can act as the proper gatekeeper to enterprise-wide services by enforcing change, security accreditation, testing and release processes. As such, a well-run SIAM function assures the readiness of all changes made to the environment. One example of this would be the ability to compel different parts of the customer organisation to purchase from tower providers as opposed to buying off-book, which could adversely impact the business case and strategy underpinning the multi-source towers model.

5. Commercial attractiveness of outsourced SIAM

One of the challenges with outsourced SIAM is making the opportunity sufficiently attractive to the market as to attract a strong field of competitive bids.

This is an area where, for example, the UK government's push for the adoption of SIAM and towers in the UK public sector initially faltered, principally because of a procurement approach that did not allow for the SIAM provider also to bid to become a tower provider (presumably on the grounds that this could prejudice the SIAM's independence and/or risk challenge under the EU regulated procurement rules by providing the SIAM provider with an unfair bidding advantage). More recently, the UK government has appeared less enthusiastic about outsourced SIAM models. It will be interesting to see how public authorities in other jurisdictions, as well as the wider private sector, tackle this issue.

Service providers will naturally assess an outsourced SIAM opportunity by weighing the reward against the potential risks. Where they are prevented from bidding for tower opportunities, that assessment will likely include a relative risk/reward analysis against those opportunities.

In order to maximise the commercial attractiveness of outsourced SIAM opportunities to the market, customer organisations should, therefore, consider bundling them with particular tower bidding opportunities where possible and appropriate. For example, SIAM and a service desk tower (dealing with end-to-end service incident and problem management) are often natural bedfellows. This is perhaps easier to achieve in private sector multi-sourcing transactions for reasons outlined above, but it is certainly not impossible in public sector deals either. Where such bundling exists, however, it will be important to provide other tower contractors with sufficient assurances of the independence of the SIAM organisation and the separation of roles. This would typically involve use of separate supplier teams, and demonstrably enforced information barriers (so-called 'Chinese walls') backed up by strong probity agreements.

Particularly where such bundling is not appropriate or possible, but even in cases where it is, some thought must also be given as to an appropriate level of risk that it is fair and reasonable to impose upon the SIAM contractor. SIAM contracts should generally seek to measure success against obligations and steps taken to ensure effective service integration and collaboration between tower suppliers. This is as opposed to measuring success by reference to a seamless service outcome. It has to be understood that the SIAM provider has only so much control and influence over such an outcome, and this approach will generally carry too great a financial risk for a SIAM supplier when measured against likely fees to make the opportunity sufficiently attractive for the SIAM supplier to want to take on.

Timing and duration of the SIAM procurement process will also be relevant in determining commercial attractiveness to the market. As discussed further below, the services of an outsourced SIAM provider are often procured ahead of those of the tower providers, but a protracted procurement process will result in greater bid costs for SIAM bidders and ultimately impact adversely on commercial attractiveness too.

6. Procurement and contracting

Getting the strategy right around the procurement and letting of contracts (tower providers, and SIAM provider too if that role is to be outsourced) is key to maximising the chances of a successful multi-sourcing.

As discussed elsewhere in this book, establishing a robust business case at the outset is the bedrock of any successful outsource. This would include an affordability analysis and a clear strategy with a solid justification for electing to adopt a multi-source model. All too often, multi-sourcing business cases and strategies have not been fully thought through, and those business cases have an optimism bias as a result – for example, situations where clients have adopted these models because they are under political pressure to do so, or because they are perceived to represent the latest thinking on best practice in all cases, or (as mentioned previously) where previous-generation single-source arrangements have not met expectations.

We have similarly encountered affordability analyses that fail to take account of what could be described as hidden costs of multi-sourcing (eg, some statistics from sourcing group ISG suggest that procurement and contract management costs could be as high as between 15% and 50% of the overall contract cost, compared to between 3% and 11% of the overall contract cost in a single-supplier scenario).

A solid understanding of the customer organisation's end-to-end service requirements, both at the time of the procurement(s) and going forward, is a key factor in ensuring that the right decision is made with regard to the sourcing approach. This can be challenging where the scope of services is broad and there is a large number of differently profiled service users with varying demands of the services. There will be a need for significant stakeholder and end-user engagement activity prior to crystallising the requirements for the purposes of the procurement. The ultimate contracts – without compromising specificity – will have to allow for scalability, flexibility, innovation, service improvement and (healthy) continuous competition among tower suppliers to ensure that the services continue to meet the needs of the customer organisation and its users.

For effective procurement, the quality of information regarding existing and future requirements will need to be high so that requirements can be properly understood, divided up among towers and articulated in procurement documentation. Often, customers are reliant (sometimes overly so) on legacy suppliers to provide this information and support the process. An appointed SIAM provider may be able to assist the customer with this exercise.

Procurement and contracting strategy should also make allowance for transition and transformation activities. So there should be consideration of such questions as:

- What provisions are there in legacy contracts around exit and transition?
- Are there timing issues created by those contracts ending at different times?
- Does that create a need for a transfer of legacy agreements, or transitional services agreements with legacy suppliers or their subcontractors?

- To what extent will there be transformation of the in-scope services going forward?
- Does any of that transformation activity need to be carried out prior to appointing the new tower providers (or would it be desirous to front-end transformation in this way) or is there an element of transformation activity in scope for the new providers?
- Will an outsourced SIAM have a role in planning/managing any transition or transformation activity?

The answers to these questions will affect the scope, timing and phasing of the procurements of SIAM and tower providers.

As regards timing and phasing, where there is to be an outsourced SIAM, the general approach has been to appoint that SIAM provider first, particularly if SIAM will have a more extensive role in planning for and negotiating the tower contracts. We would usually then advocate contemporaneous appointment of tower providers and signature of corresponding tower contracts, unless there is a compelling reason why this cannot be done (eg, where customer-side resource constraints make this too risky).

The simple rationale for this is that there will need to be a clear allocation of responsibilities and dependencies as regards overall services among the SIAM, each of the tower providers and the retained customer organisation. Where this cannot be agreed contemporaneously, there is a significantly greater risk of gaps emerging, interdependencies being missed, more complex drafting to accommodate timing issues, and greater change control to accommodate additional providers coming on board at a later date.

The allocation of responsibilities and dependencies is often achieved by agreement of a matrix or similar. However, this process of dividing up responsibilities, ensuring that there are no gaps (which might expose SIAM or, more likely, the customer organisation) and recognising hand-offs and inter-dependencies among towers, will require a significant amount of negotiation/dialogue with all of the parties concerned. Similarly, discussions are likely to be required in relation to corresponding limitations and exclusions of liability of the parties, which is linked to the extent of risk and responsibility taken on by each (liability issues are explored further later in this chapter).

All of this will, of course, take time and it will be important to make sufficient allowances in the procurement timetable and to manage the process tightly during the procurement such that the process does not become protracted to the detriment of the overall process and the participants.

This need for dialogue around responsibilities, dependencies and liability also has implications for public sector customer organisations in the European Union, subject to the regulated procurement rules, such that use of simpler procurement procedures (eg, open and restricted procedures) will not work for multi-sourced SIAM and towers procurement (although we would not generally advise the use of such procedures for anything but the most straightforward of ICT projects in any event). While there might be a temptation to use multiple simpler procedures to keep negotiation and procurement costs to a minimum, such procedures do not allow for the sort of dialogue and flexibility necessary to deal with some of the issues flagged above. There are also challenges with the use of public sector frameworks that have not necessarily been designed to accommodate a SIAM and towers model, though that may begin to change in the design of future frameworks. In reality, therefore, SIAM and towers in the public (and, indeed, regulated utilities) sectors in the European Union necessitates the use of competitive dialogue procedure, negotiated procedure (where this is an option) and, under the incoming rules, competitive procedure with negotiation.

One of the perceived advantages of SIAM and towers models is the ability to replace an underperforming tower provider to plug in another specialist provider, without undue disruption to the balance of the services, and to make re-procurement of services more straightforward next time round (assuming a broadly similar profile of services). The reality is that this will always be easier said than done, but generally speaking, the more successfully the contracts are managed, the more straightforward this will be.

7. Contract management and governance issues

As challenging as the procurement and contracting process will be, in-life governance and contract management are equally challenging.

Bluntly put, there are simply more contracts to deal with: instead of a single prime contract, with the contractor shouldering the responsibility of management of the supply chain, there are multiple tower contracts to manage. Even in circumstances where there is an outsourced SIAM provider, some of the contract management functions will remain with the customer organisation, as well, of course, as the need to manage the SIAM provider and the SIAM contract.

In addition, the use of multiple suppliers makes the overall management itself more complex. Even once contracts are executed and responsibilities and dependencies of the various parties have been determined, requirements of the customer organisation, as well as circumstances on the ground, will change over time. This will give rise to change control under the contracts, and changes under one contract can of course have a knock-on effect under one or more of the other contracts. Unless carefully controlled, this could lead to a cottage industry in change paperwork – an issue even with big prime contracts, but at risk of being exacerbated still further by the adoption of multi-sourcing models.

Given the patchwork of interdependent requirements and contracts, effective contract management software tools become essential. Such tools will be useful for:

- initial capture of end-to-end requirements in a consistent and digestible way;
- mapping of those requirements artefacts to related performance criteria, charges, reports, etc;
- assisting with the process of identifying service gaps and dependencies and supplier interface points;
- tracking changes in requirements and/or related artefacts across towers; and
- providing an up-to-date, 'single version of the truth' snapshot across the end-to-end service, which in turn will help with:
  - service and performance reporting;

- documenting change control;
- avoidance, and resolution, of disputes; and
- re-procurement of one or more of the towers.

Collaborative change boards, which not only manage the documentation and implementation of change, but additionally proactively anticipate likely changes and identify potential service improvements, will also be important.

But these boards should be only one component of a governance and contracting framework designed to foster genuine cooperation among SIAM/tower suppliers. Collaboration should be 'baked' into relevant parts of the contract drafting, as opposed to an afterthought in a well-intentioned but isolated (possibly unenforceable) light-touch cooperation clause. This will involve providing sufficient comfort for the suppliers around ownership and use of their intellectual property, and secure handling of their confidential and commercially sensitive information. Service performance and quality regimes should be designed to minimise the risk of finger-pointing and maximise service outcomes, and should be fairly administered by the customer organisation (or SIAM, as the case may be) and be seen to be so. There should be use of service incentives where appropriate to reward collaborative behaviours.

In some large-scale SIAM and towers implementations, ancillary operating level agreements (OLAs) and/or integration/collaboration agreements are entered into by all parties (alongside the bilateral tower contracts and SIAM contract, although sometimes these double as the principal agreement with SIAM). Such agreements can be used to establish the lead role of SIAM and secure the tower provider's agreement to comply with SIAM's instructions, as well as containing provisions relating to cross-licensing of IP rights between tower providers and SIAM, data and information sharing provisions and confidentiality undertakings. They will often also contain terms dealing with inter-contractor liability (see below for further consideration of this area). Sometimes, these formal binding agreements are supplemented with (or in the case of smaller implementations replaced by) 'softer' behavioural codes of conduct or operating practice manuals. While these sorts of intra-supplier arrangement can help to provide clarity as to the demarcation of responsibilities between the various service providers, they can sometimes take on a disproportionate degree of perceived importance in the context of the project as a whole, and can even result in the customer losing a degree of control over the governance of the overall services (as the various service providers look to enforce OLA remedies between themselves, and they may be more pugnacious with a perceived competitor than they would be when dealing with the customer). Accordingly, the creation of OLAs needs to be approached with caution.

Whatever the ultimate contractual structure, it is crucial that all of the contracts are managed in such a way as to focus on the objectives of the customer business and on end-user satisfaction, as opposed to service level agreement and key performance indicator metrics *per se* (of course, if properly constructed, service level agreements and key performance indicators should be designed to encourage that focus in any event). Those business objectives should be articulated by the customer organisation and understood by suppliers from the procurement stage, enshrined in the contracts (even if only at a high level in the agreement recitals, but perhaps through appropriate incentive mechanisms too), and be continuously revisited in meetings and governance. It is a feature of successful programmes that all of the parties understand and share a clear vision of service provision that will support the customer's business objectives and meet or exceed the expectations of its end users.

Overall, a culture of robust governance and contract management is essential to the success of any multi-sourced arrangement. Integration among the SIAM provider, the service providers and the retained customer organisation, and coordinated governance functions among these parties, is essential to maximising the benefits of outsourcing. In a well-coordinated sourcing transformation, the end-to-end operating model is considered before commencing the sourcing journey.

8. **Culture and resource issues**

A range of cultural considerations should be taken into account in a multi-sourcing scenario. Many of these are no different from issues arising in any outsourcing. For example, any significant outsourcing of services involves a substantial change project. That brings with it a need to secure buy-in from stakeholders and the user community by clearly articulating the rationale and benefits of the decision to outsource, sharing vision and objectives, and seeking feedback to the extent appropriate. There will also be personnel considerations including sizing and shaping of the retained team and associated sensitivities around potential redundancies or staff transfers.

However, there will be some additional considerations in a multi-source scenario. The particular rationale for embarking down a multi-vendor route will need to be explained and understood. A larger retained team may be necessary to ensure effective contract management where the SIAM function is to be retained in-house and that team would need to have specific skill sets. There may be multiple interface points with and among suppliers.

Where there is to be an outsourced SIAM function, personnel within the customer's organisation will need to be aware and genuinely accepting of the lead role of SIAM, and be prepared to follow principles and guidance enforced by SIAM (although established by the customer organisation in the first instance).

There is also an interesting and important side issue that arises within EU countries subject to the Acquired Rights Directive and derivative legislation (eg, transfer of undertakings, or TUPE, legislation in the United Kingdom). The fragmentation of a service previously provided by the customer or by a single prime provider into multi-sourced towers can affect the application of the directive, which in some cases may result in automatic transfers of personnel not applying. There is further discussion of this topic in the chapter on human resources and Acquired Rights Directive/TUPE.

9. **Liability**

As discussed above, one of the greatest risks from fragmentation of services in a multi-sourcing relates to the interaction and interdependencies between towers and tower providers. Even with the most careful and well-negotiated allocation of responsibility and liability, there are still likely to be some gaps (requirements that fall between two stools), overlaps (requirements that arguably fall within the scope of more than one of the tower providers' services) and latent interdependencies (requirements that need to be satisfied by one provider before another provider can satisfy its requirements). Delays by one provider can have an impact on one or more of the other tower providers (eg, a network tower supplier is late in providing infrastructure, which means that a cloud application provider cannot deliver services). Self-evidently, this gives rise to a greater risk of finger-pointing among the tower providers, and of the customer organisation having to resolve related disputes and claims (though the external SIAM supplier may have a role here if there is one) and ensure that there is provision for any gaps.

It is, therefore, essential to embody so-called 'fix first, settle later' principles into the governance and drafting of the various contracts. This means express obligations for tower providers to determine quickly among themselves with the customer (and external SIAM supplier if applicable) which party or parties is best placed to resolve any incidents or problems arising, and for that party or parties promptly to facilitate such resolution, regardless of initial fault or root cause, while all continue with the balance of service provision meanwhile. Thereafter, there will be a mechanism by which cross-tower claims can be resolved following a fair apportionment of responsibility.

One model for dealing with cross-tower liability claims is to provide direct determination of claims among tower providers themselves, usually in the OLA or integration agreement. In the drafting, there would be provisions allowing tower providers to make claims directly against another tower provider(s). While this might at first appear attractive from the customer's perspective given that it apparently allows the customer to avoid being drawn into claims, it raises the spectre of one of the customer's key services providers litigating against another, which would obviously frustrate entirely the principles of collaboration underpinning a multi-source model, and pose a risk to relationships and to the programme overall.

Given the difficulties in practice with direct intersupplier liability mechanisms, a better solution overall – and the one that has become generally accepted market practice in an ICT services context – is one in which such claims will flow through the customer. In other words, where one tower provider suffers loss or damage through the delay or failure of (an)other tower provider(s), it will make a claim against the customer, and the customer in turn will claim against the offending contractor(s) and flow through any resulting compensation to the aggrieved tower provider. The mechanism generally dictates that the customer would pass on only what monies it was able to recover to prevent the customer from being caught in the middle. This would not include any liability that fell to the customer itself, whereby separate compensation may additionally be payable by the customer.

If there is an appointed external SIAM provider, it will often play a role in brokering fair allocation of responsibility and compensation among the parties and informally mediating any disagreements (again the genuine independence of SIAM will be critical in order for such a model to operate – see earlier in the chapter for discussion of SIAM independence).

Regardless of the liability model selected, the customer will need to ensure that it has the right to set off any claims for compensation owing against applicable charges in each of the tower contracts. This will ensure that the customer's position is protected, as well as retaining maximum leverage and control over claims, particularly in circumstances where claims are flowing via the customer.

Contractual provisions limiting/excluding liability must also be crafted according to which model is chosen and how it is structured. In particular, where claims are to flow through the customer, the possibility of flow-through should be recognised and there must be sufficient headroom in applicable caps to allow for this. In some cases as suggested above, the customer may wish to limit the liability for flow-through claims to amounts actually recovered, though where this is the case, there will need to be a separate cap applicable to claims against the customer itself.

As alluded to earlier in this chapter, careful consideration must also be given to caps on liability for any external SIAM provider. These should be realistic, and set by reference to SIAM's performance of its obligations and what is within SIAM's control (as opposed to risk associated with failures with the totality of the services) to ensure that the external SIAM opportunity maintains the right balance between risk and reward.

For completeness, service credits (and indeed withholding of service bonuses) may also be used as part of the overall compensatory framework where there is failure/delay of a tower provider, although care should be taken to ensure that tower providers are not penalised twice for the same issue, and that service sanction regimes are not unduly complicated or incentivise the wrong behaviours.

10. Conclusion

Multi-sourcing models can offer significant advantages over larger single source models. However, in order for these to be realised, key features and success factors of multi-sourcing models need to be well understood and implemented by customer organisations. The customer's business objectives must be clearly articulated and well understood by all parties. Every aspect of programme governance, from early business case through procurement and structure, drafting, negotiation and management of contracts must be designed around these factors.

Where the selected model involves an outsourced SIAM function, there are additional considerations to ensure that the role can be performed effectively – for instance, a sufficiently attractive market opportunity to attract strong SIAM bidders, suitable delegated authority and genuine independence to empower the SIAM provider.

In short, multi-sourcing can deliver substantial benefits but will require significant investment of time and money from the customer organisation in order to realise them fully, particularly where multi-source models are adopted for the first time. This includes the proper articulation and governance of the SIAM function, which is essential for effective multi-sourcing, whether that SIAM function is carried out internally by the customer or outsourced to a SIAM provider.

Different types of outsourced services

Peter Jones
Stéphane Lemarchand

1. Introduction

1.1 Outsourcing is older than you think

The concept of outsourcing is not a recent phenomenon. While the term itself dates only from the early 1980s, for many hundreds of years governments and organisations have engaged others to undertake specific functions formerly assumed by the relevant government or organisation. The key distinctions between such arrangements and comparatively simple 'service arrangements' are, first, the degree of abrogation of accountability for the performance of a certain defined set of tasks and, second, the level of management responsibility absorbed by the person undertaking the function (and, axiomatically, the impact of this on those parts of the government or organisation formerly undertaking that function).

To assume that such arrangements were for trivial purposes or incidental is not necessarily correct. The security of the Pope was outsourced to the Swiss Guards in the early 16th century. Indeed, the Swiss provided mercenary soldiers for many a European court and army, even contributing to Napoléon I's Grande Armée's ill-fated march on Moscow.

Great Britain engaged private shipping for the transportation of thousands of convicts from the infamous rotting, rat-infested prison hulks to the (initially) inhospitable and uninviting shores of Australia. Unsurprisingly, the increased use of civilian contractors, more inclined to follow innate commercial imperatives than military orders imposed, was not without issue – as we will see in the chapter on services and service levels.

1.2 The growth in outsourced services

However, it is certainly correct to say that the breadth of outsourcing has increased dramatically over the past half-century and even more so over the past two decades – this in terms of both the geography from where outsourced functions are performed and the nature of the tasks and activities undertaken as part of those outsourced functions. Further, although outsourcing is more commonly associated with private enterprise, in some jurisdictions (eg, Australia) some of the earliest adopters have been government agencies; the ability of the private sector to undertake what were formerly and squarely considered to be government services, such as health services as part of hybrid private/public arrangements, is now better appreciated.

The fact that it is private enterprises that have embraced outsourcing more extensively is not altogether surprising given the comparative lack of political shackles and the overriding economic and stakeholder demands that they face. One of the suggestions is that the rise of the multinational conglomerate, particularly in the United States, during the growth decades of the 1950s and 1960s was met by a need to focus on core competencies and reduce management overheads in the recessionary years of the 1970s and early 1980s. Outsourcing was seen as a powerful tool in the corporate kit bag. From this initial surge has grown a global industry worth, on some estimates, $400 billion a year.

1.3 A geographically limited phenomenon?

In certain economies, there has been some hesitation in embracing outsourcing as a panacea for all corporate ills. This is perhaps best illustrated by the Korean Chaebol conglomerates (and, to a lesser extent, the Japanese Keiretsu corporate relationships). Penetration of outsourcing in other economies such as France and Germany remains moderate compared to mature markets such as the United States and the United Kingdom. Further, governments have occasionally imposed effective constraints on particular forms of outsourcing, primarily where services are to be performed outside of the customer's jurisdiction. In addition, it may be unrealistic for governments to seek to outsource certain public services.

This is not to criticise such economies or the government agencies and organisations within them. However, in an increasingly globalised world, with end-user demands for services and continually increasing requirements for efficiency, whether such arrangements will continue in the same form remains to be seen. It is also relevant to note that customers, whether public or private, that are coming to outsourcing for the first time have the ability to learn, digest and implement the lessons of earlier approaches to outsourced services.

1.4 The impact of digitisation

The extent to which data can be digitised, the rapid increase in computing power and global interconnectedness fostered by the Internet have all been major facilitators of the recent increase in the offshoring of outsourced services. Digitisation allows information to be processed almost anywhere, anytime (although the impact of privacy and data protection laws and regulations imposes a number of restrictions on particular categories of data).

When digitised information is coupled with both an appropriately skilled workforce and cross-border labour rate differentials, the opportunity for a service provider to employ that workforce as part of a compelling service offering is clear, and the strength of the commercial argument increases where the workforce is also more productive and provides a sufficient offset against risks and other concerns.

Digitisation has had a considerable impact on the growth of what is often referred to as 'business process outsourcing' (BPO). Business areas such as insurance claims processing, mortgage processing and loan processing, all of which are founded on large amounts of information and rely on substantial computing power, have seen significant growth in outsourcing. Over the past few years, legal process outsourcing for large document-heavy tasks such as corporate due diligence and discovery for litigation is increasingly being undertaken by lower-cost lawyers in different jurisdictions – often at the behest of the client. To say that this has had an impact on the established business models of law firms would be an understatement.

A widely cited article, "The Future of Employment: How Susceptible are Jobs to Computerisation" (Frey and Osborne), suggests that this wave of computerisation has not yet completely washed through all occupations, but also that there are limits to the impact this wave will have on professional occupations and those with health/emotional/welfare characteristics – at least, based on current computing power and ability. The increasingly advanced abilities of artificial intelligence could potentially impact on areas currently considered immune to technological replacement.

The short point, however, is that what is current in terms of the scope of outsourced services is not set in stone. As technology solutions evolve and adapt to mimic more human elements such as intuition and judgement, the scope of functions that are currently considered to be 'safe' from outsourcing will continue to narrow. This is even assuming that the benefits of labour rate arbitrage, which have in part driven the success of Indian subcontinent outsourced service providers over the past 20 years, cease to be as relevant.

Further increases in outsourcing, particularly where offshored service delivery solutions are included, will create longer-term challenges at a social and political level as certain skill sets are subject to automation or replacement, with the inevitable impact on labour participation and available tax base (from personal income tax at least). However, it would be wrong to suggest that such creative destruction has no positive effects on consumers, as well as corporates, in terms of costs and flexibility.

2. Why outsource anyway?

To consider the scope of services that are outsourced, it is necessary to consider the reasons for outsourcing. They include the following:

- to control and reduce operating expenditure. Prior to the global financial crisis, there was a view that broad requirements for cost reduction were being diluted by more strategic considerations such as a focus on core versus non-core competencies or development of longer-term service provider relationships and the 'relationship dividend' that would accrue. In a post-financial crisis and globally depressed economy, cost considerations are again a primary (if not sole) consideration;
- to transfer assets from the customer's balance sheet to that of the service provider, improving shareholder return on capital;
- to convert operational expenditure (eg, salary costs, lease costs) from fixed cost to variable cost based on usage volumes;
- to smooth the impact of capital expenditure by converting refresh costs from variable to fixed;
- to improve the customer's corporate direction;
- to obtain cover for internal capability, competence and knowledge gaps through engaging best-practice suppliers;

- to allow the customer's internal resources to focus skills on other areas; and
- to provide for a reallocation of business and regulatory risk.

Another reason sometimes mentioned is the need for an organisation to engage a change agent to force that organisation to confront certain problems or challenges in its business operations, although this goes against another commonly touted outsourcing mantra: "Never outsource a problem" (on the basis that the cost of correction will be opaquely embedded in future fees and the supplier receives a windfall margin).

Overall, though, the underlying theory of outsourcing is to support an organisation's pursuit of those things that it does best, to focus on its competitive differentiators as opposed to activities that can be performed more efficiently and/or effectively by an external service provider – in effect, the law of comparative advantage applied not to nations but corporations.

3. Types of services outsourced

Perhaps the common appreciation of outsourced services is limited to information technology and call centres; certainly these areas have been fertile ground for television, including sitcoms (where accent issues and cultural differences have provided a rich seam of material) and all-too-earnest dramas such as *The West Wing* (series 5, episode 19, in connection with free trade).

While these may be areas of broader public consciousness, the actual breadth of outsourced services is vast. The following diagram illustrates, at a very high level, the range of services extending from information technology, through network, infrastructure and applications layers, to business process outsourcing services, and with complementary support services operating vertically. The diagram has been based on and modified from an illustration used by NCS Pte Limited (formerly known as National Computer Systems, a Singapore-based IT company and a subsidiary of SingTel).

There are of course many different ways of slicing and dicing the outsourcing spectrum, and many sub-levels exist below the heading 'service descriptions' set out above. Also, as discussed in the chapter on service integration and management, and multi-vendor projects, the nature of multi-sourced environments also requires additional governance and often specific service integration and management frameworks, adding potentially more complication to service descriptions.

An alternative approach could be to look at outsourcing through three primary descriptions outlined below.

3.1 BPO

This category of outsourcing focuses on the contracting of operations and responsibilities of a particular business process to a third-party service provider. BPO can be further split into two main subcategories:

- front-office outsourcing – namely, customer-oriented functions such as marketing, contact centres or technical support; and
- back-office outsourcing, such as accounts receivable and human resources.

Diagram 1: Business process outsourcing services

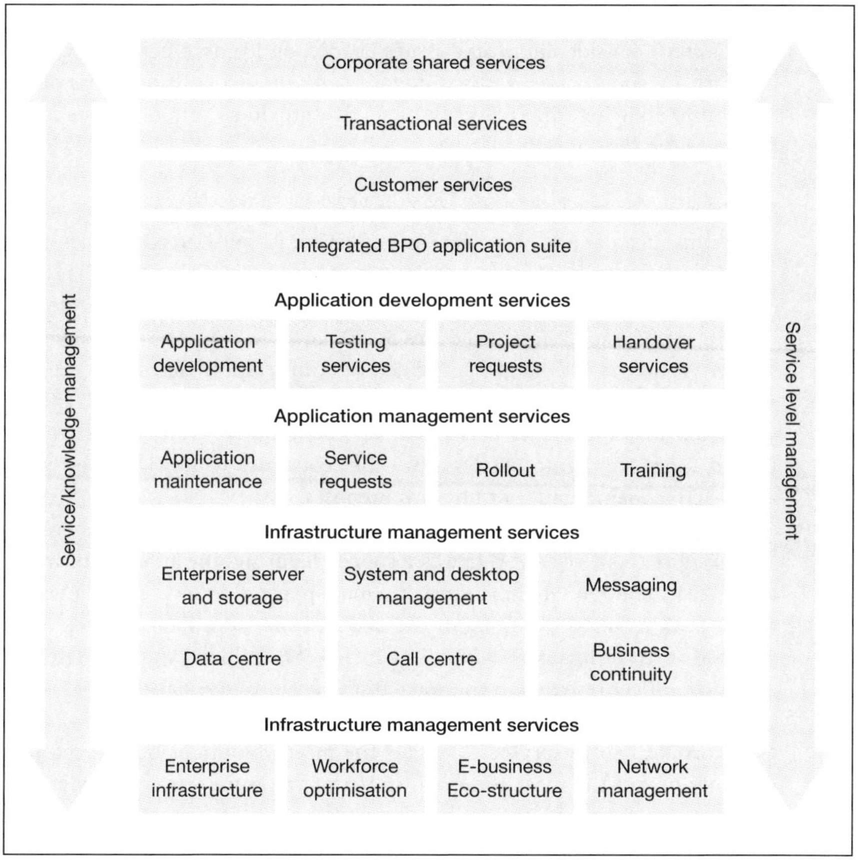

3.2 **Knowledge process outsourcing (KPO)**

This form of outsourcing is generally more complex than BPO and involves processes that demand advanced research and analytical, technical and decision-making skills. An example of KPO is a mutual fund engaging an active fund manager to run particular funds.

3.3 **IT outsourcing (ITO)**

This type of outsourcing relates to the contracting out of the customer's technology infrastructure, applications infrastructure and/or internet-related work, such as programming, to service providers. ITO also encompasses a wide range of services integral to the operation of complex IT systems, such as IT management or data storage.

In recent times, the outsourcing of application services has increased significantly. Many service providers are offering extensive application development and management services that are at the more complex end of the outsourcing spectrum.

3.4 Examples of specific types of outsourced services

While a detailed examination of all forms of outsourced services is beyond the scope of this work, reviewing examples of different outsourced services helps to illustrate the different considerations and issues in looking in more detail at certain services that are in some cases vastly different and provided through service provider environments where the maturity of service providers can vary depending on the nature of the service delivered.

Facilities management: Facilities management is rarely viewed as a particularly interesting area of endeavour, yet the market for its outsourced services is significant in terms of both overall value and the breadth and scope of service that fall into this category. Consider, for example, catering services (SATS, which provides a range of catering services to airlines, produces 80,000 meals a day), cleaning services, security services (Serco is the largest provider of immigration detention centre security services to the Australian government with contracts worth A$3.2 billion and is likewise a major provider of services to public and private sector entities in the United Kingdom, United States and other countries worldwide), and preventative and reactive maintenance of physical premises.

While these services may seem reasonably straightforward, this is not to say that there is never controversy: G4S was responsible for significant security arrangements at the 2012 London Olympics and, in what appeared to be a gross underestimation of the work required (resulting in the need for the UK military to step in), G4S was reported to have incurred a financial hit of £88 million, and ultimately the chief executive officer resigned in the wake of the ensuing scandal.

Call/contact centre services: Perhaps the most ubiquitous outsourced service and certainly one of the most common, call/contact centre services provide a customer relationship front end to manage consumer queries, issues and, in some cases, disputes. As consumer behaviour changes, including through the increased use of email and social media, the nature of the services is broadening to include those communication channels as part of the service delivery model.

A key aspect of any contact centre arrangement – as it is for all outsourcing relationships – is the pricing model: there is a tension between pricing and service quality. For example, a cost-per-call pricing model would provide a perverse incentive on the service provider not to resolve customer issues as further calls would be made, thus increasing revenue for the service provider, but also negative impacts on customer satisfaction. Related to this, service levels need to be appropriately honed to provide balance and ensure that the key outcomes are achieved. In this respect, the chapter on services and service levels provides a worked example of the development of a possible service level regime for call centre services that includes quality of service and first-call resolution metrics.

However, given the human element in this service, one of the most significant drivers of strong performance is a stable personnel base – requirements around attrition management (and attrition in this context refers to attrition from the personnel providing services to the specific customer) are key.

Network services: While this is back office, its criticality is obvious. If data is the corporate equivalent of hydraulic fluid, data networks are the hydraulic pipes and connections that allow data to flow to where it needs to. As such, network services are a base service on which almost all other outsourced services that rely on information depend. If networks are down, application access is lost. For this reason, issues such as disaster recovery and business continuity, redundancy and security are critical considerations.

Specific service levels used in these outsourcing arrangements include metrics such as data packet loss, jitter (the variation in time between data packets arriving, as may be caused by network congestion or route changes), latency (delay on a data network), data loss rate and error rate.

It is increasingly common to adopt unified communication services where all voice, video, data and mobile requirements are integrated and aggregated into a single system (a functional advantage of such systems is to allow people that rely on mobility to remain connected through softphones or wireless IP handsets even when they are outside the office or home).

Infrastructure outsourcing: Largely seen as a commodity service, infrastructure was one of the first technology domains that saw significant outsourcing activity. One of the limitations of infrastructure outsourcing is that while certain aspects such as diagnostics and testing can be undertaken remotely, there is still a need for feet on the ground (at least where the relevant infrastructure is located), providing a natural limit to the extent to which such services can be offshored. The use of cloud services, however, will affect the extent to which organisations maintain their own infrastructure, which in turn will impact on the scale of infrastructure outsourced service required by the customer.

A typical 'hot button' issue in infrastructure outsourcing is the timing of, and allocation of cost responsibility arising from, the refresh of technology equipment. Also, related to the foregoing, another consideration will be the extent of service provider relief events where underlying technology is approaching obsolescence or where the customer, for other capital-spend reasons, defers the acquisition of new technology, which leads to the service provider being required to manage 'end of life' kit (ie where the original equipment manufacturer no longer provides support with respect to such kit).

Application management/maintenance: Put simply, this is the provision by the service provider of ongoing maintenance, management, conversion, enhancement and support of an application portfolio. This will often include the undertaking of minor changes that take less than some predefined time to implement – for example, minor change arising from regulatory changes, implementation of software upgrades, installation of new release installations and break fix troubleshooting. The provision of help-desk services may also form part of the service offering, although equally this could be provided by other outsourced service providers (eg, most commonly the infrastructure service provider, which is often the incumbent outsourced service provider).

In addition to ensuring that the service descriptions are appropriate, key focus areas include the relevant service levels for response, workaround implementation and fix provision and issues as to the ability to take end-to-end responsibility for service levels where there is a need to address issues in third-party code, which may require liaison with the third party (ie, is there a 'chess clock' approach to the service level measurements, which stops the clock for the duration of any third-party consideration?).

Another requirement is frequently the provision of advice for the potential rationalisation of the customer's applications portfolio. There is a clear link here with the underlying pricing model – where pricing is linked to service volume, rationalisation will affect service volume resulting in reduced revenue to the service provider. This potentially creates a disincentive for proactive advice on this subject. Equally, if the pricing model is not volume based, the full benefits of portfolio rationalisation may not be achieved (as the service provider fees may not be subjected to an adjustment based on the decreased volume of services required for a diminished applications portfolio).

Further, and perhaps unsurprisingly, demarcation resolution regimes (where the service provider for applications and for infrastructure – and, for that matter, networks – differ) are essential in order to avoid the 'it's not the app, it is the infrastructure' reason for a fault issued by the applications maintenance service provider being met with a 'it's not the infrastructure, it's the app' response from the infrastructure service provider. The customer should be doing all that it can in terms of contractual certainty and governance regimes (including inter-service provider governance) to ensure that it does not become the meat in this unpleasant sandwich. Similar issues arise where application development is also outsourced to a different service provider.

Application development: One of the more complicated technology outsourcing areas is that of application development. It can involve a wide variety of application services including new software development for application enhancement, programming for new applications/tools and development testing. Applications development can be bundled as part of applications maintenance/management or split off as a separate silo of work. Alternatively, it is not uncommon for customers to develop panels for the undertaking of applications development activities based on different application portfolios, with one or more service providers being responsible for application development activities in respect of that portfolio.

Further to the structure of the relationship(s), there is a question as to how such work will be undertaken. Will this be via separate statements of work for specific development tasks or is a defined pool of resources (with tolerances for some flexibility) to be implemented for *ad hoc* work? Will there be a combination of both approaches? How will changes in the portfolio be managed, given that, at the time when changes are made, the customer's commercial leverage will not necessarily be as strong as when the initial deal was struck?

IP ownership is a critical consideration in applications development services as many required activities may have a significant commercial value to the customer (eg, through the launch of an end-customer tool that provides a competitive differentiator). However, the assumption that the customer pays for all the development may not be appropriate: the service provider may leverage its own background intellectual property and/or deploy proprietary processes or similar. Further, where the application is third-party code, the terms of the third-party licence will also be relevant. Constructing an effective IP ownership and licensing regime, which incorporates legitimate competitive protection and reflects respective contributions, can be a complicated and lengthy process.

Obviously, a key part of measuring whether the benefits of application development have been achieved is through testing of the development activities. The role that the customer plays in this process is critical in terms of setting acceptance criteria and other metrics that truly measure the outcomes delivered – abrogation of this responsibility to the same service provider that undertook the development effort could be seen as allowing the service provider to mark its own homework. This then requires careful consideration of the shape, size and capabilities required for the customer's retained organisation. Alternatively, another third party could be engaged to perform testing services on an outsourced basis that, as is universal in a multi-sourced environment, requires careful thought as to the inter-service provider management processes and issue escalation regime.

One final point: in both application development and application management services, it is critical to undertake internal due diligence ahead of time to ensure that the terms of third-party software licences do not preclude use by a third party – in the case of commercial off-the-shelf software products and many licence agreements that are not negotiated, this may be a default position. To the extent that issues arise, decisions will be required as to what consents are required and the process that will be adopted to obtain such consents (consent requests can often result in additional licence fee requirements arising and additional notification and security commitments).

BPO services: As noted above, the term 'BPO services' represents a huge variety of services and issues, and will often be affected more significantly by changes in law and regulation, as well as customer strategies, as it can be, and often is, easier to change human processes than embedded technology solutions.

Specific examples of BPO services include the provision of payroll services (where there is an inbuilt performance feedback loop – if people are not paid, or paid less than what they should be, this failure is identified almost immediately after a pay run. Where too much is paid, this may not necessarily be true, however) and HR services, which can be limited to issues such as talent acquisition or run through the full range of HR requirements from talent acquisition and management, remuneration, performance management and termination.

Where strong human behaviour is an integral part of the services (human resources being perhaps the best example of this), key personnel provisions are typically required. Having vetted and approved the proposed personnel of the service provider, including often through CV reviews and interviews, the customer is legitimately concerned that such personnel remain available to perform services.

Also, as many BPO relationships involve the transfer of personnel from the customer to the service provider, for good reason the customer may insist on either such personnel being included as key personnel or that certain minimum periods be mandated before such personnel can move from the customer's account.

Given the nature of information often available to such business functions (and the fact that it is often rather transparent to the relevant member of personnel), data protection – particularly for sensitive financial information – is of paramount importance. Also, there is arguably a greater risk of 'fat finger' error; in other words, where mistakes made via a single keystroke have the potential to affect the customer significantly, whether financially or reputationally (everyone will have their own horror stories of 'reply to all' or predicative address errors in email systems).

Lastly, it is important for customers to appreciate that where a business function is outsourced, the risk of errors or the impacts of certain behaviours are borne entirely by the customer. As many BPO relationships also involve the transfer of personnel from the customer to the service provider, this 'existing performance risk' is in part transferred to the service provider. The key issue is what is the responsibility of the service provider to validate its ability, with such transferred personnel operating in conjunction with the service provider's own personnel, tools and processes, to perform the services as required? Also, it is highly unlikely that any service provider would accept acting as an effective insurer with respect to all financial risk arising from any decision to outsource. The service provider's pricing will include a risk-based component that assumes that its own financial liability, with limited exceptions, is appropriately limited (see the chapter on liability and indemnities).

3.5 Final thoughts

There are two (very) broad considerations in examining the issue of what types of service can, and more importantly should, be outsourced:

- the nature of many, if not all, services defies absolute definition and delineation. As a result, most outsourcing agreements will need to include a 'scope sweeper' provision that seeks to expand the specific service definition to include obligations such as the performance of tasks and activities that are necessary and reasonably incidental to the specifically described services (see section 2.4 in the chapter on services and service levels for more details); and
- as the chapter on due diligence and transition identifies, a critical success factor in any outsourcing initiative is including clarity around transition services.

4. The future of outsourced services

What does the future hold for outsourcing? In the short term, the growth of the outsourcing market is expected to continue, both in the traditional information and communications technology areas but also in business functional areas as continued globalisation reduces the criticality of cultural sensitivities and business demands erode any internal concerns with respect to retained control. However, this is not to say that barriers do not exist and that challenges have not arisen and will not continue to arise. For example, the impact of outsourcing in terms of perception of jobs heading offshore has been a political and media football. Either expressly or tacitly, providing outsourced services to certain government agencies has required commitments that personnel performing those services will remain onshore. How sustainable this is in an era of austerity remains to be seen. Other likely impacts are outlined below:

- The 'democratisation' of information technology, through things such as bring-your-own-device programs and greater use of individually sourced applications, will create pressure on standard delivery models offered by service providers and therefore impact on the long-term cost of service acquisition (eg, if applications are sourced externally, the need to validate issues such as compatibility and security, including considerations of matters like the use of open source software).
- Linked to the above, the use of cloud technologies is already changing the way in which customers view technology acquisition and the use of technology in a business setting. Why pay for a service that is not used at capacity when the same service (or something appropriately comparable) is available on a 'as needed' basis? This trend is affecting outsourced service providers, which are increasingly looking at the use of on-demand or near-on-demand catalogues for services and self-service platforms to meet customer demand and add value.
- The ability to determine if outcomes have been achieved and, more importantly in terms of an outsourcing relationship, the extent to which any achievement of an outcome is due to factors for which the service provider is responsible is a challenge (more details on the role that outcomes-based arrangements have in contemporary outsourcing are available in section 2.2 of the chapter on services and service levels). However, the use of data analytics to establish correlations between seemingly diverse data sets has had a revolutionary impact on a number of sectors. The use of specialist data analytics by service providers to establish the positive impact of their services on the customer's business can be expected. This would affect service level regimes and pricing models – where a causal effect can be established, this might lead to service providers moving, in whole or in part, from fee-for-service arrangements to true outcomes-based pricing models such as revenue/profit sharing at an organisation-wide level or gain sharing on a project-by-project or service-by-service basis.
- While crowdsourcing is predominantly limited to specific tasks such as branding design, copy-writing and similar, there is no reason why broader global resources could not be used on typical tasks associated with outsourcing such as program development. Is this a challenge or complementary to outsourcing? Services such as Freelancer already allow for a broad range of tasks to be potentially crowdsourced; for medium-to-large enterprises, though, the administrative overhead associated with managing multiple disparate projects and providers is likely to outweigh the cost savings (at least for now), meaning that crowdsourcing as a replacement for

outsourcing is unlikely in the short term. However, service providers could look to establish their own crowdsourced ecosystem as a means to reduce delivery cost and harness global resources. From a customer perspective, issues such as data geo-location, security, IP ownership and confidentiality would create significant fetters to any service provider seeking to utilise a crowdsourced option as part of its service delivery model.

- Much has been made of the rise of the corporate venture fund, where an organisation will effectively set up an incubator and accelerator-style fund as a means of better tapping into innovation. Distancing the venture fund from the organisation itself assists in ensuring better governance in an innovation domain and avoids the taint of existing organisation behaviour acting as a brake on innovation. Partnering with service providers in the establishment of such funds and initiatives could prove useful, given the ability of the service provider to provide access to infrastructure and subject-matter expertise.
- Organisations will increasingly look at insourcing certain tasks and activities that were formerly part of a broader outsourcing relationship, given the competitive advantages in retaining knowledge internally. Application design, particularly those to be used by end-user customers, and systems architect are two increasingly common examples.
- As the world grapples with increasing rates of cybercrime and cyberterrorism, it is certain that regulators will look to enhance existing legal frameworks or introduce new regimes to better preserve data integrity and security. Also, the industry itself will continue to improve the protection of security perimeters from operational and technical perspectives. This translates into a need for contract arrangements to be sufficiently flexible to allow for evolving regulatory and technology requirements in what is an absolute business-critical area.

Due diligence and transition

Kit Burden
Tim Lyons

1. Introduction

Due diligence is the process of investigating the customer's environment, business processes, assets, contracts and employees that occurs prior to signing an agreement for the provision of outsourced services. A purchaser of a business would not buy it before ascertaining both the ability of the business to perform, after the purchase, at a level at least equal to the level at which it is currently performing, and the value of the business that it is acquiring. Equally, a service provider about to take over existing assets, employees and contracts in order to provide outsourced services will not ordinarily do so before it has satisfied itself that it will be able to provide those services to the level required by the service levels, at least to the extent that it will be reliant – in whole or in part – on using those same assets, employees and contracts in future.

The level and quality of due diligence conducted by a service provider prior to entry into an outsourcing arrangement can therefore determine the success of the entire relationship between the customer and the service provider.

A prudent customer will want prospective service providers to conduct a significant level of due diligence so that the service providers can fully understand the services to be provided and the infrastructure already in place that they will need to use to provide those services.

Service providers will thus wish to conduct extensive due diligence so that they can both properly price the provision of the services and ensure that they are capable of providing the services. The risk for a service provider in not conducting adequate due diligence is that the scope of the services may not be properly understood. In cases where the level of effort to provide the in-scope services has been underestimated, the service provider may be obliged to provide the services at a loss.

Furthermore, the service provider will often identify issues with the existing assets during due diligence or areas for improvement or remediation that are required before the service provider is able to comply with the service levels (even if this may involve activities to take place after contract signature, rather than before).

For all these reasons, it is in the interests of both the customer and the service provider for proper due diligence enquiries to be carried out prior to signing an agreement for the provision of outsourced services.

In some circumstances, it is impossible for a service provider to conduct extensive due diligence prior to contract signature. Circumstances where the customer may not provide for adequate due diligence include:

- a lack of time;
- a requirement to limit due diligence in respect of particular environments for security reasons (eg, government defence departments or police organisations);
- regulatory restrictions such as data protection requirements; and
- protection of trade secrets.

The customer must weigh up the risk of not permitting adequate due diligence against the benefits to be gained from permitting service providers to understand fully the scope of the services to be outsourced.

2. Due diligence

2.1 Due diligence by the customer

The customer must conduct some analysis and investigation in respect of the services that it intends to outsource in order to prepare the service description for inclusion in the tender documents, and indeed as part of its assessment as to the business case and feasibility of the outsource project as a whole. It should do so as early as possible after making the decision to outsource services and in any case prior to the issue of any request for tender. The greater the level of due diligence conducted prior to approaching the market to appoint a service provider, the more accurate the service description will be. In addition, the customer will be in a better position to provide disclosure of relevant information to service providers (which will inevitably end up asking for this information as part of the procurement and negotiation process). This will enable service providers to give a more accurate response including more accurate pricing, and will reduce the risk of misunderstanding and/or disputes regarding the service scope after a contract is signed. At a minimum, the investigation by the customer should involve the following:

- an assessment of all current assets used to provide the services – for example, in the case of an IT outsourcing, an assessment of the hardware, infrastructure and software including whether each is up to date. This investigation will also need to include consideration of whether the assets are used to provide services that will not be outsourced. If this is the case, then either the customer will need to retain the assets and the service provider will need to acquire new assets to provide the services, or the customer will need to acquire new assets in order to continue receiving the services that are not outsourced;
- an assessment of the third-party contracts in place – for example, whether maintenance and support agreements are in place for the relevant hardware and software that are to underpin the outsourced services in future. Consideration will need to be given as to whether these contracts may be novated or assigned to the service provider, or whether the contracts need to remain in the customer's name. In the latter case, the customer will need to consider the degree to which the incoming service provider will manage the provision of the services from the third party on behalf of the customer. If the

customer wishes to disclose the terms of these contracts to prospective service providers, it will need to consider the confidentiality provisions under the contracts and, if necessary, obtain consents from the relevant counterparties to the disclosure of the contract terms (see also the chapter on assets and third-party contracts in this regard);

- as part of the assessment of third-party contracts, the customer will need to consider specifically how it wishes to deal with licensed software. The customer may elect to assign software licences to the service provider. In many cases, software licences may be assigned to a provider of service to a customer, subject only to a requirement that the software is used solely for the benefit of the customer. Where a software licence cannot be assigned, the customer may elect to retain the licence in its name. However, the licence terms will need to be reviewed to ensure that a provider of services can use the software for the benefit of the customer (again, see the chapter on assets and third-party contracts for further discussion of some of the potential issues as to third-party software);
- the employees used to provide the services and whether any of these employees are shared across services to be outsourced and services that will not be outsourced;
- the services currently provided and whether the customer is seeking an improvement in those services or an expanded or reduced scope in the services as a result of the outsourcing;
- the service levels currently met and whether the customer is seeking an improvement in the service levels;
- transaction volumes;
- regulatory issues. In many countries, outsourcing arrangements are subject to the review or control of regulatory bodies, particularly where a customer is in the financial services sector. Consents may be required from the relevant regulatory body to the outsourcing arrangement;
- the premises from where it is intended the services will be provided. The customer will need to consider whether space has to be provided to an incoming service provider from which to provide the services. If space is to be provided, the customer may need to consider whether any consents are required from an owner of leased premises; and
- what in-flight projects are to be transferred to the service provider.

2.2 Due diligence by the service provider

Prospective service providers will normally require information in relation to the matters referred to above in order to formulate a response to any tender in respect of outsourced services. The service provider will wish to undertake its enquires in order to ascertain the following:

- the scope of the services;
- whether there is any gap between the current assets that the customer will make available to the service provider and the assets needed to provide the services scope;

- the ability to meet the service levels based on the assets that will be made available. The service provider will often request access to detailed reports on the number of incidents or problems reported over previous periods and the nature and cause of those incidents and problems, in order to assess its ability to meet the service levels prescribed by the customer;
- the employees that the service provider will be taking over. The service provider will need to ascertain both whether these resources will be sufficient in number to provide the services and whether the transferring employees know enough about the existing services to enable the ongoing provision of those services – in most cases, the service provider will need to know the terms on which employees are currently performing (see the chapter on human resources); and
- the scope of any third-party services to be provided.

Customers often make information available in a data room to assist service providers in preparing their responses to a tender to provide outsourced services.

In addition, the service provider may wish to conduct site visits to inspect the infrastructure used to provide the services. In some circumstances, the customer may not permit site visits, particularly where there is an incumbent provider of services, but in such cases the parties will need to discuss and agree on a means to enable the service provider to obtain the information that it will need in order to finalise its proposals.

Generally speaking, therefore, every outsource transaction will involve some form of due diligence prior to entry into the contract.

Increasingly, the customer may seek to include in the outsourcing contract an acknowledgement that the service provider has conducted sufficient due diligence in an attempt to preclude subsequent claims by the service provider that the provision of particular services was not included in the scope, and/or that the service provider was unaware of certain factors impacting on the provision of the services or the costs of providing them.

A standard form of words in this regard would be as follows:

The Service Provider acknowledges that it has conducted all necessary due diligence in relation to the Services and Deliverables and its obligations under this Agreement prior to the Commencement Date.

The Service Provider acknowledges and agrees that it has entered into this Agreement in reliance on its own due diligence alone and, in entering into this Agreement, has not relied on any representation, warranty, condition or other term, express or implied, statutory or otherwise (including as to condition, quality, performance or fitness for purpose), save for those expressly provided in this Agreement and those which cannot be excluded or limited by law.

The effectiveness of such a clause may be limited depending on the law of the jurisdiction governing the contract. In any event, even if the service provider has done a diligent and professional job, there may still be limitations on what it can commit to – for example, with regard to the actual accuracy of information provided to it, either by or on behalf of the customer. As the quality of due diligence information provided by customers is also often somewhat less than ideal or if service providers feel uncomfortable with the amount of data disclosure, service providers can be put in a difficult position if the procurement process leads them to face pressure to agree to such wording. In such circumstances, they may feel driven to include heightened risk premium elements to their pricing, which may operate to the ultimate detriment of the customer.

In addition to the above provisions, the customer will usually seek to include a 'sweeper' clause in its contract. While the customer will attempt to define all of the services in the schedule containing the service description (see the chapter on services and service levels) sweeper clauses are included in the contract to ensure that even where a specific reference to a particular service is not included in the services description, it does not necessarily mean that the service provider does not need to provide that service. As the name suggests, the sweeper clause seeks to sweep up additional obligations or aspects of service provision that might not have been explicitly stated in the contract, but that the customer expects the service provider to perform. Although somewhat contentious when first introduced into outsourcing contracts, such provisions are now very common.

Service providers may, however, raise concerns as to the way in which such a clause could operate. For example, it may be the case that the services are intended to change/transform, and that in order to do that and to provide the agreed pricing to the customer, the service provider has specifically modelled its envisaged set of tasks/activities on the basis of a set number of people being available to undertake them (be they from the service provider's existing pool of employees or transferred from the customer's staff). If new tasks are then found for the transferring employees to undertake, the service provider may have to allocate additional staff to fill the gaps.

The bigger service provider concern, however, is its relative inability to ascertain what these additional tasks might be, which relates directly back to the quality of the due diligence exercise. The acceptability of such a clause will accordingly be heavily influenced by the extent of the service provider's familiarity with the customer's operations and its plans concerning the retention of the transferring workforce.

2.3 Pre- and post-contract due diligence

In most cases, data room information will be available to all prospective service providers prior to formulating their final bids to provide the services. In more complex or larger transactions, sometimes more detailed due diligence and clarification responses are provided to shortlisted tenderers only. Following this process, the customer may request 'best and final' offers from the shortlisted service providers.

In circumstances where the customer cannot make all information available to a potential service provider prior to entry into the contract, the parties may agree that due diligence can be conducted during a transition-in period (sometimes prior to service commencement, but equally often as part of the start-up phase for the services themselves) to define the services better. It may also be the case that the customer simply has not tracked matters or statistics of relevance to the service provider (eg, as to the service levels achieved by a previously internal service delivery function). The service provider may then argue that it has no choice but to start such measurements as from when it takes responsibility for providing the services in question.

The risk to the customer in such an approach is that the service provider may state that various particular services were not identified or known prior to contract signature, or that the historic level of service performance was much lower than what the customer now wants, and that these changes in scope and/or requirements for improvements will involve additional cost to the service provider and, accordingly, an additional price payable by the customer. The risk here for the customer is that the measurement of the service levels will then be dependent upon the service provider itself, such that if it performs poorly during the relevant measurement period (which is not so unusual or unexpected, given the fact that it will still be relatively new to the arrangements and will be getting up to speed with the outsourcing as a whole). This might then lead to service levels being set at an artificially low level for some or all of the rest of the contract term.

This post-contract verification approach can be validly used in the circumstances described above where full disclosure cannot be given to the service provider prior to contract signature. Various boundaries can still then be placed upon the size of scope change, the most obvious being that the agreed contract price cannot change by more than a fixed percentage; the service provider must bear the risk of any increase in cost to it outside of this fixed percentage. Alternatively, the approach can be switched round the other way, such that the service provider has to bear any additional costs insofar as they are not material, which can be left subject to further discussion, or linked to an express threshold in terms of pound, dollar or euro value (see also the discussion on post-contract verification provisions from a charges perspective in the chapter on charges and charging models).

To deal with the service level issue referred to above (eg, where the service level performance is affected – to a greater or lesser extent – by factors associated with the new service provider itself rather than what it has inherited from the customer), additional factors to consider will include whether to seek to impose a minimum required level of performance that would not be breached in any event (eg, by reference to more general market standards), or whether to provide that the service provider must in any event improve the historic service levels up to the level required by the customer, within a set period of time.

An alternative may be that a service provider will seek warranties as to the adequacy of various assets, contracts or employees where it cannot satisfy itself as to the nature and/or quality of what will be provided by the customer to the service provider. The customer will naturally seek to avoid giving any warranties in respect of any of these items, particularly where they are not under the control of the customer but reside with an existing supplier. There would then in any event be uncertainty as to what would happen if the warranty is breached – that is, the extent to which the service provider could then gain relief from its contract obligations, or vary its pricing.

2.4 Trade secrets, tools and methodologies

Contention may arise where an existing supplier is replaced through a tender process (ie, as part of a second-, third- or subsequent-generation outsourcing) with regard to the intellectual property of the existing supplier. Ideally, prospective service providers will be given access to all information in relation to the current services. However, some of that information will include the incumbent supplier's tools and methodologies – that is, its way of providing the services. These tools and methodologies are often the way that service providers differentiate themselves from other suppliers and, therefore, they are treated as trade secrets.

The incoming service provider should have its own internal tools and methodologies. The grey area is where the documentation relating to the existing services includes the incumbent supplier's method of providing the services.

A customer will need to ensure that its contract with a service provider allows for disclosure of all information that an incoming provider must have access to in order to provide the services on an ongoing basis and without risk to service continuity. In most cases, this need not extend to the incumbent service provider's method of providing the services, but just that which relates specifically to the customer's ways of working.

3. Transition

A service provider cannot usually immediately commence providing outsourced services once a contract is signed. There is generally a period of time between signing of a contract and when the outsourced services begin. During this period, the services are transitioned, either from the customer to the service provider or from an outgoing service provider to the new service provider. The objective of the transition is simply to move the provision of the service from being internally to externally provided (or from an incumbent provider to a new service provider), while not compromising service continuity.

The period for transition will depend upon the complexity of the outsourced services, and the underlying service delivery model. At its simplest, a transition could involve the transfer of some assets, the assignment of third-party contracts and the transfer of employees currently employed in the provision of the services. Once these steps have been taken, the service provider is hopefully in a position to provide the services to the level prescribed by the service levels. Any remedial work is then to be undertaken during the transition period to ensure that the service levels can be met. Another option is for the services to be transitioned on an 'as is' basis, with a subsequent period following transition during which remediation will take place. This period is often accompanied by a service level holiday during which the service provider may not be bound to provide the services in accordance with the service levels, or else may report against the service levels but not be subject to service credits in the event that they are not met. Lastly, and increasingly in the world where cloud services are becoming more far reaching, the service provider may not require much of the customer's legacy infrastructure and so may be able to switch directly to its own model of service delivery with much less in the way of transition services.

For a more complex transition process there will be a further key element, which is knowledge transfer. Knowledge transfer is the process by which the service provider will fully understand the existing assets and services, and be in a position to provide the services from the service commencement date successfully. This will involve the customer in freeing up some of its staff (and potentially those of its incumbent suppliers) from their day jobs so that they can explain how they undertake their functions and be available to answer questions from the incoming service provider (see section 3.2 below).

Transition periods are usually programmes of works in their own right. One thing common to all transition periods is that there must be a fixed deadline for completion of the transition services so that the services commencement date is met. In the absence of a fixed date, there may be a lack of continuity of service, particularly if an outgoing service provider will cease the provision of the services on a particular date.

3.1 Transition-in plan

Generally speaking, the service provider must provide all transition-in services in accordance with a transition-in plan while reaching the milestones in that transition plan by the fixed milestone dates.

The transition-in plan will clearly define all the tasks required for transition, any deliverables and responsibilities for those tasks. This will also include any responsibilities to be placed back upon the customer, either regarding its own resources or in respect of obtaining the assistance and cooperation of its incumbent suppliers. In any event, the service provider must be in a position to provide the outsourced services by the service commencement date.

In the case of any delay by the service provider, the contract will normally provide for immediate notification to the customer of any such delay, along with details of the cause of the delay and the steps that the service provider intends to take to overcome or minimise the delay. There may also be a provision for liquidated damages to be payable in respect of delays caused by a service provider. Liquidated damages will be intended to compensate a customer where the service provider is not ready to provide the services by the relevant service commencement date, and will inevitably be open for debate as part of the negotiation process.

3.2 Knowledge transfer

Knowledge transfer is an extension of the due diligence process referred to above. However, knowledge transfer should not be seen as being a process by which the service provider may seek to vary the contract, but rather a process by which the service provider will gain a full understanding of the existing systems and processes employed by the customer in order for the service provider to continue to provide those services. Often, the primary process by which this knowledge transfer occurs is by face-to-face interviews with subject-matter experts and workshops with existing employees, a handover of documentation and, on occasion, shadowing of the personnel currently providing the services to understand how those services are delivered.

A strong governance structure throughout the transition is crucial to ensure that any impact on the customer's existing business is minimised, while giving the service provider sufficient contact with key personnel and subject-matter experts so that it fully understands the provision of the services. Where this may involve some degree of disclosure of information that may be confidential to the incumbent suppliers, there may be a requirement for the incumbent and the incoming service provider to enter into some form of non-disclosure agreement so as to provide the incumbent supplier with assurance that its information will not be misused in future.

All knowledge transfer should ideally be completed prior to contract signature; leaving it to be completed post-signature leaves the parties open to all of the uncertainties relating to post-contract verification as referred to above.

3.3 Staff transfer

Depending on the jurisdiction involved, the transfer of staff may be either compulsory or a voluntary process whereby the supplier will make offers of employment to various personnel that it considers necessary for the ongoing provision of the services.

In any event, there will be a separate schedule setting out the terms applicable to staff transfers (see the chapter on human resources).

3.4 Asset transfer

Asset transfer may involve the transfer of particular hardware and also the assignment of software licences. It could also involve the assignment of third-party contracts for the maintenance and support of the relevant assets used to provide the services.

The full nature and extent of the assets to be transferred should be identified through the due diligence processes referred to above. The details of the issues associated with asset and contract transfer are set out in more detail in the chapter on assets and third-party contracts.

3.5 Governance and procedures manual

Specific elements of service delivery may also be developed or finalised during the transition period. Occasionally, the ongoing governance framework for the day-to-day management of the services is developed or finalised in detail during the transition-in period.

Even more common is the definition or finalisation of the procedures that will apply to service delivery. These procedures will be set out in a procedures manual (also known as a 'service delivery management plan'). The service description is the 'what', the procedures manual sets out the 'how'. Often the contract is entered into with a draft procedures manual or table of contents for the procedures manual included in the contract. The final procedures manual governing the provision of the services is prepared by the parties during transition-in. It is generally approved by the customer and it then governs how the services will be provided following completion of transition.

Services and service levels

Kit Burden
Peter Jones

---

1. Introduction

The services schedule and service levels schedule form two parts of what is often referred to as the 'Holy Trinity' in any outsourcing arrangement (the third limb being the charges schedule); they are crucial to the engagement between customer and service provider in that they are the basis for determining what will be provided, and to what level of ongoing quality/service delivery.

However, legal advisers often overlook or neglect the services description in particular as being not legal in nature or not as important as the front-end terms and conditions. As such, the schedule can frequently be left to the business or commercial teams to complete, even though these teams may have had limited experience of contract preparation and drafting. The result can all too often amount to little more than a collection of bullet points, with hardly any context or underlying detail. While the customer and service provider representatives who noted all of this down at the time will no doubt have had this understanding in their heads and may have presumed that it was obvious, they may well move on and no longer be available to help with interpretation in future (and, in any event, may turn out to have different recollections, once disputes as to scope arise in future and money and/or sanctions for alleged non-performance are at stake).

Accordingly, any negotiator and drafter of an outsourcing contract should be at pains both to understand the scope and nature of the services that are to be captured in the services schedule and to be heavily involved in the drafting of it, and likewise to ensure that the service level schedule maps closely against it. The remainder of this chapter seeks to highlight the specific drafting issues to be considered in so doing.

2. The services schedule

2.1 Capturing the service requirements

It may be tempting to think that the process of describing the services to be outsourced would be easy. After all, surely the customer knows what services it wants to acquire, and the service provider knows what it is going to provide? The reality, however, is that the process is far more complex than might appear at first. Indeed, it is probably fair to say that the perfect outsourced service schedule has never yet been written, and probably never will be.

Let us illustrate the issue with a simple example whereby the outsourced service is "to make a cup of tea". This sounds straightforward enough – but is it really? Strictly speaking, to make a cup of tea all that is needed is to dip a tea bag for long enough into a cup of boiling water. However, most people might also expect the task of making/offering a cup of tea to include enquiring as to whether the recipient takes milk (and adding it if he does) and sugar (and again adding it – and stirring the spoon thereafter – if sugar is indeed required). To add a further level of complexity, does the recipient expect:

- full-fat, skimmed or semi-skimmed milk?
- sugar or artificial sweetener?
- Earl Grey tea or some other form (eg, peppermint)?

This does not even take into account cultural difference in interpretation (eg, in parts of the United States, tea would be expected to be served in iced form), how long the tea bag should be left to brew, or the vexed issue of whether the cup of tea should be accompanied by an offer of biscuits.

If such a simple task can involve so much complexity, imagine the potential for confusion or debate in the context of a major outsourcing engagement. Equally, the example above amply demonstrates how the potential differences of opinion can have an impact upon both time and cost (eg, in the fuller interpretation of scope in the tea example above, the service provider would also have been obliged to procure various different forms of both milk and sugar/sweeteners, all at its own additional cost).

It is essential, therefore, to take the time to set out the service descriptions as fully as possible. If external legal or sourcing advisory services have been engaged, it is possible or even likely that they will have detailed precedent service descriptions available for most of the standard forms of outsourced services (eg, regarding the operation of a service desk, the provision of application development and/or maintenance services, or the operation and maintenance of local/wide area networks), but it would be unwise to conclude that a precedent will ever be a perfect fit for an organisation's requirements. A lot of work will accordingly be required to adjust any such templates to fit with the particular circumstances and requirements of the individual project and client. This will inevitably be time consuming and can accordingly be a considerable drain on the subject-matter experts within the customer organisation, who will frequently have to juggle this with their day jobs. However, it will pay dividends not just during the negotiation of the contract, but also over the lifetime of the contract itself.

2.2 Prescriptive or descriptive?

Initially, the description of services typically adopted high levels of prescription, mirroring the status quo of tasks and activities and reflecting a 'command and control' approach to outsourcing by customers. This is unsurprising, as early service providers confronted the need to establish the necessary levels of assurance as to their ability to perform at the required level, while customers naturally sought to minimise the impacts of outsourcing on the organisation.

The challenges in this approach are largely twofold. First, if one of the expected benefits of engaging an external service provider is to benefit from that service provider's experience, knowledge and processes, the stipulation that the service provider mimics the existing organisation – or largely does so – defeats that purpose. Expected productivity gains will not follow and efficiency dividends may not arise as the service provider will charge for a tailored solution rather than apply the pricing of its standard service delivery model.

Second, the effort required to translate existing behaviours to contractual commitments is significant and rarely results in complete alignment, meaning either service overlaps (where the retained organisation and the external service provider consider that each is responsible for a particular task) or service gaps (where the retained organisation believes that the external service is responsible for a particular task, a belief with which the service provider disagrees).

One of the responses to these challenges was to adopt what is known as an 'outcomes-based' approach, focusing on what the customer's business outcomes are rather than the service inputs for which the service provider is responsible. Another way to look at this is not to prescript the 'how' but to describe the 'what'. This approach is reflected not only in terms of service descriptions, but also more broadly including service levels (eg, a service level based on end-user experience rather than a service level based on, say, the time within which documentation is required to be updated following changes in process) and the broader contractual commitments and governance regimes. Diagrammatically, an outcomes-based contract can be represented as:

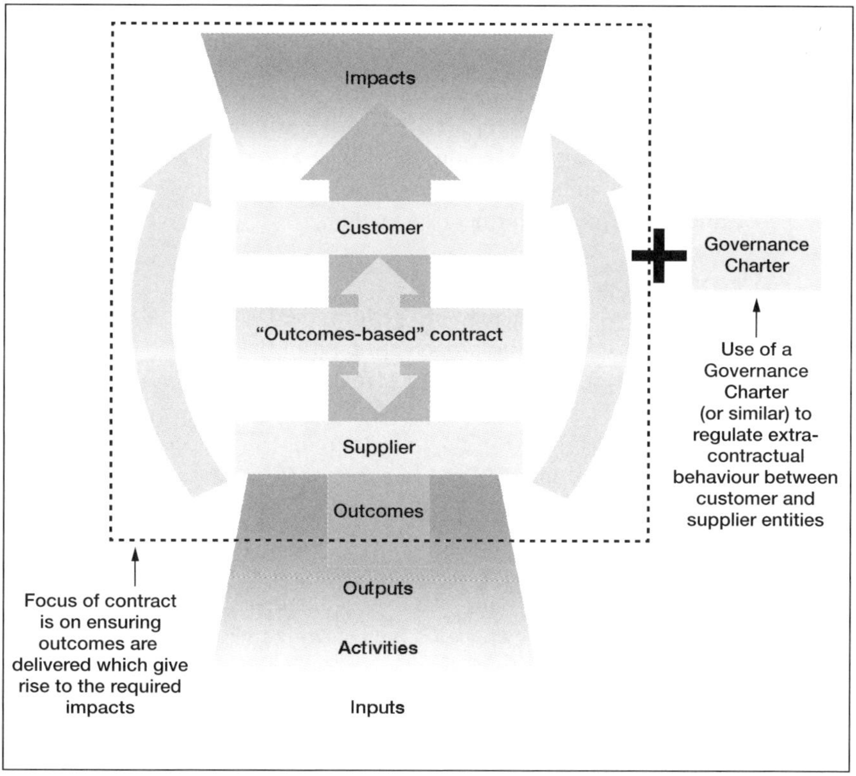

However, an outcomes-based approach is not without its challenges: developing clear, cohesive and cogent outcomes is difficult. There is an inherent ambiguity in describing outcomes and attempts to do so often revert to high-level descriptions of outcomes that are then cloaked in what is perceived to be the safety and security of more detailed service inputs. In this case, all things in moderation is not necessarily a recipe for enduring success.

Further, where a true outcomes approach is ultimately implemented, the risk of interpretative differences in terms of outcome definition demands strong governance and relationship management, recognising the interdependence between customer and service provider.

There are also issues in determining whether outcomes have been achieved and, if so, the extent to which the achievement was a result of the service provider and/or other externalities.

The reality is that the precise approach to service definition will depend on the customer (including its retained organisation and internal corporate governance), the industry, the extent of regulatory oversight and direction, the services outsourced and the delivery model of the selected service provider. There is no 'one size fits all' solution in outsourced service description.

2.3 Example of a service description

Below is a description for a service agnostic document management service (ie, a necessary service but one that is complementary to a core service such as applications development or infrastructure management).

It adopts an outcomes-based approach, setting out a number of higher-level requirements and allowing the service provider, within these parameters and subject to other quality assurance requirements such as service levels and general quality warranties and commitments, to determine itself how to undertake the required task.

Annotations provide further explanation.

1.1. Description

The service provider is required to perform the Document Management Service. All the tasks, activities and processes set out in this Service Description must be performed as part of the Document Management Service.

Document Management means the tasks, activities and processes required to coordinate and control the flow of electronic and paper Documentation in a secure and efficient manner, and to ensure that the Documentation is accessible only to persons authorised by the customer as and when required. Without limitation, Document Management includes the following tasks, activities and processes: [This definition is intentionally not exclusive to minimise any arguments that the specific service requirements are strictly based on the following. This inclusive approach is a recurring theme throughout this clause as it applies to the tasks, activities and processes that the service provider is required to undertake. Further, the following could also be subject to greater definition; however, as this services description is prepared within the context of an outcomes-based arrangement, it is intentionally not prescriptive in terms of all tasks, activities and processes]

(a) Document storage;
(b) Document retrieval;
(c) Document processing;
(d) Document printing;
(e) Document routing and distribution;
(f) release management;
(g) version control; and
(h) access control.

1.2. Outcomes

The service provider must achieve the following Outcomes for this Service: [The outcomes are intentionally broad in scope, though with specific details on key issues (eg, version control)]

(a) Document Management is planned, communicated to customer and performance is measurable.
(b) a centralised online library is implemented in accordance with the requirements of the agreement.
(c) all Documentation may be quickly and efficiently retrieved as and when required.
(d) the Document Management System in place enables effective collaboration between dispersed groups of users.
(e) only personnel authorised by the customer are able to view, access, modify or destroy Documentation.
(f) effective disaster recovery strategies are in place with respect to all Documentation.
(g) Incidents of lost and damaged Documentation are minimised (and the service provider must take all reasonable steps to minimise such loss or damage).
(h) only the latest version of a particular Document is available through the Document Management System by default, however superseded versions of Document are also readily available.
(i) Documentation that is up to date, current and accurate.
(j) the Document Management System ensures that customer's confidential material is at all times held in a manner that is confidential.

1.3. Supplier Responsibilities

The service provider responsibilities for this Service, which must be performed in accordance with the prevailing policies, standards and procedures of the customer in connection with document management [There is also an obligation to ensure that the customer's own policies, standards and procedures are observed. However, this raises a legitimate issue for the service provider – in the event of any change in customer's requirements, how is this communicated, and how is the impact in terms of cost, service levels etc regulated? In the context of this agreement, a separate overriding clause exists to provide for the impacts of policy compliance requirements], include the following:

1.3.1. Document management system [Not only are specific requirements outlined, but also the underlying process for providing assurance that such requirements will be undertaken, in this case through a requirement to implement a system and, below, a requirement to implement a specific plan]

(a) implementing and operating a Document Management System that:

(i) satisfies the requirements of the agreement with respect to data protection and confidentiality;

(ii) stores all Documentation in a secure and fail-safe environment;

(iii) organises and indexes Documentation to assist retrieval via indexes or other tools;

(iv) enables Document browsing and searching to facilitate Document retrieval via search tools;

(v) only enables access to Documentation by persons authorised by the customer; and

(vi) ensures Documentation is secure and unauthorised persons are prevented from viewing, modifying and destroying Documentation;

(b) providing disaster recovery services for Documentation stored in the Document Management System to minimise disruption to delivery of any Outcomes or to the customer's business operations;

(c) identifying which Documentation must be:

(i) returned to the customer and any other supplier nominated by the customer after the agreement terminates or expires;

(ii) held confidential after the agreement terminates or expires; and

(iii) retained by the service provider after the agreement terminates or expires;

(d) archiving Documentation to maximise performance or reduce cost by taking Documentation offline or through any other method after a defined period signed-off by the customer;

(e) managing and enforcing version control, release control and Document traceability to ensure only current versions of Documentation are in use (other than where superseded versions of a Document are specifically requested or required);

(f) tracking modification date and users of Documentation to provide transparency with respect to any changes to a Document; and

(g) ensuring Documentation is managed under the guiding principles defined by the Knowledge Management Service.

1.3.2. Document Management Plan the service provider's personnel [There is a separate obligation that the plan is subject to a customer review and approval process (see below). There is, however, a balance to be struck – namely, the extent to which a customer acts as an approval body (with the potential absorption of risk as a result) and the confidence in the service provider being able to regulate its own performance]

(a) developing and accordingly documenting a Document Management Plan that:

(i) documents a Document Management System, including by detailing the process, tools and methods required by that Document Management System;

(ii) allocates to the service provider's personnel roles and responsibilities with respect to Document Management; and

(iii) sets out the manner and methodology by which the service provider's performance of Document Management Services may be measured; and

(b) ensuring that all the service provider's personnel comply with the Document Management Plan; and

1.3.3. Manage Documentation

(a) developing and maintaining the Documentation contemplated by or specified in this Service Description and amended in accordance with the customer's requirements as contemplated by or set out in this Service Description;

(b) providing access to and or copies of the Documentation as specified by the customer;

(c) regularly reviewing and updating the Documentation as specified in this Service Description and the agreement;

(d) amending the Documentation as reasonably requested by the customer;

(e) conducting periodic audits (no less than monthly) to determine whether or not the Documentation under management is complete and current; and

(f) returning, retaining and holding confidential Documentation in accordance with the Document Management Plan.

1.4. Customer Tasks

The customer's tasks are as follows for this Service: [A separate process exists where the service provider is able, subject to certain notification and mitigation obligations, to obtain relief in the event that the customer does not undertake a particular task that affects a service provider commitment]

1.4.1. Document Management System

Signing-off on the Document Management System or otherwise providing feedback on the Document Management System to the service provider.

1.4.2. Document Management Plan

Signing-off on the Document Management Plan and other Documentation related to Document Management Services or otherwise providing feedback on the Document Management Plan and such Documentation to the service provider.

1.4.3. Manage Documentation

Signing-off on Documentation or otherwise providing feedback on such Documentation to the service provider.

1.5. Supplier Document Deliverables

In addition to any other requirements to provide Deliverables under a Contract, the service provider must deliver the following Document Deliverables for this Service:

1.5.1. Supplier Document Deliverables

(a) Document Management Plan which is substantially in the form set out in the relevant customer policy or standard (where available) or as agreed with the customer and which otherwise meets the requirements for this Document Deliverable contemplated by or set out in this Service Description.

(b) A report which lists all current versions of all Documentation under Document Management. The report must contain the following fields:

(i) Document Identifier (if available);

(ii) Document Name;

(iii) Document Version;

(iv) Document Revision Date; and

(v) Document Author,

and otherwise meet the requirements for this Document Deliverable contemplated by or set out in this Service Description.

2.4 Request for proposal documentation

Assuming that – as is usually the case – the customer will run a bidding process involving some form of request for proposal to potential service providers (see the chapter on the overview of the procurement, negotiation and delivery process), one of the immediate pay-offs of the work done in preparing the service description will be the inclusion of part or all of its content in the bidding instructions sent out as the basis for the proposals to be submitted by the service providers. The service providers should then be able to assess the nature of the customer's business operations and requirements, and assess whether they have the capability to provide the envisaged outsourced services in future.

This leads on to an important consideration: what relevance/use (if any) should any such request-for-proposal document have when the contract comes to be signed?

One view has it that the request-for-proposal documentation should be of no significance, and that the parties should have exhaustively negotiated the contract documents themselves so as to include in the relevant schedules all of the service requirements, porting across as necessary such parts of the original request for proposal as may be relevant. Proponents of this view point to the advantage of having 'a single view of the truth' in the form of the finally signed contract, without risk of ambiguity or conflict in looking back to try to interpret previous documents. It is also said (with some validity) that while a customer may have originally stated a set of service requirements in a request for proposal, these requirements may have been set out only at a relatively high level (perhaps even at the 'make a cup of tea' level as referred to above in secion 2.1) and have been subject thereafter to elucidation and clarification during the subsequent bid and contract negotiation process; there may then have been elements of the original request for proposal that the customer has dropped or changed, or that the service provider has indicated it could not provide or would need to provide in a manner that is different to that envisaged in the original request-for-proposal documentation, all of which could more accurately be covered in the final contract schedules. Service providers will also be aware that customer's request for proposals are often stating 'aspirational' requirements (eg, for 'best in class' service provision) that may be risky to give contractual effect to.

By contrast, a customer might argue that it has put a lot of time into creating the service requirements as stated in the request for proposal, and that these requirements consequently form the best description of what the customer wants. Accordingly, it can be said that – at least in the absence of a specific statement from a service provider that it cannot deliver part of the required services – the request for proposal should form a part of the contract or even take precedence over any other document (ie, on the basis that this is the document against which the service provider has based its promises and pricing in the contract).

What then about the possibility of looking instead to incorporate the service provider's response to the request for proposal, either on its own or by way of an amendment or addition to the proposal itself? This may have some merits; it would help to resolve the issue of the service provider stating what it could not do or would do differently, and would potentially also help to contractualise another level of the service provider's commitments so as to capture not only what it would be doing for the customer, but also how it would do it – for example, in relation to technology and processes to be employed, service locations and internal governance structures. The service provider might argue that its own proposal document is also an even better reflection of its detailed pricing and contract commitments than the customer's request for proposal as it will set out in more detail what the service provider's solution and services will consist of.

However, simply incorporating the service provider's proposal document is also not without risk or downside, for both customer and service provider alike. A customer may be concerned about potential omissions from its detailed requirements; if the service provider's response is silent on a particular requirement, would this mean that it is accepted/included, or not part of the services being offered? Equally, the customer may want to insist on some aspects of its original requirements being provided (eg, something that the service provider could do, but might have preferred not to or failed to price for); if these are then picked up in the subsequent negotiations, the customer would have to take great care in ensuring that they were expressly stated in the contract service schedule itself, or risk them being lost. From a service provider perspective, the contract negotiators will be wary that much of the response to any customer request for proposal will have been created by the service provider's sales/business development team, all of whom will have been keen to win the project work and to have put the best possible spin on the service provider's delivery capabilities. There is a risk, therefore, that some marketing speak may have been used, which could be quite onerous if given express contractual effect.

In relation to both the request for proposal and the service provider's response documents, there is the additional challenge of how best to capture any further clarifications or negotiations of these documents during the bid and negotiation phase; for example, there may have been any number of PowerPoint presentations, workshops, subject matter experts' meetings, emails and conference calls to discuss and refine the requirements and service offers further, which may in turn have changed the nature of either the requirements or the proposed solution, potentially to a material degree. If the original documents are to be given express contractual effect, then these subsequent discussions and documents would presumably need to be as well.

The traditional approach to these challenges has tended to exclude both the customer's request for proposal and any service provider responses, both by avoiding any express contract provision to incorporate them into the contract (whether by attachment to the contract or by incorporation by cross reference) and by including in the contract a 'whole agreement' clause to state expressly that the provisions in the contract constitute the entire agreement between the parties as to its subject matter, to the express exclusion of any other pre-contractual documentation, discussions or representations. This has the not-inconsiderable benefit of creating a clean and certain entry point for the contractual relationship between the parties, and hence tends still to be the default option in most outsourcing engagements. However, another option that can be used and that seeks to strike a compromise between this approach and those referred to above is to allow for reference to the pre-contractual documentation (eg, both the customer's request for proposal and the service provider's response(s) to it), but expressly only in the circumstances where there is ambiguity in the contract drafting/description of the services, and then only to the extent necessary to resolve such ambiguity.

2.5 The service description

Whatever approach may be taken to the inclusion or non-inclusion of pre-contract documentation, there is no substitute for taking time to record the service description in as much detail as possible. Hopefully, the customer will already have done much of the legwork in this regard in the course of ascertaining the service requirements as described in section 2.1 above, but the process of negotiating with the service provider will undoubtedly have resulted in clarifications and further detail, and also additions from the service provider as to how it will go about service delivery, all of which will need to be catered for and captured. A debate as to whether to take a descriptive or perspective approach will also need to be had and concluded (see section 2.2 above).

The service descriptions will obviously vary depending on the nature of the outsourced services themselves, and as a general rule of thumb should be defined to such a level of detail that someone reasonably skilled/experienced in the relevant subject matter would be able to understand not just what is to be done, but also the general scope/size of the task involved. By way of example only (and building upon the lengthier example already set out in section 2.3 above), below is a form of words dealing with a particular element of a desktop IT and hosting services outsource deal concerning batch management.

1.1 Batch Management

The Supplier's responsibilities will include:

1.1.1 manage and control a secure batch scheduling environment on a 24×7 basis;

1.1.2 implement change to planned and current schedules;

1.1.3 manage yearly diaries and calendars as defined by the batch owners;

1.1.4 provide support for application development teams on how to best exploit the environment;

1.1.5 optimise batch to ensure that there are no unnecessary linkages or dependencies;

1.1.6 clearly instrument the batch to make external dependencies clear;

1.1.7 provide Centre of Competence (CoC) for all batch scheduling for the Customer and third party service providers;

1.1.8 publish and enforce Customer standards for all batch runs scheduled;

1.1.9 automate all batch activities to include critical batch alerting ensuring all critical deadlines are adequately signposted;

1.1.10 manage and support all operations applications that support the processing of batch and the broader operations environment.

In this example, the service provider's responsibilities in respect of batch management include those listed out in the clause, which of course raises the prospect of the customer arguing that other tasks that may be associated with the general duty of batch management would also still be within the overall scope of the services and, therefore, fall to be performed by the service provider. This reflects the reality that – for most outsource projects at least – the nature and scope of the outsourced services will be so multifaceted as to be impossible to define down to the last potential detail so as to be truly incapable of debate as to precise scope.

There are therefore residual risks for both customer and service provider. For the customer, the concern will be that once the contract has been signed (and when the customer will be fully committed to the project and its bargaining leverage will be correspondingly diminished), the service provider will seek to exploit any ambiguities as to the service descriptions so as to allege that aspects of the customer's requirements on a day-to-day basis are out of scope and therefore subject to change control (and by implication, agreement as to additional fees to be paid to the service provider) – a process only half-humorously referred to as 'death by change control'. Suspicious customers may even form the view that service providers may allow poorly crafted service descriptions to pass through the negotiation process and into the final contract knowing that they will be well placed to exploit any uncertainties thereafter.

Service providers may, however, have a different perspective. Far from feeling that they have the whip hand in discussions about change control post-contract signature, service providers may feel beholden to the customer in agreeing that the 'new' activity is, in fact, a change at all, and in the absence of such agreement may find themselves facing the prospect of being compelled to perform an enlarged role (or at least one beyond what they had planned and costed for) without additional payment – a phenomenon usually referred to as 'scope creep'.

There is unfortunately no magic wand or silver bullet solution for this issue. Effort and attention in detailing the services will clearly mitigate the risk, but will not avoid it altogether. Outsourcing agreements have therefore developed to seek to further close the gap between the parties by means of a series of implied services, usually contained in what is sometimes known as the 'sweeper clause'.

2.6 The sweeper clause

As the name suggests, the sweeper clause seeks to sweep up additional obligations or aspects of service provision that might not have been explicitly stated in the contract, but which the customer expects the service provider to perform. Although somewhat contentious when first introduced into outsourcing contracts, such provisions are now very common and – from a customer perspective at least – probably part of best practice in contract drafting.

The clause breaks down into several component parts.

The first part is the least contentious, and relates to the additional tasks that are a 'reasonable and inherent part' of the overall outsourced services (the idea being to capture the kind of thing that a reasonable bystander with knowledge of the kind of outsourced services in question would ordinarily have expected to see detailed as being part of the service provider's responsibilities). A typical form of words in this regard would be as follows: "[The Service Provider shall also undertake and perform] any services, functions and responsibilities (including any incidental services, functions and responsibilities) not expressly specified in this Agreement as being within the scope of the Supplier's responsibilities but which are reasonably and necessarily required for, and related to, the proper performance and provision of the Services."

From a service provider perspective, one might accept the logic of the approach (recognising the difficulties of creating a perfect services schedule, as discussed in this chapter), but seek to negotiate some kind of boundaries for it. Examples include a time limitation within which the customer must have identified and notified any such 'additional' service requirements to the service provider (so as to try to get to a point when a line can be drawn under the scope of the services, and using the logic that any discrepancies should come to light reasonably quickly after commencement of the services, even though the customer may argue that the full annual business cycle would need to be completed for it to be able to say with any certainty that this would be the case), and/or a limitation on the additional cost to be borne by/effort to be undertaken by the service provider in supplying the 'implied' services, before it is able to raise a change control note to recover any additional amounts (on the basis of an argument that the clause is intended to pick up more minor or incidental matters only, and that if more significant costs are being incurred, one might surmise that the service description itself was flawed/inadequate and therefore in need of re-negotiation).

The second part looks at the individuals undertaking the services immediately prior to the commencement of the outsourced services, who may then transfer across to the service provider's employment (whether by agreement or by operation of the Acquired Rights Directive – see the chapter on human resources and the Acquired

Rights Directive) or be replaced by the service provider's own personnel or those of its subcontractors. The form of words that one might then see utilised could read as follows: "[The Service Provider shall also undertake] any services, functions and responsibilities that the Customer can reasonably demonstrate were ordinarily provided by the Employees and/or any individuals employed and/or engaged by an incumbent supplier in the twelve (12) months prior to the Service Commencement Date."

The customer's argument here is that it is outsourcing the function that those employees were previously undertaking. It follows that the customer is intending to continue to receive at least the same scope as was being provided before (if not more/to a better standard), and that therefore the service provider should be obliged to continue to undertake such services, even if not explicitly stated in the services schedule.

There is considerable logic to this approach, especially for those deals modelled on a service provider taking on the customer's existing function on pretty much a like-for-like basis, and then looking to run it more efficiently/cost effectively thereafter so as to reduce the cost to the customer (and possibly also improve or commit to service levels). If the individuals in question have transferred across to the service provider, it is likely that they will continue to perform pretty much the same tasks as they did prior to the transfer of their contracts of employment, and so the customer's expectation as embodied in this form of words should be fulfilled.

Service providers may however raise concerns as to the way in which such a clause could operate. For example, the services may be intended to change/transform, and in order to do that and to provide the agreed pricing to the customer, the service provider has specifically modelled its envisaged set of tasks/activities on a set number of people being available to undertake them (be they from the service provider's existing pool of employees or those previously employed by the customer). If 'new' tasks are then found for the transferring employees to undertake, the service provider may then have to allocate additional staff to fill the gaps.

The bigger service provider concern, however, is the relative inability of the service provider to understand/find out what these additional tasks might be. To give two real examples:

- In an outsource transaction we were involved with in Scandinavia, it transpired that one of the transferring personnel used to drive in to the office via the local post office, and so would drop in to pick up a mail sack each day. He was made redundant shortly after the outsource agreement was signed (on the basis that his role would be undertaken in future by India-based staff), but the service provider was told that it had to keep on picking up the mail and delivering it to the client's offices (which it had to do by way of paying ongoing courier fees).
- In an IT outsourcing project in the United Kingdom, a team of three administrators transferred across with the core IT services. It subsequently came to light that they had habitually undertaken procurement activities not just for the IT department (which was the subject of the outsource deal), but

also for other parts of the business (eg, office supplies, furniture etc), and the customer required that these procurement activities be continued.

The acceptability of such a clause will accordingly be heavily influenced by the extent of the service provider's familiarity with the customer's operations and its plans concerning the retention of the transferring workforce.

The third potential element of the sweeper clause relates to third-party contracts that are to be novated or assigned to the service provider. A form of words to cover this issue might read as follows: "[The Service Provider will provide] any Services within the scope of any contracts assigned and/or novated to the Service Provider directly in connection with the provision of the Services."

For the customer, the attraction of such a clause is clear; it had previously been receiving a set scope of services from a particular supplier, and now that those contracts have passed across to the outsource service provider instead, it will not expect to see any diminution in them. Again, there is undeniable logic in such an argument, but not to the point that it will necessarily apply on a blanket basis to every deal. For example, the parties may have discussed and agreed that a third-party supplier will be retained for only a short period of time, with the service provider then being understood to be changing to a new mode or location of service delivery. In such circumstances, it might be always understood and agreed that there would be a change in the scope of services from those described in the transferring contracts, which would then need to be accounted for.

For both the second and third elements of the potential sweeper clause, one might again find service providers arguing for time limitation periods and/or cost caps regarding the identification of additional tasks to be undertaken, over and above what is expressly stated in the contract. These tend to be hotly contested and negotiated between the parties.

2.7 Customer responsibilities and relief notices

It should not be forgotten that in order for the service provider to perform the services, it is likely that the customer will have to do a few things as well.

Such customer responsibilities can be seen in contracts at a very high/broad brush level – for example, by way of a statement to the effect that the customer will provide the service provider with all such information or assistance as it may reasonably require in connection with the provision of the services. However, whether such a catch-all provision exists, it is likely to be in the interests of both parties to have included in the contract a more explicit/detailed list of any particular obligations or duties that the service provider will need the customer to fulfil. Although the customer might at first question why it might be best advised to accept additional contractual obligations in this manner, it is worth taking a moment to reflect upon what the customer really wants from an outsourcing agreement; in our view, its objective is not to get sanctions or remedies against the service provider simply for the sake of having them (although clearly such remedies need to exist). Instead, the better-advised customer will be aiming to have a contract that best supports the prospects for the outsourcing being a success, and this will mean one that reminds the customer that it must do certain things as well (even if this is by way of a pointed reminder that the service provider will be relieved from liability and may be able to claim additional costs if the customer fails to do so). See also the chapter on the role of the client in this regard.

Accordingly, having a relatively detailed list of customer responsibilities can be a good thing from a customer perspective (usually as set out in a separate 'customer responsibilities' schedule in the relevant contract). As with the service descriptions themselves, care must however be taken to ensure that the responsibilities are carefully crafted and scoped, can be readily understood, and are linked to 'relief notice' provisions.

'Relief notices' are a relatively recent innovation in outsourcing agreements in the sense of only becoming truly common in the course of the past five or six years. They were borne out of experiences with many failed or failing outsourcing engagements, in circumstances where the project appeared to be proceeding on track with no major issues being flagged, and then all of a sudden when the service provider seemed to be on the point of failing to meet a date or to deliver on some other obligation, it would allege that the 'true' cause of the problem was not its non-performance, but something that the customer either had or had not done some time previously (and sometimes some period of months previously). Although this would be a point of fact to be determined, the practical reality is that records and documents needed to ascertain the true picture might not have been retained or might be difficult to gather, memories may have faded or people with relevant knowledge may have moved on to new employment, all leading to increased uncertainty as to the outcome of any dispute between customer and service provider. All too often, what would happen would be a forced agreement between the parties on terms that could be equally unsatisfactory for both, and with lasting damage to the relationship between them.

This is clearly an unsatisfactory state of affairs. The outsourcing market has accordingly borrowed from a long-standing approach used in the construction industry, whereby if a supplier wishes to allege that its performance of its obligations has been effectively prevented by reason of the non-performance of the part of its contract counter-party, it must serve a written notice to that effect upon becoming aware of such non-performance.

In the outsourcing context, a clause to embody this approach might read as follows:

> 1.1 The Supplier shall only be entitled to relief in respect of any failure to meet any obligation imposed by the Agreement if and to the extent:
> (i) the Supplier's non-performance results directly from a Relief Event;
> (ii) the Supplier uses all reasonable endeavours to mitigate the Relief Event and to perform the Services notwithstanding the Relief Event; and
> (iii) the Supplier notifies the Customer's Contract Manager as soon as reasonably possible (and in any event within 7 calendar days) after the Supplier becomes aware of the Relief Event via a notice in the format specified in Schedule XX (Pro Forma Relief Event Notice) (a "Relief Notice").

Although this clause may at first appear to be relatively advantageous to the service provider in that it is providing it with an express right of relief vis-à-vis its contract non-performance, closer examination shows that it is an obligation placed upon the service provider itself and a limitation of its rights. If the service provider were to fail to notify the customer of the alleged relief event (which would usually be defined as a failure by the customer to perform any of its express obligations under the outsourcing contract), then it would be denied the ability to raise the customer's acts or omissions as a shield or defence against any corresponding failure on its own part to perform in accordance with the contract requirements (eg, if it incurred liquidated damages for failing to hit a contractual milestone, or incurred service credits vis-à-vis resulting failures to meet service levels).

This may seem harsh, but in reality there is good reason for it. If the service provider did not face such consequences, there would be serious doubts as to whether it would be sufficiently incentivised to serve any such notices upon the customer. After all, there is a risk that the issue of a relief notice might prompt a debate or argument with the customer that the service provider might prefer to avoid from the point of view of maintaining good client relations, and if the service provider knows that it can still claim a defence by reason of the customer's original non-performance of its obligations, whether it serves a relief notice or not, it will likely err in favour of keeping things sweet on the customer relationship front. The customer, however, will want to know if there are failings on its side that are preventing the aims of the outsourcing agreement being met (which takes us back to the point that the customer ultimately wants a working service, not a contractual sanction against the service provider).

A number of points will remain to be negotiated in respect of such a clause. In particular:

- will the notice be required to be given in a prescribed format (as is the case in the example cited above) or will email or some other format suffice (eg, by noting the issues in the minutes of a weekly progress meeting)?
- will the service provider be able to recover any additional costs, either as a result of its mitigating actions or by reason of the relief event itself?
- what is the time period within which the relief notice must be served?
- is the provision of relief under the clause the sole and exclusive remedy of the service provider, or can it also claim damages (or even potentially seek to terminate the contract if it has a contractual right or means to do so – see the chapter on termination and step-in rights)?

2.8 Other services obligations

The contract may include various service obligations that sit outside the services description (and aside from the entry and exit relation tasks associated with transition and termination assistance, as are dealt with in the chapters on due diligence and transition, and renegotiations, retenders and termination assistance). Some non-exhaustive examples may include:

- an obligation to comply with the customer's policies and processes;
- obligations to comply with applicable laws and regulations (and potentially

with any post-signature changes to them, which will usually be a vexed topic for negotiation vis-à-vis the charging arrangements for this – see the chapter on charges and charging models);
- provisions to require the service provider to improve the services continuously (usually without being too specific as to how this is to be done); and
- an obligation to replace elements of the customer's infrastructure with more up-to-date versions/releases of the applicable software or hardware (usually referred to as 'tech refresh' obligations).

The service provider in particular will need to consider such provisions carefully so as to ensure that it is capable of performing them and caters for them in its financial model.

3. Service levels

3.1 Introduction

An integral part of any outsourcing agreement is the service level regime implemented to measure performance at a quantitative and, in contemporary contracts, increasingly a qualitative level. The service level regime forms one of the four pillars of an outsourcing agreement along with the service description, pricing details and governance requirements.

There is also, however, often confusion as to how best to develop and subsequently manage service levels to drive the correct service provider behaviour, and a tendency to seek set-and-forget positions that do not respond to the one constant in any long-term contract of interdependence – namely, change. Equally, customers sometimes fall into the trap of seeking to specify too many service levels or to require measurement and reporting on rather peripheral or unimportant aspects of the service, thus running the risk of making the whole regime cumbersome, uncommercial and sometimes even unworkable.

What, then, is a service level regime? At its most basic, service levels are pre-determined and usually measurable performance requirements that the service provider must meet in its performance of the service and where any failure to meet such performance requirements typically generates a credit (or rebate) in favour of the customer – usually by way of a deduction from the service provider's ongoing charges for the outsourced services – and, increasingly commonly, providing a bonus payment where other performance thresholds are exceeded (see in this regard section 3.7 below).

An effective service level regime therefore creates disincentives (and, increasingly, incentives) for the service provider to ensure that the services performed meet the customer's requirements, and reflect the quality of services promised by the service provider during the initial procurement and negotiation process.

A simple example is a service level aligned to problem resolution for critical problems, as shown below.

Service level	Definition	Required metric	Service level credit
Problem resolution – Severity 1	Permanent resolution of a Severity 1 problem or customer-approved workaround to a Severity 1 problem.	95% of problems resolved within 4 hours of the problem notified to service provider or otherwise identified by service provider and 100% of problems resolved within 8 hours of the problem notified to service provider or otherwise identified by service provider	2% of monthly charges

Unsurprisingly, service levels rely on defined terms in the outsourcing agreement itself – in the above example, terms such as 'problem', 'resolved' and 'Severity 1'.

3.2 History

The use of commercial drivers to encourage certain behaviour is not a new phenomenon. To return to the example given earlier in this book of the British government using private contractors for the transportation of convicts, reformers raised concerns with the high mortality rates of those being transported (which significantly exceeded already high rates of mortality for transcontinental travel). One hypothesis suggests that a key reason for this was the fact that if a person died in transit, an equal weight of rum could be acquired and then on-sold to the colonies on arrival, providing a windfall gain for the ship owner. To counter this, the government introduced a bonus payment that was paid following the verification of the health and wellbeing of the persons transported in addition to prosecuting the worst cases of ill-treatment – the commercial carrot and the penal stick, as it were (though prosecutions were rare and no such prosecution was ultimately successful).

More contemporary approaches exist in the telecommunications services contracts from the 1980s onwards where the concept of service levels as currently understood were initially implemented, or were probably initially implemented (although these were not necessarily accompanied with a rebate or credit arising where there was non-performance).

From here, given the criticality that service level regimes play in outsourcing relationships, an industry now exists around the development, implementation and management of service level frameworks, either as part of the outsourcing advisory business or as specific standalone assistance and training. Organisations have also developed internal supporting capabilities. However, developing an effective service level regime remains a delicate balancing exercise between the legitimate interests of the customer and those of the service provider.

3.3 Broader context

"Not everything that counts can be counted and not everything that is counted counts". This quote, commonly attributed to Albert Einstein, shows that even in a world increasingly geared towards data analytics, quantitative analysis has limitations – intangibles continue to exist, qualitative considerations continue to arise and an over-reliance on multiple service level metrics can result in analysis paralysis.

While an incredibly useful tool to drive preferred service provider behaviour, service levels remain just that: a tool as part of a bigger toolbox of contract commitments and broader relationship governance. Any service level regime is part of the outsourcing agreement generally and should not be divorced from a relationship with other terms, especially those of a liability-related nature.

For example, what is the relationship between service levels and:

- termination rights? Should a certain number of service level failures, the impact of each of which in isolation is manageable but in aggregation may represent a more systemic problem, give rise to a right to terminate the agreement? If so, and given that not all service levels necessarily represent the same level of importance, how should any such termination right be defined?
- remedial obligations? Rather than, or perhaps in addition to, a specific termination right, should specific service levels or aggregated service level failures result in a requirement for the service provider to develop a draft remedial plan that is subject to the customer's approval and sets out the specific steps that the service provider will take to correct the underlying cause of service level failure(s)? If so, what is the remedy if the remedial plan itself is either not complied with or does not ultimately result in rectification of the underlying issue?
- reporting? How and when is the service provider to report on service level performance? What is the format of reports? Should raw performance data be provided or otherwise made available? What verification rights should the customer have?
- benchmarking? What consequences arise if a benchmarking exercise indicates that the service level metrics are less than market?
- relief events? Should *force majeure* events result in a suspension of any service level liability? Similarly, if a customer fails to perform certain obligations, what is the impact on service level liability? How is the causal nexus between any prescribed relief event and a service level failure to be determined? Or has the likelihood of such relief events arising already been factored in to the setting of service level metrics?
- liability? What is the relationship, if any, between service credits that may arise and the service provider's overall liability limit? Should service credits paid reduce the available cap or exist separately, as a form purely of adjusting the amount of the charges?

3.4 Setting service levels

(a) *Who should do the setting?*

The setting of service levels has powered many debates between customer and service provider, and even between different business units within the customer. In the information and communication technology context, the debate was often between the IT department and 'the business' as to which unit was better placed to determine the required service levels. It is probably fair to say that this debate has been settled largely in favour of the latter.

Given that the intention of any outsourcing is ultimately to provide some benefit to the business organisation, and the increasingly common view that internal support departments such as information technology exist to support the commercial operations of an enterprise, it is unsurprising that the personnel who will be most affected by any decision to outsource certain services should be fully engaged (although often facilitated by external, specialist consultants) in setting the performance parameters of the incoming service provider.

Of course, with the aim of service levels being to define measurable service targets, this process sounds easy. But in certain service areas, in particular those requiring significant human interactions and relying on personnel making qualitative decisions (eg, human resources), agreeing quantitative measures is not necessarily simple.

(b) *An example*

Even in what might be seen as comparatively simple services, the process can give rise to different considerations. Imagine that you have been tasked with setting meaningful service levels that can be quantitatively evaluated for call centre outsourced services. Now assume – not unreasonably – that your own key performance indicators are in part driven by customer satisfaction results.

The starting point might be to align your own internal key performance indicators with what you require the service provider to meet. However, the service provider might respond with the (not unreasonable) view that your own indicators are not quantitative, that they fail to take into account adequately other aspects of the organisation's performance (apart from the specific call centre experience) that might affect customer satisfaction, or that the service provider has its own tried and tested customer satisfaction measures.

You might therefore instead start to think about the sorts of things that drive good customer experiences and which therefore might reasonably be anticipated to be likely to affect overall customer satisfaction. In a call centre context, this might lead you to think about the following:

- How fast are calls answered? Or, to put the same issue another way, what is the maximum time a customer should be expected to wait until the call is picked up?
- Your customers are also busy people who do not want to spend ages on the telephone. So you might consider including a measure of the period of time that it takes to complete a call. But not all calls are the same and different

issues are experienced. What to do? Maybe some form of averaged time is the solution.

- However, your own customers are presumably calling about an issue that they want resolved without the need to call back. So you might think about a call resolution rate to measure the extent to which a customer calls back within a period of time after the initial call (this itself can raise other issues of course. What if the end customer simply had another unrelated issue? Often this might be managed through setting a target that allows for such variability).
- There is a tension, however, between a resolution requirement on the first call (which might take time) compared to a service level based on a required handling time. What is more important? Do you need to weigh the requirements? Do you impose different credit amounts if the service level is not met? Do you impose a credit only on the service level that you consider to be the most important?
- Of course, the end customer's resolution might occur only if the call centre representative then logs the required action in your own organisation's systems. So you might include another service level requiring relevant inputs to your own customer systems within a period of a call being completed.

And so on.

Then you have to consider the required performance targets, and whether these apply on a 24/7 basis (which will relate in turn to the call centre's required hours of operation). You might then return to the issue of customer satisfaction and require this to be included, although you may have to look at the methodology used or consider an alternative path to the imposition of credits if performance falls below a certain level.

A simplified version of the output of this hypothetical exercise could therefore be similar to the version below.

Service level	Service credit weighting	Measure
Call acceptance	25%	85% of calls answered within 10 seconds, 95% of calls answered within 15 seconds.
Average handling time	10%	The average time that it takes a consultant to answer and handle a call to be less than or equal to 2 minutes.

continued on next page

Service level	Service credit weighting	Measure
First call resolution	50%	The percentage of all issues resolved on the first call must meet or exceed 75%. An issue is deemed to have been resolved on the first call where there are no repeat calls from the same customer within 48 hours as measured by the relevant system.
Escalation	20%	Where tickets are required to be logged to the customer's CRM system as a result of a call, 95% of such tickets are logged within 1 hour of the relevant call being completed and 100% of such tickets are logged within 2 hours of the relevant call being completed.
Customer satisfaction	N/A – see measure	The customer will commission an external market research company to gauge end-customer satisfaction in accordance with the details set out in Annexure X. The service provider will provide the research company with a random list of 50 end customers who have dealt with the service provider in the last month. The results of the interviews are collated monthly, and a report is provided to the customer by the 10th business day of the following month. The survey will measure end-customer satisfaction based on the manner in which the service provider delivers the services, and not end customers' satisfaction with the customer's products or services specifically. The supplier must meet or exceed the customer satisfaction service level based on responses by customers to the following question, which will be scored out of 10, where 1 is the lowest score and 10 is the highest: "Thinking about all

continued on next page

Service level	Service credit weighting	Measure
		aspects of your most recent call centre experience, how would you rate the service provider's handling of your call?" The service provider's service level is that the average mean score from end customers is equal to or greater than 7. If the service provider does not meet this service level, it must provide to the customer a rectification plan that sets out the processes and steps that the service provider will take to remedy the non-performance. Any failure to comply with the rectification plan is deemed to be a material breach of this agreement, and if the service provider fails to meet this service level in 3 consecutive months or 5 months in any 12-month period, the customer may terminate this agreement for cause and the provisions of Clause XX will apply.

Where applicable, service credits will be determined by the following formula:
SC = MC × W × Lim
where:

- SC = the amount of the service credit to be credited to customer;
- MC = the amount of the charges payable by customer;
- W = the weighting that applies to the relevant key performance measure, expressed as a decimal (eg, 50% would be expressed as 0.50); and
- Lim = 0.10, being a percentage limit on the allocation of monthly charges in respect of a service Level failure, expressed as a decimal.

All of the above has a direct impact on the underlying commercial model. Put simply, the service provider will find it easier to commit to more testing service levels if it is able to apply more resources/people to the underlying services, but all of this needs to be paid for. The customer may accordingly have to balance out the service levels that it might ideally want against what it is prepared (or able) to pay for.

(c) Baselining and service level holidays

One of the issues that commonly arises in the transition phase of any outsourcing relationship is determining what the service level target should be.

Accurate historical customer data, where it exists, can be useful – although it is rarely determinative; after all, a skilled provider of services is usually expected to be able to perform services at a level higher than that of the existing internal personnel of the organisation, or possibly its legacy service providers/suppliers. Even where such personnel may be transferring to the employment of the service provider, the service provider's tools, processes and supervision may be expected to result in better and more efficient performance.

So, the view might be that the service provider's own historical performance with its wider customer base becomes the appropriate litmus test for setting targets. In some circumstances, where the service provider is deploying its standard service delivery model into an organisation that has sufficiently comparable systems, facilities and infrastructure as those of its other customers, this might well be appropriate. Or where effective market intelligence exists in the form of performance benchmarking, this also could provide an effective litmus test to guide the setting of service level targets.

However, there may be an aspect of transformation as part of the outsourcing initiative where systems and/or processes will be changed. What confidence exists in historical performance information in this case? Further, certain services may not have clear comparable environments – for example, where an application management service is being provided in a specific environment or over niche applications. Alternatively, the outsourcing arrangement may be fundamentally based on continual use of the customer's existing infrastructure or facilities, such that the service provider may not be able to effect improvements in historic levels of performance very quickly (if at all). In such circumstances, a 'baselining' process may be required as part of transition and where the service provider undertakes the services for a defined period, measures its own performance and then the resulting performance data is used to determine the service level targets. There are, though, a couple of key issues to consider in any baselining process:

- Given that the performance data will be used (at least in part) to set future service level targets, there is a perverse incentive for the service provider to underperform during the baselining period. Adequate contract protection and post-execution management can mitigate this risk, however.
- Once the baselining process is completed and the data provided, how will the targets be set? Should the data themselves automatically set the targets – for example, through averaging the relevant months of data or perhaps averaging but with highest and lowest performance months excluded to remove outliers (the latter being the service level equivalent of ice skating scoring)? Or should the data trigger a further negotiation between the customer and service provider? If so, what occurs if there is no resolution? Should an independent expert be used? If so, who?

Related to the transitional issue of the setting of targets is the question of when performance against those targets should be measured and from when any negative consequences of failing to meet those targets (eg, service level credits) should commence. Many outsourcing initiatives allow the service provider a period to 'bed down' its delivery model, tools and personnel before any negative consequence arises from any failure to meet service levels – often referred to as a 'service credit holiday' or similar.

There is nothing necessarily objectionable about holidays where a genuine need exists to bed down complex services or manage the results of a transformation programme (ie, on the basis that the service provider's focus will be on that rather than hitting service levels, which may well be a stretch target in any event). There is less justification for such holidays, or at least certainly ones of any significant length, where the services being performed are essentially generic and where no or limited transformation activities have been undertaken. As in all aspects of outsourcing, there is not a right or a wrong answer.

(d) Dealing with change

Unfortunately, 'set and forget' service level positions in long-term outsourcing contracts are questionable for at least two key reasons. First, what if the customer's requirements change over the duration of the term of the contract? Second, what if the market moves such that the service provider's competitors are providing better service at comparable prices (and, where those competitors are providing services to the customer's own competitors, the impact of this is not a palatable one)? This may, for example, result from improvements in the underlying technology being used to deliver the services, as opposed to the service provider having to work harder. Service levels therefore ideally need to be dynamic.

The tension here is obvious. The service provider has entered into the contract based on the agreed terms and conditions (and, indeed, it will have priced its services based on a certain risk allocation). If the customer requires flexibility around service levels, how is this risk of change to be priced? What should be the parameters of change? In a microcosm, this issue as it applies to service levels shows one of the most significant challenges in implementing effective outsourcing contracts and relationships: effective measures for dealing with change.

One approach to managing customer-required changes is to implement an ability to change the service credit allocation over time, allowing the customer to weigh service levels differently. This approach can be effective where the service provider may have been performing very well against certain service levels, but perhaps not as well in respect of others. This approach is often referred to as the 'pool allocation percentage' model.

The diagram below is an example of an adjustable pool where, in year 1, 20% of the potential amount of service credits payable has been spread across Service Levels A to J. Initially, this would suggest that the customer considered that Critical Service Levels A and E were particularly important, and so a greater proportion of the available service credits were allocated to those particular service levels.

Now, let us assume that in reality the service provider's performance against Critical Service Levels A and E turned out to be particularly strong, while performance against Critical Service Levels B and C was poor and required a greater level of focus. Under the pool allocation percentage model, the customer could address this by reallocating some of the potential service credits away from Service Levels A and E, so as to increase those for B and C.

As indicated in the diagram below, a key issue in any such adjustable pool is the timing of change – how regularly can the customer alter the allocation of service credits (once per year in the example below, which is common in the market although quarterly or biannual adjustments also occur). A further issue is whether the extent of change is entirely discretionary (as it is below), or whether there should be limits placed on the extent of change (eg, in the following diagram, the service provider may require a limit that the allocation of service credits can change only by a single percentage point. So, if this rule applied, the change in Service Level C from 2% to 5% would not arise and it could only be raised to a maximum of 3%).

	Allocation of potential service credit – Year 1 (% of monthly charge)	**Allocation of potential service credit – Year 2 (% of monthly charge)**
Critical service level A	5%	3%
Critical service level B	2%	4%
Critical service level C	2%	5%
Critical service level D	–	1%
Critical service level E	4%	1%
Critical service level F	2%	1%
Critical service level G	1%	–
Critical service level H	1%	–
Critical service level I	–	2%
Critical service level J	3%	3%
Total	**20%**	**20%**

Customer elects to exercise its annual right to adjust service credit weightings

What about the relevant service level targets themselves (ie, the actual levels of performance that the service provider is to achieve)? Should a customer be entitled to vary these and if so how? Again, this may depend on the leverage positions of the customer and the service provider, the requirements of the customer and the representations made by the service provider in any request for proposal or similar competitive offer process. However, mandated changes in targets – for instance, moving an application availability target from 99.5% to 99.6%, 99.7%, 99.75% etc each year – is not without precedent (and may arise because the project involves specific transformational obligations that should in due course improve service quality, or simply because the service provider is confident of its ability to improve upon the level of performance inherited from a previously in-house function. However, the customer will of course pay for the change through the pricing model developed by the service provider, so a key question should be whether a move from 99.5% to 99.75% over a four-year term reflects genuine value.

The ability of a customer to change the required targets unilaterally, without any form of limit, is understandably rare. Likewise, the ability of a customer to introduce new service levels and targets without consent is also rare. It may even give rise to considerations with respect to unconscionable conduct or similar concepts in certain jurisdictions. This is not to say that provisions cannot be included at least to frame a discussion with respect to such changes – for example, as part of an annual or quarterly review process where both parties are required to act reasonably, however typically the potential impact of such changes on the service provider's delivery model will result in a requirement of negotiation and formal amendment.

Similarly, general obligations on the service provider to ensure continuous improvement in its performance against service level targets are common, though the ability to rely upon such commitments from a legal, rather than commercial or relationship perspective is often questionable given the 'motherhood' nature of many such provisions. In any event, customers often fail to manage the service provider's performance adequately in light of such broader considerations (where the immediate focus is on the strict service levels imposed, not such wider, and more difficult to manage, concepts).

However, certain outsourcing models now seek to give such soft commitments some real teeth by adopting a mechanism where the service provider's actual average performance against the service levels over a year is measured and if it turns out to have been in excess of the required service level targets, the service provider's performance in the subsequent year will be reset to its immediate past performance level (or at least adjusted by some percentage of the delta between the original service level and the actual level of performance achieved). To go back to the application availability service, if this is set at 99.5% without any automatic adjustment, this model would hold that if the service provider's performance over a year averaged to 99.6%, 99.6% would be reset as the new service level target. There are, however, some important limits to this model that should be carefully considered:

- A rational service provider would be encouraged to do all it could to ensure that performance meets but does not exceed the existing service level target (and might argue in negotiations that it would be unfair for it to be penalised for better performance, by having its service levels increased). Improvements would then be unlikely to accrue. Attempts to remove this disincentive could be introduced, however, through a payment of a bonus for over-performance in the previous year. This raises complex financial modelling questions, however, and if the amount of the bonus is insufficient, the same prisoners' dilemma arises. Further, as noted elsewhere, where a primary driver of many outsourcing relationships is to reduce costs, the payment of bonuses could be seen as being anathema to that objective, even leaving aside the often difficult issue of internal budgeting for potential bonus payment.

- Even if the relevant incentives were adequately determined, the price impact of the service provider being subject to increased levels of performance might well see upward adjustments to the service provider's pricing model. So, if increased performance is not achieved, the service provider may not receive a bonus, but the customer may still be paying an increased amount for the potential increased performance (on the basis that the service provider will have factored this in to its pricing model at the point the contract was signed). Further, if increased performance is achieved and a bonus is paid, does the increase in the service level target reflect any genuine business value? If the business has agreed to a service level target of, say, 99.5% for application availability, that may simply indicate that a move to 99.6%, 99.7% or higher will lead to limited improved productivity and, therefore, no added value for the customer – in which event the payment of a bonus may make little business sense.
- Lastly, difficult discussions on the impact of externalities also commonly arise. In other words, to what extent should the service provider be able to rely upon improvements in service level performance that have occurred for reasons not of their making?

In terms of broader moves in the market, where other service providers are offering comparable pricing but better performance, benchmarking can provide an effective mechanism to ensure that comparability is maintained (see the chapter on charges and charging models).

3.5 A word on service credits

Service credits can easily be confused with liquidated damages. In many jurisdictions, parties to contracts are entitled to agree the amount of damages that will be paid in the event that a certain event does not arise. One of the better-known examples of liquidated damages is in the construction industry where liquidated damages are often paid for late completion.

However, there is also often a legal requirement in many jurisdictions that the amount of damages agreed by the parties be a "genuine and reasonable pre-estimate" of the loss that would arise from the relevant event. If the amount is more than that, the amount could be deemed a penalty with the consequence that the amount is unenforceable.

To use the building example, if a landlord had a completion date of January 1 and had lessees ready and available to take premises from that date, if there was any delay a genuine and reasonable pre-estimate of the landlord's losses might be determined by considering the expected rental income. If the specific amount of liquidated damages was more than that, in some jurisdictions the landlord would be unable to claim those liquidated damages. In short, liquidated damages are a measure of loss.

Should service credits be seen in the same light? Given that the intention of a service credit is not to compensate the customer for losses suffered as a result of a failure to meet the corresponding service level, but rather to reflect the decreased value of the services provided, an alternative is to view service credits as nothing more than a price adjustment. In other words, if you agreed to pay $100 for a service and if that service was performed late, $5 difference if reducing the price to $95 is no attempt to compensate the customer for the impact of the late service; it is a mere reflection of the diminution in value of the service provided.

There is danger, therefore, in assuming that liquidated damages, penalties and service credits are interchangeable terms. This needs to be assessed jurisdiction by jurisdiction in order to consider the potential impact upon the legal enforceability of the service credit regime.

The accrual of service credits can be calculated in many different ways. Below are a few examples.

Simple monetary amount: For instance, if Service Level A is not met, the service provider will pay the customer $X.

Percentage of fees/charges: As with simple monetary amount, but instead of $X, the amount then incurred as a service credit is expressed as a percentage of the relevant charges (usually calculated on a monthly basis) – for instance, 0.5% of the monthly charges per individual service level breach.

Pool allocation percentage model: This is alluded to in section 3.4 (d) above. Under this model, the total amount of potential service credits (again, usually expressed as an overall percentage of the service provider's monthly charges) is spread/allocated across the total number of service levels. From a customer perspective, the size of the pool to be allocated in this regard should ideally be more than the 'at risk' percentage, as otherwise the full 'at risk' amount will never be incurred by the service provider unless it fails to achieve all of the relevant service levels. Having an allocatable pool of between 150% to 250% of the 'at risk' amount is accordingly common (although the service provider will never have to pay/deduct more than 100% of the 'at risk' amount, even if more than 100% is notionally accrued); from a service provider's perspective, it will equally be important for the pool not to be too large, as this would materially increase the risk of the full 'at risk' amount having to be paid out in a given month.

One of the advantages of this model from a customer perspective is that it will often be set up on the basis that the customer can change the allocation of the overall pool across the various service levels so long as the maximum size of the pool itself does not increase. See again the example in section 2.4 above.

Service credit point model: This model starts with the assessment of the amount placed at risk to service credits in a given month (or other measurement period), but then divides that monetary amount by a denominator so as to create the value of a single service credit point. Knowing then the value of each such point, the customer and service provider will agree for each service level how many points should accrue if the service level is missed (often on the basis of more points accruing, the further below the required service level the service provider may fall). Thus, if a service level required a workaround for an incident to be provided within eight hours, a service credit point-based scheme might then state that five service credit points per hour would accrue for the eight to 16-hour period after the incident was logged, then 10 service credit points per hour for the 16 to 24-hour period, and then 15 per hour for each hour thereafter until the workaround is provided.

3.6 Service bonuses?

It is certainly not uncommon for service providers to position their response on service levels as one that includes statements similar to the following:

> *While appreciating that there needs to be an effective regime for ensuring service assurance and performance, where we are subject to a model which imposes a financial impact on certain levels of performance, there should be an equivalent opportunity for us to receive a financial benefit where levels of performance are exceeded. As a result, we propose a service bonus regime which mirrors the service credit regime.*

There is certainly no issue with any service level regime that includes bonuses where there is actual value derived from the payment of a bonus (ie, the payment of a bonus provides an incentive for a level of service performance or other outcome that the customer organisation considers is more valuable than the amount of the bonus) and the budgeting impact of a potential bonus payment has been factored in. This is ultimately a business call.

However, if no value arises from performance in excess of a service level target, should the service provider be entitled to an additional amount? Has the customer not already determined the level of performance that it requires and paid for that through service charges? Perhaps cynically, has the service provider not already included a risk buffer in its service pricing in the event that any service credits are not achieved so, in fact, there is no need for such mutuality? To give an example, if a service level requires that a call to a service desk be answered within an average of 30 seconds and the actual average time for answer is 27 seconds, the customer may well be pleased with how the service provider is performing, but will it have derived any additional financial benefit?

It is arguably more effective to divorce service bonuses from the detailed service level credit regime and apply such bonuses to less quantitative and more outcome-based measures such as customer or executive satisfaction.

Ultimately, however, the payment or not of bonuses is part of the customer's outsourcing philosophy – some organisations take a very firm view that in no event will bonuses be paid (perhaps linked to the primary rationale for outsourcing being cost savings). Other organisations may take a different approach. The customer should make its position clear, whatever its approach.

3.7 Linkages to termination rights

One of the other advantages of a detailed service level regime is that it can be used to pre-define the points at which poor performance will trigger a termination right (and so as to avoid a potentially difficult debate as to whether a failure to meet the service levels is a breach of contract and if so, whether it constitutes a material breach so as to justify contract termination). Detailed service level regimes may accordingly set minimum levels/thresholds of performance for truly critical service levels – and usually at a level some way below the point where service credits will start to accrue – on the basis that if such threshold is breached, a termination right will arise.

Aside from debating which critical service levels this kind of threshold should be attached to and the setting of the threshold itself, service providers can be expected to challenge whether a one-off failure should trigger termination, or whether it should be required to be repetitive (eg, a breach of a minimum service level two or more times in a rolling six-month period).

Other service level-related termination rights commonly seen are those relating to a repetitive breach of the same service level, or where the aggregate accrual of service credits over multiple measurement periods exceeds a set amount (eg, if more than 75% of potentially accruable service credits are in fact accrued across a six-month period).

For more in this regard, see the chapter on termination and step-in rights.

Charges and charging models

Kit Burden
Joris Willems

---

1. Introduction

Charges and charging models are a fundamental part of any outsourcing agreement – for the customer, because charges and the right charging models are often key to the decision to outsource certain operations, and for the service provider, because this dictates how much it can earn on the project, and what kind of profit it might then hope to generate.

For a charging regime to be successful in the context of an outsourcing contract, it must achieve a number of things:

- The customer should have a clear understanding of its existing costs for the services that it wishes to outsource, and how the costs after the outsourcing may differ. The charging regime must therefore set out as clearly and precisely as possible the price that the customer is required to pay for the various services.
- The charging regime must anticipate the wide variety of circumstances, both internal and external, that could affect the cost of delivering the services. Which circumstances should alter the price paid by the customer for the services and how will such price adjustments be calculated, and which circumstances should be for the account of the service provider?
- The charging regime must also interact properly with other important parts of the agreement – for example, liability provisions (as liability caps are often linked to charges on a 'risk versus reward' basis), service credits (which may operate as an automatic price adjustment) and termination (to enable the calculation of any termination payments).

There is no 'one size fits all' charging regime. Instead, a range of options must be combined in a way that meets the underlying objectives of each party, the nature of the deal in question and available budgets. This chapter accordingly considers some of the key parameters and options available to the parties in this regard.

2. Process for establishing the right charging regime

When parties are discussing which charging regime is the best one for their outsourcing project, they should (as a minimum) consider the following factors:

- the customer's top-level requirements. For example, a charging model that provides cost certainty is quite different to one that prioritises flexible charging for flexible service demands;

- existing costs. It is obviously essential that the customer does not procure an unaffordable service. Therefore, the customer should have a clear understanding of its existing costs for the services, and how the costs after the outsourcing may differ (and the service provider will likewise be keen to understand what such baseline costs are, both to know what target it has to aim at, and also to form a view of what kind of cost reductions are likely to be achievable, given the overall construct of the deal – for instance, the personnel or assets that it has to take on and the service levels that it has to meet);
- the service provider's expectations. The service provider should be given sufficient certainty of cost recovery and profit as early as possible in the negotiations. A brittle contract, caused by a charging regime that unduly penalises the service provider, does not ultimately benefit either party as a service provider under constant pressure because of narrow margins will inevitably be less flexible in terms of accommodating change (or at least more insistent on being paid for it);
- ease of use. The agreed charging regime should be clear, easy to understand and straightforward to use. Without this, it will prove difficult to track whether payments are being correctly requested and made;
- transparency. If variations to the charges are to be allowed, then the parties should ensure that there is a method for verifying these in a way that gives confidence to both sides;
- flexibility. It is inevitable during the course of the project that external factors will influence the cost of provision of the services. The chosen charging regime should anticipate these factors and decide whether and how these will impact on the price that the customer will pay.

3. Charging models

Various charging models are commonly used in outsourcing projects (with endless detailed permutations), each of which will need to be treated differently from a contract drafting perspective. When choosing a charging regime, probably the most significant issue is to strike the correct balance between certainty and flexibility. Another significant factor is whether the pricing will be calculated by reference to inputs or outputs.

Input-based pricing directly links the price to the amount of resources used by the service provider to deliver the service. Examples of inputs include day-rate pricing and pass-through of third-party costs. Input-based pricing is relatively transparent and easy to calculate. However, a service's input cost might not reflect its value to the customer. Also, the service provider may be less incentivised to develop efficiencies under this model.

Under output-based pricing the service provider is paid on the basis of what is delivered to the customer (eg, calls handled, computing power provided, numbers of transactions processed). This is an increasingly common model in outsourcing transactions, since it enables the customer to align the pricing more closely with the value to the business, and encourages innovation by the service provider, while also adjusting automatically to fit in with fluctuations in volumes in demand (subject to some caveats that we consider in more detail below). However, ensuring that the unit price is set at the right level and that payments are made only for the correct outputs can prove challenging.

What, then, are the primary charging options?

3.1 Time and materials pricing

A time and materials model is often used where the scope of the services is unclear or likely to be highly variable. It benefits from being flexible and easy to understand, but if used completely unrestrained, it shifts all of the pricing risk onto the customer. This model operates most effectively in combination with upper charging limits and strong contract management to ensure that the costs do not escalate out of control. It can in some cases be accompanied by an 'open book'/'cost plus' mechanism (whereby the service provider discloses its actual costs of providing the services, on the basis of being guaranteed to be paid a margin on top of them, albeit at a fixed/capped level), to give some greater control over the pricing; this model often incorporates a discounted rate for services as volumes increase.

A particular subject of time and materials charging is 'bodyshopping' or 'resource augmentation'. Under this model, the customer simply requires the service provider to provide personnel with particular skill sets (and hourly/daily rates) to work at their direction, usually then as part of a larger team together with the customer's own staff. Although sometimes described as a form of outsourcing it does not involve the service provider taking on any defined delivery responsibilities or any transferred business risk from the customer, and so does not qualify as outsourcing as discussed in the context of this book.

Depending on the type of services involved and nature of the commercial deal, a time and materials pricing model will need to include considerations of:

- rates applicable to different levels of experience (both in terms of seniority and types of skill set/specialism);
- splits between onshore/offshore rates (on the assumption that staff based offshore at locations with a lower cost base – such as India or the Philippines – will attract lower rates);
- minimum periods of notice required for personnel to be added to the services, or thereafter removed from them (if demand is ongoing rather than linked to the delivery of a more fixed scope of work, such as the completion of specific Application Development projects).

3.2 Fixed price

A fixed-price model has, on its face, certain obvious advantages. It is a simple model to understand (certainly compared with some of the other potential models where usage or other variables must be measured) and it should provide certainty for both sides. For example, the customer could agree to pay a fixed amount for the provision of an outsourced call centre, or set of support services for a particular set of software applications.

However, a poorly designed fixed-price model can fail to deliver either certainty or clarity. This is particularly so where the scope of the fixed price is too narrow, or a large number of assumptions in the contract prove to be incorrect. In these circumstances the service provider might seek additional charges that were unanticipated by the customer and (more importantly) fall outside its project budget. Such a scenario is difficult for both parties; the customer faces an increased bill and the service provider risks a deterioration in its relationship with the customer (and/or an impact on its margin, if the customer simply refuses to release additional budget).

In addition, a fixed-price model may not represent the best deal for the customer. The service provider will typically (and reasonably) build a premium into the fixed price to cover unexpected cost variations and the risk that its actual cost of delivery is greater than it had estimated. It follows that where the anticipated unexpected does not happen, the fixed cost might be higher than the total cost would have been under a time and materials model. What is more, the fixed-price model does not benefit from the flexibility inherent in a unit-based pricing model to ramp down the services (and therefore the cost) if demand falls; equally, renegotiation of the fixed fee will be required if scope or volumes increase.

Therefore, when considering a fixed-price model:

- the customer should allow the service provider to carry out sufficient due diligence to understand properly and fully the nature of what is to be priced for (which will minimise the number of assumptions built into the model) and so reduce the scope for future disagreements or debate;
- both parties should ensure that the boundaries of the fixed-price contract, and the implications of over-stepping such boundaries, are well defined. For a fixed-price contract, it will be even more important than usual to ensure that scope is tightly defined (along with, for example, any retained customer responsibilities) so that both parties have clarity as to what they will receive/have to deliver in return for the fixed fee;
- both parties should ensure that the services description is properly aligned with the chosen charging regime – for instance, without aspects being left for later agreement or subject to other variable factors, such as the need to comply with future changes in customer policies or changes in law or regulation (which will become an even more fraught area for negotiation than might otherwise be the case); and
- the control management procedures should be precise and sufficiently robust to prevent abuse of the change control mechanism. For example, knowing that the mechanism will be almost certainly called into play means that the parties will be sensitive to the negotiation of the costs of assessing requested changes and preparing change request notes (which would ordinarily otherwise be done without charge to the customer), and the customer will be particularly concerned to ensure that there is a pre-agreed rate card to apply to change control work, and possibly a means of referral to an expert for binding determination if parties are unable to reach an agreement.

3.3 Transactional/variable/unitary pricing

Often known as 'pay as you go', 'transaction-based pricing' or 'unitary pricing', this model focuses on assessing the charges upon a particular type of unit that is either a component of the services (eg, the number of devices to be supported) or an output from them (eg, number of transactions completed) – the key to this charging model being to ensure that the correct unit is chosen and is then expressed in the contract. For example, if the unit for the charging model in question is a call to a helpdesk:

- does this capture all calls that are made or only calls that are answered?
- does it include emails?
- is there a way to prevent double counting if there is more than one call on the same issue (eg, if the service provider's personnel hang up, or cannot resolve the call first time)?
- does it exclude calls that are a result of service provider failures (eg, if the call is being made to complain about a previous interaction)?

Equally, from a service provider perspective, it will be essential:

- to have a complete and accurate view of all input costs (including those being inherited from the customer in the form of transferring personnel, assigned or novated contracts etc); and
- to be sure that the selected units are, in fact, directly linked to the real cost of providing the services. For example, if a unit is chosen that has no real bearing on the service provider's underlying costs, it will not recover additional compensation when there are increases in volumes in respect of whatever it is that incurs additional expense (and so leave it increasingly out of pocket and without a means to recoup payment for its increased costs).

Getting this definition wrong from a customer perspective can result in the charges being considerably greater than anticipated, and from a service provider perspective can rapidly turn an attractive project into a loss maker.

The baseline volume for each unit should also be well understood in advance, as neither party will welcome actual volume levels that differ widely from expectations (and, indeed, the baseline volumes will usually be used as a means of calculating what the initial unit prices should be – eg, by dividing the base underlying costs between the baseline number of units – such that having an incorrect count at the outset could materially prejudice either the customer or service provider). Ideally, the outsourcing project should include mechanisms for forecasting volumes and ways to deal with spikes in demand. This will in particular help the service provider to ramp up or down its required resources without having to keep potentially expensive additional resources on hold for a level of additional demand that may never materialise (and that comes with a cost which would ultimately be passed on, at least in part, to the customer). Such forecasting provisions will then often link through to the service level regime as well, as the service provider may argue – with some justification – that if there is a sudden and unexpected increase in demand, its ability to deal with the increased volumes may be dependent upon its ability to assign more personnel to the services.

Most transactions-based models include lower and upper thresholds. The service provider will seek a minimum volume/payment at least to cover its fixed costs and the customer will argue for a price ceiling. Such models are often based on what is called an 'ark and rook' model, where the 'ark' is an additional resource cost (ie, the additional fee for each upwards adjustment in volumes with the actual unit cost then often decreasing in line with different bands to reflect the ever-increasing economies of scale) and the 'rook' is a reduced resource cost (eg, the amounts by which the charges will decrease, as volumes decline). As volumes decrease, however, there will come a point where the service provider will argue that its overheads and fixed costs cannot flex downwards any more, such that there is effectively a floor or minimum price. The customer may conversely argue that if volumes increase far in excess of the initial estimates, then in effect the overall deal has become very different such that a renegotiation should be triggered (with the potential of a low/no-cost exit, if the parties cannot then agree on revised financials).

Some models take into account unit volumes, but charge according to set bands. In these partially variable models careful consideration needs to be given as to where to set the banding. Once this is agreed, the customer should monitor its position to avoid needlessly underusing the capacity that it has (therefore overpaying) or blindly exceeding the banding (and, therefore, potentially, exceeding its budget).

3.4 Open-book pricing

Open-book pricing is now relatively rare in outsourcing transactions, but had a brief surge in popularity, particularly with deals involving public sector entities.

The principle behind open-book pricing is relatively simple. The service provider fully discloses all its actual costs in providing the services; it then gets to charge a set, pre-agreed margin on top of such costs. The service provider therefore can never make a loss, but the customer will equally be comforted that it should not find itself in the situation where the service provider is making 'super profits' (ie, a level of profit in excess of what might have been reasonably anticipated) at its expense.

The chief downside of open book (and probably the reason for its decline in popularity) is that it removes any incentive to innovate or improve, or to strive to find ways to reduce costs or streamline operations. The service provider knows that it will not suffer financially if it performs inefficiently, and in the same vein will not be rewarded if it improves its cost base so as to reduce its underlying costs. The customer may also have lingering doubts as to whether it will ever get a complete picture of the financials from the service provider, irrespective of what level of audit or reporting obligations the contract may contain.

4. Price variations

4.1 Cost of living adjustment and indexation

Across a multi-year arrangement (as most, if not all, outsource engagements will be planned to be), the service provider's underlying costs will be affected by a variety of inflationary factors. To take a few obvious examples, salaries of personnel are likely to go up and the cost of consumables will also be likely to increase, broadly in line with inflation.

What then is to be done regarding the charges? Should they also increase, in line with such underlying costs? Some outsourcing contracts will provide for this, such that the initial quoted charges will be subject to a periodic cost-of-living adjustment or other inflation-related index. If this is to be incorporated into the contract, the specific factors to be considered by the parties include:

- point of assessment – for example, is it following the first anniversary of contract signature, or at some later point?
- relevant charges to adjust – if, for example, the majority of the service provider's underlying costs are staff related, it would make sense to apply an index to those cost elements that relate to increase in salaries over the relevant period. By contrast, in a networks outsource deal, for example, bandwidth and IT-component costs are just as likely to go down than up and it would accordingly make little sense to apply the same kind of inflationary index to those cost elements as is applied to the salary-related ones. The solution may be to apply either different indices to different components of the charges, or a compromise index;
- indices to apply – if there is an agreement to adjust an element of the charges, there will be a choice of which index to apply. To take a UK example, two commonly seen indices are the Retail Price Index and Consumer Price Index, but they can produce markedly different rates of increase in the charges. Care must also be taken to apply an index that is relevant not only to the type of underlying costs, but also to where they are being incurred (eg, so as to apply an index that is relevant to the Indian labour market to costs associated with personnel based in Bangalore but a different one to those based in Boston); and
- whether there is to be a cap. In order to provide for an increased degree of budgetary certainty, many customers will in any event press for an index-related increase in the charges to be subject to an overall cap – that is, to no more than X% in any given year.

A customer may in the same vein seek even more budgetary certainty by refusing to allow for index-related adjustments to the charges at all, at least for the initially envisaged term of the agreement. In such circumstances, one of two things will likely happen:

- the service provider will effectively factor in what it assumes will be the required cost increases to its overall charges calculations, so as to show a charges profile that increases year on year (even though this may be tempered or even discounted altogether by cost savings or efficiencies that the service provider expects to be able to realise over the same period); or
- the charges will not show any particular uplift year on year, but the base charges will themselves have included an element of risk premium as applied by the service provider to help to guard against inflationary price pressures (eg, so that a unit price or day rate is increased by X%, as from the service commencement date and throughout the term of the agreement).

4.2 Contract extensions

Outsourcing contract procurements and negotiations are time consuming and expensive undertakings. If the service provider is generally performing well, therefore, and the customer is happy with the services being provided, the customer may prefer to have the option of extending the existing contract rather than having potentially to renegotiate it, or do a fresh procurement exercise. As such, many outsourcing contracts now contain rights for the customer to extend the initial term of the outsourcing deal, often by allowing up to two separate extensions, each of up to a maximum of 12 months.

This can be good news for the service provider in that it is securing new/extended work, and without having to compete for it via a new procurement process. However, the question will arise as to how much the customer should pay for the services during the extended period, at least unless the original contract allowed for year-on-year indexation increases to any extent. If it did not, then it would be prudent (from a customer perspective at least) to avoid leaving the charges to be negotiated and to include instead a provision defining what the charges will be in the extended period (or the mechanism to be applied to calculate them).

4.3 Changes in law and regulation

Quite aside from the service-orientated issues of the duty to comply with applicable laws and the division of responsibility for monitoring and notifying changes to them is the question of who should pay for any change to them if this impacts upon the services.

The more extreme customer position might be that any such changes should fall within the ambit of the transfer of risk associated with the outsourced servicer across to the service provider, such that the service provider should bear all such costs associated with changes in law or regulation. At the other end of the scale, the service provider might argue that its pricing reflected what it knew to be the position when the contract was signed, and that as the customer would have in any event picked up the costs associated with changes in law or regulation before the services were outsourced, it should have the same obligation to do so afterwards.

Both positions have some potential merit and it is thus perhaps no surprise that outsourcing contracts will often reflect a negotiated compromise, whereby the customer picks up costs of changes specific to it or its business sector (eg, whereby a bank would bear the costs of changes in financial services regulations), while the service provider would bear the costs specific to it as a supplier of outsourced services (eg, changes in minimum wages or regarding visa requirements for personnel dispatched to work in foreign jurisdictions). The middle bucket of costs, however – that is, those relating to changes in law that are general in nature and apply to organisations of any nature (eg, laws relating to health and safety, data protection etc) would still need negotiation and allocation, depending on the commercial construct of the relevant outsourcing engagement and the relative bargaining power of the parties.

4.4 Foreign exchange adjustments

Depending on the currency of payment in the applicable outsourcing contract and the country or countries in which the service provider incurs its main costs associated with its provision of the services, the service provider may be exposed to a degree of foreign exchange rate risk.

Different service providers approach this issue in different ways. Some of the larger suppliers will enter the international money markets and hedge their foreign exchange exposures (and their costs associated with doing so will form part of their corporate overheads and, hence, indirectly impact upon their base charges). Alternatively, the service provider may commit to bear the cost impact of variations between stated exchange rates (eg, US dollar and Indian rupee), provided that they remain within a set tolerance band by reference to exchange rates as at the date of contract signature, but on the basis that the charges may vary according to a set formula thereafter.

4.5 Assumptions and post-contract verification

Ideally, the pre-contract due diligence process will have provided the service provider with a clear picture of the required services and the likely costs associated with providing them, such that it can put forward clear and un-caveated pricing proposals (and the contracts prepared by the customer will often seek to enshrine this in contractual terms by expressly precluding the service provider from using any perceived defects in due diligence as a basis for seeking to vary the charges, post-contract signature).

However, the reality is that the due diligence information provided by the customer is often not as comprehensive as the service provider would like, or may even contain gaps or areas of ambiguity acknowledged by the parties. This can be addressed in the following ways:

- 'price for it' – a customer might take a more aggressive approach and require that the service provider simply add an element of contingency into its pricing so as to cater for the perceived risks associated with the gaps in due diligence. While this will result in budgetary certainty for the customer, it can leave the service provider facing the age-old 'how long is a piece of string' question, which may in turn lead to it having to include more contingency into its pricing than would be ideal (and may therefore result in the customer paying more for the outsourced services, overall, as such amounts will be payable regardless of whether the potential risks associated with the due diligence exercise come to pass or not).
- post-contract verification – if there is a good reason to believe that the information that was not available during due diligence will become available in a reasonably short period after contract signature (as might be the case if cost information is dependent on volumetrics, or information needs to be obtained from third-party signatories to transferring agreements), then the parties may agree to do a reconciliation/true up of the charges at the end of that initial period after contract signature. While such a process can in many cases be fair or appropriate, it is to be approached with caution as it will be performed after contract signature, when the parties have already bound themselves contractually to the outsourcing process.
- assumptions – alternatively, a service provider might identify certain issues where clarity is still lacking post-due diligence, and make specific assumptions as to what the 'true' position may be. For example, if the total

number of devices within scope for a break-fix service has not been definitively established, there may be an assumption that there are no more than [x] number of them. If the assumption is thereafter proven to be correct, the charges remain unchanged. If, however, the assumption turns out to be wrong, then a price variation is triggered (ideally, according to some kind of pre-defined metric so as to provide certainty, but often as an 'agree to agree' basis where the parties will need to have some further negotiation as to what the pricing impact may be).

5. Other considerations

5.1 Pass-through costs

A service provider may, in the context of the outsourced services, incur a number of costs other than those associated with its personnel. Some are fairly fundamental and therefore capable of being factored in to the main charges (eg, costs associated with key subcontractors, or software or hardware to be procured in order to deliver the required services). Others, however, may be more incidental and/or hard to predict (eg, travel and accommodation costs, courier charges or costs of office supplies and consumables in the content of many business process outsourcing-style engagements).

A customer may take the approach of requiring that the service provider's charges be framed as being inclusive of all such third-party costs. This is certainly simpler and provides budgetary certainty, but runs the risk of resulting in the customer paying more than it ultimately needed to (as the service provider will need to factor an assumed level of such costs into its charges – plus a risk margin/contingency – and will then benefit if it incurs a lesser level of such third-party expenditure).

Alternatively, the costs could be added on to the base charges, as and when they are incurred. In such circumstances, the contract will need to consider and specify whether:

- any particular policy is to be followed in the incurring of such costs (eg, as per the customer's or service provider's published policies);
- the customer's prior (written) consent has to be obtained; and
- the costs and expenses are simply passed through as incurred and without mark-up, or whether the service provider is entitled to apply any kind of margin or administration fee in relation to them.

5.2 Taxes

The service provider will expect to be able to add services/value-added taxes to its invoices, and the customer will equally expect not to have to bear any element of tax burden associated with the service provider's income.

However, often taxes may arise that will have to be provided for in the agreement, such as import/export duties and – more significantly with regard to multi-jurisdictional deals – withholding taxes. Service providers will typically want to have their payments grossed up so as to insulate them from the impact of any withholding taxes, while conversely the customer will want to avoid having to do so, even though it would at least be reasonable to expect the customer to provide some assistance to the service provider in its endeavours to obtain recovery of any withheld amounts that might otherwise lead to double taxation – for instance, by providing relevant documentation and proof of payment for production to the relevant tax authorities.

5.3 Overtime/out-of-hours working

Even in fixed-price or transaction/unitary-based charging models, there will likely be a need to account for payment for hours worked by service provider personnel out of normal business hours.

The first principle in this regard is that such payments should arise only for work done in addition to what the service provider is contractually obliged to do. For example, if a service provider is falling behind schedule against transition or transformation-related deadlines and needs its personnel to work longer hours to catch up, the customer would not expect to bear the additional costs of any related overtime. By contrast, if a customer asks a service provider to undertake a particularly urgent piece of application development work under an AD outsource contract, or a rushed-through installation, move and change under an infrastructure outsource deal such that the only way to meet the customer's time requests is to have staff work longer than normal hours, then overtime may be payable.

The contract will accordingly need to specify:

- what constitutes overtime. For example, what are the hours of normal work (which may vary depending upon the shift patterns for the relevant personnel, and may also need to be adjusted according to the country where they are based, which can be dependent on where the customer is located);
- what rates apply to overtime work. Will there, for example, be an uplift to a normal rate card, and if so how much?
- how overtime will be controlled. Does it, for example, need customer approval in writing? Is there a certain, specific individual on the customer side who has to give such approval?

Warranties and delivery commitments

Paul Allen
Jonathan Rofé

---

1. Introduction

Risk allocation between the customer and the service provider is a central focus of outsourcing contract negotiations, with the warranties and delivery commitments being two of the most critical components of this discussion. Put simply, the warranties articulate the key promises of each party to the other party, which, if breached, will allow the innocent party to claim at least damages for losses suffered as a result of the breach. It is this risk of being held liable for damages that at least theoretically, if not always practically, incentivises the parties to ensure that they keep their promises. One of the most important promises typically made by a service provider, outside of delivering the services to the service levels, is that it will honour certain delivery-related commitments, such as providing equipment, software or some other deliverable by a specified date and to specified requirements. Given the central role played by warranties and delivery commitments in risk allocation between the parties, significant attention is given to them in the outsourcing contract.

2. Warranties in outsourcing agreements

2.1 Background

Outsourcing transactions are complex contracts that require strong warranties to apportion specific risks and liability properly. While the definition and interpretation may differ from one jurisdiction to another, a 'warranty' may be defined generally as a guarantee given on the performance of a product or of the doing of a certain thing. In fact, contractual warranties ensure that risk is apportioned between the parties, that each party discloses known problems to the other, and that contractual protection exists where the law does not offer protection. In other words, it is a contractual promise or commitment, which if breached may lead to a claim for compensation or even give rise to a termination right.

In relation to the last stated purpose, it is important for parties to an outsourcing agreement to be aware of what local statutory laws may apply to the terms of its agreement as, commonly, such statutes will offer some level of protection. For example, for the sale of goods the French Civil Code grants buyers a mandatory warranty against latent defects that prevent or affect the use of a product to the point that one would not have purchased it had one known of the defect at the time. Similarly, the UK Sale of Goods Act 1979 provides implied warranties as to the quality of goods supplied and its fitness for purpose, while the Supply of Goods and Services Act requires that services be provided with reasonable skill and care.

Such implied warranties aside (which, depending on the terms of the relevant statute, may or may not be excludable by agreement between the parties), parties to outsourcing contracts usually negotiate a very broad range of contractual warranties that strike a balance between each party's rights and obligations, and that are more specific to the details of the outsourcing project in question. Hence, these agreements often include usual contractual representations and warranties – such as that each party has the authority to conclude the agreement – as well as a limited disclaimer of other warranties not intended to be part of the contract (eg, implied warranties or conditions of merchantable quality and fitness for a particular purpose or arising by law).

In practice, approaches differ when acting for the service provider or for the customer. A service provider should consider offering warranties that are relevant and meaningful to its customer, which means warranties that protect the customer from a risk better managed by the service provider – and vice versa for the customer. Whatever side of the table one is on, warranties should be specific to the deal at stake, objectively measurable and relevant to the concerned services.

A very long list of warranties may be included in an outsourcing agreement, depending on factors such as the scope, the complexity, the parties themselves and the risks associated with the outsourcing. Nevertheless, the most common warranties in outsourcing contracts are related to the performance and quality of software and services, data protection and security, intellectual property and legal compliance.

2.2 Performance warranties

The objective of performance and quality-related warranties is to ensure that the technology and services will be provided in accordance with certain criteria, which are set in reference to market practices (eg, warranty to perform services in accordance with state of the art) or contractual indicators (eg, warranty to conform to the service level agreement). The latter warranties generally aim to ensure that the service provider meets technical requirements such as a certain speed, availability, quality, access, interoperability, scalability or level of service. Performance indicators are usually specified in the contractual appendix named 'service level agreement', which sets forth different levels depending on the concerned phase of the outsourcing (ie, transition, run or exit). For further information, see the chapter on services and service levels.

The experience and skills needed from the service provider to design and supply the concerned services, or for the customer to receive and use them, are also often subject to specific warranties. For example, it is common for the customer to require the service provider to warrant expressly that the individuals performing the services will have the necessary skills, qualifications and experience to perform the services in accordance with the agreement. A service provider may in turn seek to caveat this warranty, if and to the extent that some of such individuals may be transferring across from the customer pursuant to the EU Acquired Rights Directive (ie, on the basis that it would be unfair for the customer to claim that the service provider is in breach of such an obligation, simply because of deficiencies in the quality of personnel that it has inherited from the customer).

2.3 Warranties regarding IP rights

IP rights should be properly defined and identified before drafting IP warranties to ensure that the service provider owns the appropriate rights and authorisations to provide the technology or service, including patents, trademarks, confidential information, trade secrets and/or any licence from third parties owing such rights.

By doing so, the service provider acknowledges that the technology or services provided by it do not violate or infringe the rights of any third party in any applicable jurisdiction. In case of assignment of ownership in new materials/ deliverables to the customer, the service provider must certify that it has the right to make such assignment and/or has obtained the relevant consent to make any such assignment from the relevant authors (eg, its employees).

The customer shall also be aware of any restrictions pertaining to the deliverables that it will get from the provider. In particular, the increasing use of open-source software in IT projects raises issues as to the limitations that the customer may face in its receipt and use of the services. It is therefore essential that the service provider warrant that either it will not include open-source software in the products and/or services, or that it will get the customer's prior consent before doing so. Any such consent will be subject to the customer knowing the type of open-source licence concerned and associated restrictions.

The service provider will often want some IP warranties from the customer too, particularly concerning rights of use for any third-party materials that it is required to access or use on the customer's behalf in the course of supplying the services (eg, third-party software products). The customer will need to have undertaken a thorough due diligence process in respect of the relevant licence terms in this regard so as to ensure that it has such rights and thus can safely give such a warranty.

2.4 Warranties concerning certain information

Security and data protection warranties have become common in complex contracts such as outsourcing ones. Such warranties concern the level of security, confidentiality and protection expected from the service provider, and refer to the measures of protection implemented by the latter in order to avoid (or limit) any threat to the customer's confidential information to ensure absence of viruses, backdoors or any other unanticipated IT risks.

As a consequence, outsourcing contracts usually set out obligations to remedy (or to use "commercially reasonable efforts" to remedy) any threats that may be detected and to put in place written and comprehensive recovery plans and security policy documents that include appropriate administrative, technical and physical safeguards to ensure the safety of confidential information, including in particular customer and personal data.

The service provider may also be requested to provide the customer promptly with notification related to any failure of security measures and security breaches, and/or to engage in planning of periodical audits of the service provider's physical, logical and information security controls. Such 'required notification' provisions may be more difficult to enforce in practice, however; what, for example, would be the customer's loss for a failure to notify of a confidentiality breach, over and above what it would in any event have been entitled to receive in respect of the breach of confidentiality itself?

Legal compliance warranties may also be needed to ascertain that the performance of the project will not violate applicable laws and, conversely, that the customer will operate in accordance with statutes and regulations of the specified jurisdictions. Discussions are usually held as to the laws that are within the scope of any such warranty. Typically, the parties will agree that the service provider shall comply with the law applicable to its business and the provision of the services while the customer complies with those applicable to its activity and the use of such services, but different approaches will apply depending on the nature of the outsourced services.

2.5 Remedies

Different types of remedy may be sought from a party in case of breach by the other party of a warranty. Remedies are usually set forth in the contract, but may otherwise apply in line with the governing law chosen by the parties.

Service credits are the most common remedies applicable to any (material or not) failure by the service provider to comply with the contractual service levels. Level of service credits may depend on the failure at stake, the consequences attached thereto for the customer (eg, costs associated to any delay), but more generally to the negotiation strengths of the parties. Discussions about service credits relate to:

- the indicators that may give rise to service credits;
- the formula allowing the calculation of such service credits;
- the cap above which the customer may not claim for such credits;
- whether such credits constitute the customer's sole and exclusive remedy; and/or
- whether such credits count towards the liability cap.

See the chapter on services and service levels for further analysis on this topic.

Remedies for breach of a contractual warranty also refer to the breach of any term of the contract that thus entitles the claimant to terminate the contract for cause and/or sue for damages representing loss by reason of such breach (see the chapters on liability and indemnities, and termination and step-in rights).

Indemnities constitute the other example of contractual remedy as an enhanced means of recovering financial loss, over and above what a damages claim would allow for. Several questions should be asked when negotiating them. Who does the indemnity apply to? Should it apply only to the contracting parties or be extended to other parties such as the party's directors, officers, agents, subcontractors, affiliates? What is the scope of the payment? Should it include only claims that have been proved or also those that have not been settled and damages related to third-party claims? What is the indemnity for and how far will it extend? Do parties have any other options such as receiving notice of a claim or the ability to conduct and control any related lawsuit? (See the chapter on liability and indemnities.)

If information provided is incorrect (when it had been warranted that it would be correct), the remedy sought may be different again. If a service provider was relying on a warranty of accuracy of customer information provided during due diligence, it will not want to sue the customer for damages, and instead will want a contractual right to vary its charges and contract commitments (ie, to be in line with what it would have said that it could do and how long that would take/how much that would cost, had it had the right information at the outset). Conversely, if the customer has the benefit of a warranty as to the accuracy of the service provider's original proposal (which is a warranty that most service providers will resist giving), then the remedy that it may want if the information is found to be (materially) inaccurate could be the right to rescind the whole contract.

3. Delivery commitments

3.1 Introduction

Whatever the service provider is responsible for delivering (eg, a turnkey telecommunications network, support for a series of software applications or a monthly performance report), the customer will want to receive some assurance that these responsibilities will be fulfilled successfully, especially in terms of quality, timeliness and price. The precise written terms of the outsourcing contract will have a strong influence on the likelihood of such fulfilment, and on what remedies will be available to the customer if such promises are not fulfilled. While this may sound ominous for service providers, those service providers with expertise in the relevant outsourcing market (and in contracting for such services) will not be put off by the prospect of such consequences as they will know what they can commit to, what inputs they will need from the customer to meet those commitments and where it is fair and reasonable for them to bear the risk of failure if things go wrong. Such service providers will treat delivery commitment discussions as an opportunity to set the project up for success, and will encourage a transparent discussion between the parties in relation to such matters. It is best for customers always to take this approach themselves, and to be wary of any service provider that does not do the same.

3.2 First principles

A delivery commitment, in an outsourcing context, is typically a commitment to achieve a certain outcome that meets a set of specified requirements by a specified date in return for a specified price. The main difference between the delivery commitment and a service commitment, therefore, is that the delivery commitment focuses on achieving an outcome at a set point in time, whereas the service commitment is continuous over a period of time.

How delivery commitments are described in contractual terms will depend on a range of factors, including the type of outsourcing, the jurisdiction in which the outsourcing is taking place, the extent to which the outsourcing involves delivery commitments, the fees payable in respect of achieving those delivery commitments and the importance of those delivery commitments to the overall success of the outsourcing programme. If, for example, the outsourcing involves the turnkey design, build, implementation and operation of a telecommunications network, the attention given to delivery commitments will be far greater than in the case of an application maintenance outsourcing that is primarily and almost exclusively concerned with service delivery (putting aside the 'book end' processes of transition and exit). At the heart of any outsourcing where delivery commitments are of substantive importance, it is normal to see references being made to:

- 'deliverables' (the tangible and/or intangible output to be provided by the service provider to the customer);
- 'milestones' (the definition of the outcome that must be achieved – eg, provision of specified deliverables, or the issuing of a final acceptance certificate for telecommunications network, or the completion of an interim milestone such as completion of the design phase in a waterfall-based software development project); and
- 'milestone date' (the date by which the relevant milestone must have been satisfied).

These terms, as described, will be used in the remainder of this chapter. They are unlikely to be defined in this way in the context of an outsourcing contract. The definitions given here are simply to provide a brief explanation of concepts that are fundamental to a discussion of delivery commitments.

3.3 Delivery commitment failures and remedies

Imagine the chief executive officer of a major financial services organisation waking one morning to newspaper headlines that his profits have fallen dramatically because customers have abandoned his company for competitors after repeated invoicing errors. Due to these errors, customers have been charged interest incorrectly, they have not received statements and they have found errors in their statements including purchases that they have not made, and so on. The reason for all these errors is a delivery commitment failure by ther outsourced service provider: it implemented a system that did not meet explicitly stated requirements, even if it conforms with the technical specification included in the contract. What can be done? The first step would be to reach for the contract, as it should, if properly negotiated and drafted, define the remedies available for the service provider's failure.

The above example, while fictional and extreme, is not absurd – outsourcing disasters of this nature occur from time to time. Far more common, however, are smaller failures that nevertheless have an impact on the overall success of the outsourcing programme (and consequently upon the customer's wider business). How such failures are dealt with will, at least in part, depend on what has been written in the contract. A poorly prepared outsourcing contract will cover only the most common contractual remedies – namely, damages for breach of contract and termination. While these two remedies may well be the most appropriate in a doomsday scenario, they are the least appropriate in terms of managing day-to-day risk associated with an outsourcing programme. After all, if one milestone date is missed by a handful of days, are you really going to sue your service provider or seek termination of the contract? Probably not. Indeed, unless you have incurred losses as a result of the breach, or the delay is deemed to be one that gives rise to a material breach of the contract, you will not even have such claims; you may just have to put up with the less than satisfactory performance. Equally, pressing for such draconian remedies will also increase the service provider's perception of the overall risk associated with the contract, which will then likely lead to higher risk premium being built into the charges.

Understanding what remedies are common in the context of an outsourcing agreement is an important step in determining what remedies to include in a particular situation and how the risk associated with the remedies is apportioned between the parties. Such remedies, and the risks that they present for the service provider, are set out in the following table.

Table 1 – Delivery failure remedies

The explanations provided in this table are illustrative only. The precise terms and governing law of the contract will dictate whether the customer has a right to enforce a remedy and will govern what the customer can expect to receive as a consequence of a successful enforcement.

Remedy	**If the service provider fails to fulfil a delivery commitment, then the customer has a right to:**	**The risk for the service provider is that use of the remedy:**
Escalation	escalate the matter to a senior member of the service provider's organisation so that it is brought to that person's attention in the hope that the person will, because of his position, have the necessary authority and inclination to fix whatever is causing the poor performance.	could become a nuisance for the service provider leading to organisational disruption, and potentially a lot of wasted management time if matters are escalated unnecessarily.
Rectification	• require the service provider to rectify the situation at its own cost; • undertake the rectification work itself, at the service provider's cost; or • engage a third party to undertake the rectification work, at the service provider's cost. In each case the intention is that the customer will ultimately receive the intended benefit of the original delivery commitment.	will add to the costs of the service provider, thereby reducing the expected profit to be made from the deal.

continued on next page

Remedy	If the service provider fails to fulfil a delivery commitment, then the customer has a right to:	The risk for the service provider is that use of the remedy:
Liquidated damages	be paid an amount of money calculated in accordance with a stated formula, such amount ordinarily representing a genuine pre-estimate of the loss that the customer has suffered as a consequence of the relevant delay (although whether this is an absolute requirement will depend largely upon the chosen governing law).	will reduce the fees payable to the service provider, thereby undermining the expected profit to be made from the deal, and may expose the service provider to such compensation even if the customer's actual financial loss was much less.
Refund	return whatever deliverable has been delivered and obtain a refund for any monies already paid for the relevant deliverables such that, while the customer does not benefit from intended delivery commitment, it at least has not paid for what has not been delivered.	will reduce the fees payable to the service provider, thereby undermining the expected revenue to be made from the deal, and also creating revenue recognition challenges from an accounting perspective (which are outside the scope of this book).
Step-in	increase the monitoring of, or even take over (to some extent) the operations of, the service provider as they relate to the outsourcing (see the chapter on termination and step-in rights) so as to increase the chance of the relevant failure being rectified.	depending on the terms of the step-in arrangements, may reduce the fees payable to the service provider, thereby reducing the service provider's revenue, and in any event, is likely to lead to a situation where the customer is in a better position to terminate the contract.
Performance bond claim	as a beneficiary under the performance bond, receive money under the terms of the performance bond from the issuing bank, such monies being compensation to the customer for the relevant failure without the need to go to court to prove any losses.	will result in the service provider losing the equivalent amount of money paid by the bank to the customer under the performance bond.
Breach of warranty claim	sue the service provider for the losses that it suffers as a consequence of the delivery commitment failure, with the amount of that claim being dependent on a range of factors including the liability and indemnity provisions of the agreement (see the chapter on liability and indemnities).	will result in dispute resolution activity that will incur costs and, if the customer is successful in its claim, will result in a damages payment to the customer. However, the service provider will also know that the threshold level of proof and litigation risk for the customer will mean that a damages claim is not a step that it will take lightly.

continued on next page

Remedy	If the service provider fails to fulfil a delivery commitment, then the customer has a right to:	The risk for the service provider is that use of the remedy:
Indemnity	make a claim under the indemnity for the losses that the customer suffers as a consequence of the delivery commitment failure, thus compensating the customer for the relevant failure (see the chapter on liability and indemnities).	will, if successful, result in a payment to the customer on an indemnity basis (ie, likely to enable a higher quantum of recovery than for a damages claim); plus, if the claim is disputed, the incurring of additional costs in connection with the dispute.
Termination	terminate the agreement for cause (the so-called 'nuclear option'), resulting in the relationship between the parties being brought to an end (see the chapter on termination and step-in rights).	if the termination is valid, loss of the relevant deal including some or all of the revenue expected to be received for the period post-termination.

In crude terms, the more likely it is that the customer will have the contractual right to enforce remedies of the type described above, the greater the risk for the service provider and, at least from the customer's point of view, the more incentive there is for the service provider to meet its delivery commitments. However, before customers take the approach of trying to have its service providers bear unreasonable levels of risk, they should be mindful that such an approach can be counter-productive and lead to undesirable results, and in any event to the service providers looking to increase their pricing so as to account for the increased risk profile of the overall deal.

The role of the customer is to ensure the success of the outsourcing programme. This requires that the customer ensure that a reasonable level of risk sits with the service provider. To a customer, it may therefore seem appealing to engage a service provider that simply accepts delivery commitment provisions which allow the customer to inflict a broad and severe range of remedies in the event that such commitments are unsatisfied. However, if such provisions are not aligned with market practice, one must question the motive behind the service provider's willingness to accept such a level of risk. Is it because it is desperate to win the work (and, if so, why)? Is it because it is building-in a high-risk premium that means inflated prices for the customer? Or is it because the efficacy of the risk transfer provisions has been undermined in some other way? If the answer to one or more of these questions is yes, the customer probably needs to rethink its approach. We would always recommend an apportionment of risk that is fair in the context of the individual outsourcing project.

3.4 Defining the delivery commitments

Given the significant harm that either party could suffer in the event of a delivery commitment failure, it is probably unsurprising that the related provisions of the contract are particularly hard fought in any contract negotiation.

Whether a delivery commitment has in fact occurred will depend, first and foremost, on how the delivery commitments have been described in the contract.

Common matters to be considered when preparing and negotiating this aspect of the outsourcing agreement are set out below.

3.5 Input versus output-based delivery commitments

Broadly, when it comes to the way in which delivery commitments are defined, the parties can choose between three common models – namely:

- input-based delivery commitments;
- output-based delivery commitments; and
- a hybrid of the two, with one taking precedence over the other.

For the purpose of explaining the three models, it is useful to consider the example of an outsourcing agreement that involves the delivery of a mobile telecommunications network on a turnkey basis. A mobile telecommunications network is a highly complex system made up of hardware, software and infrastructure that must be assembled and configured in a very precise manner so as to ensure that the network, once completed, can carry the intended network traffic and achieve the intended key performance indicators. If it does not, then the mobile telecommunications operator is unlikely to make its intended return on investment.

If the parties were to agree on an input-based model, then the service provider would be under an obligation to deliver to the customer only what is stated in the bill of quantities (ie, a long itemised list of equipment and software). Provided that these inputs are delivered to the customer at the time and place and in the condition required by the contract, the obligations of the service provider would be fulfilled. The risk associated with constructing the network so that it meets the necessary key performance indicators would thus rest with a third party, either the customer or another supplier. Therefore, this input-based approach carries a lower risk for the service provider than if the service provider was responsible for constructing the network.

In an output-based scenario, the customer is concerned only with the outcome, with this outcome defined by way of a set of output-based requirements that details at great length the functional and non-functional requirements of the network (ie, what will the network be able to do once it has been commissioned and is operational). The customer is unconcerned with how these requirements will be fulfilled, and so the inputs are irrelevant. In this case, the entire risk of fulfilling the output-based requirements sits with the service provider, even though the customer's position would be very uncertain, unless there is also a description of how the requirements will be satisfied. This type of approach is uncommon in the context of telecommunications networks, but is common in the context of application (software) development.

The hybrid option, where both the output-based requirements are defined and the service provider also provides its technical solution – that is, a description of the inputs and how the requirements will be satisfied (ie, bill of quantities, project plan, high-level design documents, etc). This approach is typical of IT and telecommunications network projects delivered on an outsourced basis. Where a hybrid option is chosen, the parties will still need to agree which of them carries the risk of the technical solution not satisfying the customer's stated requirements. For instance, if the telecoms network does not meet the key performance indicators because of a flaw in the design of the network, will it be the service provider that is responsible for correcting the design flaw and rectifying the failures at its own cost, or is this a cost that the customer must bear? How this issue is resolved will depend on a range of factors, not least of which will be the strategic value to the service provider and buying power of the customer.

3.6 Ambiguity

If a delivery commitment is unclear, then it becomes more difficult to conclude whether or not there has been a delivery commitment failure. Such an ambiguity may benefit either the service providers or the customer, depending on the circumstances. However, in either case, it is likely to result at least in some level of dissatisfaction because expectations of one party are not met or, in a worst-case scenario, a major dispute between the parties. Both parties should therefore endeavour to detail the delivery commitments as objectively and comprehensively as possible so that they contain no material ambiguity.

With the best will in the world, however, some level of ambiguity often creeps into the statement of delivery commitments. It is for this reason that the parties will sometimes agree that where there is an ambiguity within the delivery commitments, the service provider will raise it as an issue with the customer and resolve the ambiguity before proceeding (and hopefully, therefore, before any issues have a chance to develop). This is a common-sense and practical approach to dealing with low-level ambiguities or ambiguities that can reasonably be expected to be managed through operational or technical discussions during the outsourcing.

The precise terms of such an agreement present their own challenges. What happens if the ambiguity results in additional cost for the service provider? What if resolving the ambiguity to the customer's satisfaction will require more time than originally planned? What happens if the ambiguity, although apparent, is not raised by the service provider at the correct time (ie, when it first became apparent)? How these questions are answered will, as is often the case, depend on the circumstances. Needless to say, discussing such issues will be easier where the level and degree of ambiguity in the delivery commitments is minimal.

3.7 Reasonable endeavours

Where a service provider does not wish to commit itself to an absolute obligation, it will look to negotiate into the contract qualifying words as to the amount of effort required by it in relation to the obligation. As an example, an absolute obligation may be written as: "The Supplier shall achieve the milestones by the applicable milestone dates."

Subject to the other terms of the contract, the above obligation would mean that if the service provider either does not meet a milestone at all, or meets a milestone only after the applicable milestone date, it will have failed to meet is delivery commitment and will be in breach of contract such that the customer will have enforceable remedies against the service provider.

Where, by contrast, the service provider wishes to create a qualified obligation, it may seek to use wording along the following lines: "The Supplier shall use its reasonable endeavours to achieve the milestones by the applicable milestone dates."

By way of example, under English law, where the words 'endeavours', 'reasonable endeavours', 'all reasonable endeavours', 'best endeavours' or the like (sometimes these phrases replace 'endeavours' with 'commercial' or simply insert 'commercial' before 'endeavours') are used, even if the milestone is not met or met but after the milestone date, there may still be no breach of the contract if the service provider has satisfied the necessary level of endeavours as prescribed by the contract and relevant case law. The same or similar position exists in a number of other jurisdictions around the world. It is beyond the scope of this chapter to explore the case law in all of the main jurisdictions in the world in this regard. Suffice to say, customers and service providers alike will at times need to consider whether the obligation should be an absolute one or whether there is good reason to qualify the obligation through the use of such language. As a rule of thumb, if satisfying the delivery commitment is not entirely within the control of the service provider, there may be an argument to qualify the obligation in the way described, although a more precise approach would be to qualify the obligation by reference to whatever specific dependency it rests upon.

3.8 Milestones and milestone dates

Commonly, delivery commitments are defined by reference to milestones and milestone dates. It may be that the milestones include the delivery of specific deliverables, or the occurrence of some other form of outcome – for example, the completion of implementation of a system, system go-live or end of transition. Whatever makes up the milestone, it is critical to the enforceability of the delivery commitment that the milestone is properly described. It is equally important that the date for the achievement of the milestone is also defined.

There is sometimes a temptation to leave milestones and milestone dates to be defined after contract signature. While there can be good reasons for this, it is sometimes an area that is forgotten, especially if the parties are not incentivised to ensure that agreement on the milestones and milestone dates is reached in a timely fashion after contract signature. The consequences of ultimately not defining the milestone and milestone dates can be disastrous for the customer (as Case study 3 in the chapter on the role of the customer highlights) and can also adversely affect the service provider, particularly where payment is tied to achieving the milestone.

If it is impossible for whatever reason to define the milestones and milestone dates properly ahead of contract signature, the parties should consider what mechanism will help to incentivise them to reach an agreement in this regard post-contract signature. It may be that the contract is a framework agreement, in which case specific work orders or statements of work will contain the relevant details, with both the customer and service provider being suitably incentivised to conclude those documents by reason of the fact that no delivery or payment will take place until such agreement is reached. If that is not the case, it may be worth simply making such agreement a condition precedent to the commencement of any delivery or payment obligations.

3.9 Warranty periods

In an outsourcing agreement involving the delivery of some form of IT Services, the service provider typically commits to fixing deliverables that are defective during what is known as a warranty period. This is akin to being able to have broken parts of a new car repaired under a warranty for a period of time after the car is first purchased. Of course, there are important differences between cars and information technology that make the terms of a car warranty unsuitable in this context, however, the principles of the warranty are not dissimilar.

In the IT context, it is almost inevitable that when a solution becomes operational, defects will appear that were not identified during testing, no matter how exhaustive the pre-go live tests may have been. Because of this, the parties will either agree to some form of maintenance arrangement in respect of the solution, or that the solution will be subject to the warranty period, or both. Where a warranty period is chosen, the parties will need to agree on:

- the length of the warranty period;
- the defects that will be corrected under the warranty period (all defects, or material defects, material defects that cause particular severity levels of incident or something else); and
- the extent of the obligation of the service provider to correct the defect, including in terms of timing.

3.10 More on remedies

Assuming that the parties have drafted the outsourcing contract to the highest standards so that the delivery commitments are clear, comprehensive, objective and free of ambiguity, and the service provider then fails to deliver, the customer will still have to consider whether the remedies as specified in the contract are available. Of the remedies stated above but not covered elsewhere in this book, customers and service providers should be aware of the following important issues when preparing the relevant provisions of the outsourcing agreement.

(a) Escalation

Customers view escalation as an important early intervention tool that allows them to reach out to senior representatives of the service provider in order to resolve problems before other remedies need to be invoked. While nothing prevents a customer from making such approaches even where the contract is silent on the matter, incorporating the remedy explicitly in the contract gives the service provider a level of comfort by offering a named stakeholder to approach. For such provisions to be effective, they should:

- identify when they may be used;
- stipulate who within the service provider's organisation the customer may contact, certainly by title and perhaps by name also; and what action the service provider representative should then take to resolve matters.

(b) Rectification and refund

Rectification and refund are considered here together as these remedies may be considered in life at the same time or consecutively in respect of the same failure. A clause in this regard may read as follows:

If the Supplier fails to achieve the relevant milestone following any tests and such failure is due to a Defect in a deliverable, the Customer shall have the option to:

(a) require the Supplier to continue to cure the Defects at its own cost as soon as possible; or

(b) engage a third party to correct the outstanding Defects, in which case the Supplier shall reimburse the Customer for the charges of that Third Party which exceed the Fees the Customer would otherwise have paid to the Supplier for the relevant deliverable;

(c) reject any particular deliverable in which the Defect(s) exist and the Supplier shall refund in full any monies paid by the Customer which are directly attributable to such rejected deliverable(s); or

(d) accept the deliverable as partially complete/delivered but with a reasonable adjustment to the Fees in respect of that deliverable.

(c) ***Liquidated damages***

Perhaps the most common form of remedy for delay, liquidated damages provisions are often the source of significant contention and will give the customer a right to be paid money by the service provider where the service provider fails to fulfil its delivery commitment (irrespective of the customer's actual loss). This obligation to make a payment, even if it is just a reduction of the fees payable, is a key risk for service providers and also creates certain accounting complications. A typical liquidated damages clause reads as follows: "Each time the Supplier fails to achieve a milestone by the milestone date, it shall pay the Customer liquidated damages to be calculated in accordance with the formula set out at clause [x]."

Putting the commercial elements of the liquidated damages remedy to one side for the moment, this is one of the remedies where the law governing the contract is particularly relevant to the way in which the provisions of the contract are drafted. For example, a well-established English common law rule states that penalties are unenforceable, meaning that if the court were to determine that the payment of the liquidated damages would amount to a penalty on the service provider (ie, an amount in excess of what level of loss the customer might reasonably have expected to have as a result of the breach in question), the service provider would not be obliged to make such payment. Broadly, the courts will not make this finding if the amount payable is held to be a genuine pre-estimate of the loss likely to be suffered as a consequence of the breach. Accordingly, contracts governed by English law will often contain the following language:

The Supplier acknowledges and agrees that liquidated damages payable by the Supplier under this Agreement are a genuine pre-estimate of loss or damage likely to be suffered by the Customer as a result of any delay in the achievement of the milestones by the applicable milestone date.

However, even if a contract contains this language, it is no guarantee that a court will not determine that the amount payable as liquidated damages constitutes a penalty. For that reason, it is important for the customer to consider what losses it will suffer as a result of the service provider's delay, and to ensure that the method of calculating the liquidated damages will reflect this amount.

As for the commercial considerations, key matters to be considered include:

- the method of calculating the liquidated damages;
- whether the liquidated damages should be capped and, if so, at what amount;
- whether there are any circumstances where the liquidated damages would not be payable (ie, because the service provider is relieved from liability for the delay – see the chapter on services and service levels for a discussion of relief events);
- whether the customer will have a right to have liquidated damages paid directly to it or to deduct them from the fees or both; and
- whether the amount payable for liquidated damages will sit inside or outside of any cap on liability.

(d) *Performance bond*

In certain jurisdictions, customers will often mandate that service providers offer a performance bond as a condition of contract award. Understandably, this requirement may make service providers nervous, especially if coupled with all of the usual commercial and legal leverage tools commonly found in outsourcings contracts. Some might argue that performance bonds are a step too far, acting as a Sword of Damocles that instils fear in a supplier rather than focusing on strong delivery. Such arguments aside, performance bonds are common in some procurement settings (most notably public procurement in the Middle East), meaning that customers and service providers alike must negotiate their terms in order to close deals.

A performance bond is a financial instrument issued by a bank in favour of a beneficiary (ie, the customer), under which the bank promises to pay monies to the beneficiary in certain circumstances and up to a certain amount. Sometimes a different name is given to these instruments, such as a 'bank guarantee' or, where they are given as security for an advance payment, an 'advance payment guarantee'.

In public procurements, applicable procurement laws may also make it impossible to circumvent performance bond requirements. In either public or private sector procurements, service providers should not feel that they must blindly accept the requirement, because they may be able either to offer an alternative or at least negotiate the terms on which the performance bond is issued. In this regard, numerous elements of the performance bond and the supporting language of the related contract can be discussed between the parties in an effort to reach a mutually acceptable position.

Typically, customers (and banks) prefer the performance bond to be unconditional/on demand, meaning that the customer need only call on the bond for the bank to then be obliged to make that payment. As an alternative, pre-conditions can be attached to the performance bond such that, unless those preconditions are fulfilled, the bank will have no obligation to pay. Such preconditions might be as simple as a notice sent to the service provider, right through to a court order for damages having been issued against the service provider.

The merits and practicalities of including preconditions need to be considered by the parties at the time of negotiation.

Although it is not essential, it is not uncommon for the related outsourcing contract to include performance bond-related provisions, including the:

- value of the performance bond. Customers should be aware that the cost to the service provider of the performance bond will increase with its value, and that such costs will more than likely be passed on to the customer. Accordingly, coming back to the Sword of Damocles image, increasing the size of the sword does not necessarily benefit the customer once the sword is already large enough to destroy the deal for the service provider if it is swung;
- duration of the performance bond, commonly tied to such things as milestones, the term of the contract or a period after the contract ends to cover potential post-completion claims; and
- contractual conditions to be satisfied before the customer may call on the performance bond. If such contractual conditions are included but not satisfied, a bank that has issued an on demand bond will still be obliged to pay once it is called upon (ie, the performance bond operates independently of the contract). Inclusion of conditions, however, has relevance if the service provider wishes to restrain payment under the bond.

Irrespective of what is negotiated, circumstances may arise in which the customer wishes to call on the performance bond. When a performance bond is called upon (or when the threat of doing so is great), a service provider may (depending on applicable law) seek an order from the court against the bank in order to delay payment until a substantive case regarding any underlying dispute can be heard. Any unmet conditions contained in the contract may support the relevant court application. If such conditions are not met and payment is made or threatened under the bond, the service provider may also bring or threaten a damages claim against the customer for breach of contract. Given these possibilities, both the customer and the service provider should be aware of the local laws relevant in such proceedings and ensure that its contract management practices will support any such proceedings.

Calling on a performance bond is in any event likely to have grave consequences for any customer/service provider relationship, making it a remedy often considered to be of last resort. If the performance bond sword is swung, the terms of the performance bond and the related contract may determine whether the sword lands where it is meant to or misses the mark completely.

4. Conclusion

In the context of outsourcing, one size does not fit all, and so no cookie cutter approach can be taken to the definition of warranties, delivery commitments and corresponding remedies in outsourcing contracts. The parties to the contract should seek to understand precisely what it is that the customer requires and fashion warranties and delivery commitments to support those requirements in a way that apportions risk appropriately for the deal at hand.

Confidentiality, intellectual property and data

Jan Geert Meents
Duncan Pithouse

1. Introduction

Data and information are everything. They encompass product designs, trading data, accounting records, customer records, bank account details, supply chain structures and much more. If this data and information are lost, the party to which they belonged will likely struggle to do business – either efficiently or at all – and will quite possibility be exposed to significant claims from customers and censure from regulatory authorities.

Even businesses that do not trade in information, such as manufacturing companies, have significant and valuable databases that need protecting.

Businesses that are reliant on data, such as financial services businesses, put the protection of data at the forefront of everything that they do.

Moreover, businesses are forced by an increasing raft of legislation and regulation to ensure that data is protected.

Businesses therefore face a triple threat if they cannot protect data and information properly:

- their business is harmed because either they do not have the information on which they relied to trade, or the value of their business is diminished because secret information is now disclosed to competitors, removing their own competitive advantage;
- lost data and information can upset customers, who can then take their business elsewhere and bring claims against the company; and
- regulators have a keen, and increasing, interest in the protection of data and information, with the ability to levy material fines for data breaches.

With any outsourcing deal, the service provider is likely to have direct access to, or at least the means of accessing, the customer's confidential information. Such confidential information could well be the lifeblood of the customer's business activities, and probably contains at least some of the customer's own end clients' information. Losing or disclosing such information would create material issues for the customer in terms of being able to service those end users, and for the end users to maintain trust in the customer – trust being key to enabling the customer to grow its business.

There is, then, little option but to ensure that appropriate protection is afforded to information and data at all stages of an outsourcing engagement.

Protection of intellectual property is the more traditionally obvious focal point for any business that appreciates the concept of ensuring that no one can use what is valuable.

But outsourcing contracts are not simplistic IP rights assignment documents or licences. Outsourcing arrangements encompass a wide range of different IP rights and different use scenarios. Outsourcing arrangements generate different IP rights at different times and require parties to merge their own IP rights to generate an output or services for the customer. And then the agreement comes to an end and the parties need to part ways, but this cannot lead to a simple packing of suitcases and going their separate ways; the service provider's intellectual property is likely to have become an integral part of the customer's business organisation and activities such that stripping it out would likely have a material impact on the customer's ability to function successfully or at all.

So outsourcing contracts need to look at intellectual property as it exists in various states and at various points in time; they should include provisions that will afford appropriate protection to both the service provider's intellectual property, which is arguably the very reason that the service provider exists, and to the customer's business operations.

This chapter looks at the following topics as they apply to an outsourcing arrangement:

- confidentiality;
- IP provisions, especially in connection with how the customer and the service provider can reuse material generated as part of the relevant services;
- data security provisions; and
- the data protection provisions.

2. Confidentiality in the bid process

Confidential information will be disclosed and shared during the bid and procurement process for an outsourcing contract. As it is doubtful that all bidders will sign a contract with the customer replete with confidentiality provisions at the outset of any request for proposal process, it is important to set some parameters around the disclosure of information at as early a stage as possible.

To enable potential service providers to make meaningful submissions, the customer will need to disclose matters such as the fact that it is interested in outsourcing and details of its operations, staff and levels of services historically received, among other things. The service provider would disclose, in any bid response, details of its service delivery model, of its technological solution, of pricing and so on. Both the customer and the service provider will consider all these elements confidential.

It would be usual therefore for the customer either to issue and require the return of a non-disclosure agreement prior to sending out any bid documents, with such agreement covering the continued exchange of information up until signature of the agreement (if any), at which point the outsourcing agreement would supersede, or to include in the tender documentation robust confidentiality terms and to be clear that continued participation in the tender process is deemed to be acceptance to these terms. The latter solution, however, might not work in some continental

European countries where silence regarding proposed terms does not necessarily mean consent to those terms.

The terms would probably need to have particular nuances against a standard series of non-disclosure and non-use provisions in respect of confidentiality obligations.

First, often the provisions would be one way in favour of the customer only, such that only the bidder is bound by the terms. If the customer is bound by the terms, it will need to be clear that it can use and disclose the bidder's confidential information to its own advisers.

Second, there will usually be a clear prohibition on bidders disclosing the information to anyone at all without the customer's consent. This is to control the confidentiality risk, but also to give the customer control over the make-up of the service provider and who would be involved in the delivery of the services to it. This restriction will often expressly extend to other bidders in the same process as to remove the possibility of any collusion between the bidders.

Third, if the customer is subject to the terms of the confidentiality restrictions, it will often make it clear that it can take the ideas and proposals made by the bidders and use these as part of the broader procurement process, including – expressly or implicitly – asking the other bidders to consider bidding on the same basis or to incorporate these ideas in their own proposals.

Clearly, there will be some degree of reticence on the part of the service providers to enable competitors to understand and then leverage their own ideas, especially if this would likely put them at a disadvantage in the bid process.

It would be preferable to avoid negotiating the terms of participating in a bid process when there is likely to be detailed negotiation on the terms of the agreement itself. So, if the bidders raise concerns about these provisions the customer can be faced with three options as to how to approach it:

- It can simply say that the terms "are what they are" and if the bidder wants to participate, the bidder must accept them. There is then a risk that the bidders do not participate, or that the process starts off on an unnecessarily adversarial basis.
- It can concede the point, but this is likely to cause some issues in terms of getting the benefit from a multi-party bid process designed to get the overall best solution from the process.
- It can draft the provisions in the first instance so as to be clear that it is the general concept of the ideas that would be shared, but not the specifics of any service delivery model and not the specifics of any charging model that might, for example, give an insight into the other bidder's commercial offer. The generality of this approach is usually enough to avoid any disputes as to the terms of participation.

3. Confidentiality in the outsourcing agreement

Duties to protect confidential information exist even if there are no clauses requiring information to be kept confidential. For information to be kept confidential, the information itself must have the quality of confidential information and it must have been disclosed in circumstances that indicated that it should be kept confidential. Further, in some countries business secrets are protected by specific laws (deliberately leaving open what a business secret is exactly).

There can, therefore, be debates and disputes as to whether the information had the necessary quality and whether there was an intention behind the disclosure that it be kept confidential. While marking documents 'private and confidential' can clearly assist in this process, not all information is disclosed in documents and not all documents will or can be marked 'private and confidential'.

On the basis that one of the fundamental purposes of a contract is to avoid disputes by providing for a clear set of ground rules for the relationship, it is normal and appropriate to state clearly the nature of information to be kept confidential and the basis on which it would be kept confidential.

3.1 What is confidential information?

A common definition of confidential information in an outsourcing contract might read as follows:

"Confidential Information" means all information which is disclosed by one party to the other whether before or after the date of the Agreement, which is designated in writing as confidential or would appear to a reasonable person to be confidential and which relates to a party's (or any member of that party's Group's) business and including its products, operations, processes, plans or intentions, developments, trade secrets, knowhow, design rights, market opportunities, personnel, suppliers and Customers of the party disclosing it, all Customer Data and all information derived from any of the above together with the existence or provisions of the Agreement and the negotiations relating to it.

Note how in the drafting above the information still needs to have the quality of confidence – that is, not all information will fall within the definition of 'confidential information'; to qualify as confidential information, it still needs to be either marked 'confidential' or appear to a reasonable person to be confidential, or it needs to fall within one of the defined classes of information in the definition.

One area of debate on the definition of 'confidential information' is whether IP rights and know-how should be included. Their use is often subject to the IP provisions and, thus, they arguably neither fall within the definition of 'confidential information' nor are they subject to the confidentiality provisions for fear that one set of provisions cuts across the other and so removes some benefit of rights granted under – most probably – the IP licensing provisions. We cover this issue in more detail below.

3.2 Whose information is protected?

The very first issue to consider is who is covered by the confidentiality provisions. Some customers will assert that only their own confidential information is protected, such that any provisions within the agreement are one-sided in favour of the customer only. This argument is largely predicated on the size of the customer organisation, the lack of appreciation of what is confidential and the consequent unwillingness to accept the risk that it might be in breach of provisions, which in turn could expose it to liability.

More common, though, is a general reciprocal set of confidentiality provisions, albeit with some special treatment for the use by the customer of confidential information that it receives (see below).

3.3 What do the confidentiality provisions say?

In terms of the confidentiality provisions themselves, it is usual to include a standard series of confidentiality clauses detailing:

- an obligation to ensure that confidential information is kept confidential;
- an obligation not to disclose the confidential information to any third parties with some limited exceptions (see below); and
- exclusions from the definition of 'confidential information', usually in relation to:
  - disclosure with the prior written consent of the disclosing party;
  - information that was already in, or goes into, the public domain other than by reason of a breach of the agreement; and
  - independently developed information.

One other common exception to the obligation to keep confidential information confidential is where the information is required to be disclosed by a court or regulatory authority. The rationale for this is, fairly obviously, that if a court or regulatory authority directs a disclosure, then it would be impossible to refuse this on the basis of confidentiality obligations and, yet, it would not be reasonable to be put in breach of those obligations when responding to such a direction. However, this should not be treated as a carve-out from the definition of 'confidential information' since this would mean that, whatever information the court or regulatory authority requires to be disclosed becomes non-confidential and, therefore, could be disclosed more widely. Instead, it should be clear that disclosure to a court or regulatory authority does not constitute a breach, but that the information itself is still confidential.

3.4 Permitted disclosures

There are two principal exceptions to the obligation not to disclose the other party's confidential information. The service provider will need the ability to disclose the customer's confidential information to its own subcontractors, contractors and representatives. It will of course be important for the customer to understand the definitions of these classes of recipients so as to keep control over the disclosures both in terms of keeping an audit trail of the identities to whom the confidential information has been disclosed, and also to minimise the probability of the confidential information being inadvertently released – that is, the more people it goes to, the higher the probability of a disclosure.

Moreover, the customer will want to be clear that the service provider is responsible for the compliance with the confidentiality provisions by the relevant recipients so as to ensure that the customer can bring claims against the service provider for the recipient's misuse of the confidential information.

The customer should ensure that:

- it has the ability to use and disclose the service provider's confidential information to enable it to gain the benefit of the deliverables; and
- it can pass the service provider's confidential information to the customer's other suppliers, to the extent required for the other suppliers' provision of goods and services to the customer.

The first point is intended to ensure that notwithstanding the licence granted to the customer in respect of any pre-existing intellectual property that may be in the deliverables, the service provider cannot seek to restrict the use of that element of the deliverables (and, therefore, in likelihood all the deliverables) by claiming that its use is subject to the confidentiality provisions, which themselves prohibit the use and disclosure of the service provider's confidential information by/to third parties.

The second issue is often a hard-fought point with the service provider itself. On its face, it enables the customer to ride roughshod over the confidentiality provisions that it has just committed to by permitting the customer to disclose the service provider's confidential information with some degree of impunity and to the precise class of person that the service provider is likely to be concerned about – namely, its competitors.

For a customer, however, it is all about facilitating a joined-up supply chain that can support its business operations without fear of tripping over confidentiality restrictions. For example, in an IT outsourcing, there is a real possibility that the customer might have to disclose information with regards to the service provider's confidential processes or system infrastructure to enable other IT providers to supply their goods and integrate them into an overall IT service.

Conversely, a service provider will want to limit the scope of these exposures even though many suppliers recognise the customer's need to disclose some elements of its confidential information. Principal among the service provider's concerns will often be the protection of its commercial model and details of its pricing, and protection of proprietary systems and processes that it considers are its 'crown jewels' or market differentiator. A fine balance needs to be struck. The important issue is to explore what the customer really needs to be able to disclose and seek to achieve an appropriate right for the customer to disclose that class – bearing in mind that the provision needs to subsist for a number of years and so needs to consider the potential of change in circumstances, not just the immediate and prevailing circumstances. What this means is that the customer usually agrees not to disclose details of the service provider's charges, and seeks to give the service provider comfort as to the scope of the likely disclosure by virtue of being able to disclose the service provider's confidential information only to the extent that it needs to do so to enable another supplier to provide goods and services.

3.5 Return of confidential information

Typically, there will be an obligation to return each other's confidential information, either when it is no longer required and certainly at the end of the contract term. This is to mitigate the possibility that the receiving party pays less attention to the importance of keeping the information confidential when the relationship is at an end such that a disclosure is more likely, and also because the confidential information probably has some inherent value such that it should not be used when the outsourcing relationship is at an end.

In respect of this obligation:

- the customer should not be obliged to return confidential information that it continues to need to gain the benefit of the services and deliverables. Likewise, it is important that the continued application of the confidentiality provisions does not affect the ability to use the deliverables, as discussed above;
- the parties may well need to keep a copy of the other's confidential information for audit and regulatory purposes – especially if they retain obligations to auditors to disclose information relating to the transaction for some time after. Therefore, it will be important for a party subject to these provisions to ensure that the obligation to return is qualified by the ability to retain a copy for these reasons, albeit subject to continued compliance with the confidentiality provisions;
- there can be a risk that having returned confidential information, it becomes more difficult to understand and build a picture of any rights to bring claims against the disclosing party. For example, if the receiving party has returned working documents that do not constitute deliverables (which the customer is entitled to retain and use), its ability to understand whether the services were provided in accordance with good industry practice will be more limited because this requires an analysis of what the service provider actually did and how it did it, which can be ascertained only by looking at working files. So, having to rely on disclosure exercises will be less advantageous to a party;
- the references to the term in this context should properly encompass any termination assistance period so that the customer is not obliged to return information that it continues to need to use. As above, it will therefore be important to ensure that the continued ability to use with the customer's other providers includes replacement providers and any advisers on a re-procurement exercise; and
- in reality, it may simply not be practicable – either from a reasonable point of view or from the sake of what is actually possible – to return confidential information, especially if it is within an IT system in a disseminated form. It might therefore be appropriate to settle on the fact that the recipient will not use the other's confidential information, save for the point made in the first bullet point above. Alternatively, the parties can agree that confidential information is to be deleted instead and that the deleting party must confirm in writing to the other party that the confidential information was actually deleted.

3.6 How long do the duties of confidentiality last?

One school of thought is that the duties of confidentiality last for a finite period of time, and that such period would be set out in the agreement. This approach comes from a perspective that information maintains its quality only for so long before it is superseded – especially from a business value perspective – by market developments, which effectively removes the information's inherent confidentiality. Accordingly, past that point the information should no longer benefit from the confidentiality provisions, even though in order to remove the risk to the receiving party that disclosures will be in breach of confidentiality clauses, the information is no longer confidential.

The other school of thought is that the mere passing of an arbitrary period of time does not, in and of itself, mean what was once confidential is no longer confidential. This is likely to be particularly relevant where customer data is involved.

Any decision to cap the time period of the application of the confidentiality provisions will need to be made following a confident assessment of what is going to be disclosed over the entire life of the agreement.

In either case, one should make it clear that the confidentiality provisions continue to apply after the expiry or termination of the agreement, via the usual 'survival of clauses' provision in the agreement. In this regard some competition law issues might come into place and might limit the time period that certain confidential information is to be kept confidential.

4. Enhanced confidentiality obligations

In certain industries, market participants are subject to enhanced and often regulatory-imposed obligations to maintain the confidentiality of information that they handle and come into contact with. Banking secrecy obligations are among the most obvious examples of such a regime.

It is, therefore, necessary to ensure that the customer understands whether it is subject to any such regulatory requirements, and takes appropriate steps to ensure that the outsourcing agreement will enable it to comply with these obligations, or at least will not put it in breach of those obligations.

5. Intellectual property in the bid process

Just as with the confidentiality provisions in the request-for-proposal (RFP) document described above, the parties need to consider what will be provided as part of the bid process and how this material may be used by each other.

The customer will probably make available certain information and data, maybe in the form of information about the company that the bidders will need to be able to use to respond to the RFP. In strict terms, then, the service provider will need a licence to use this material. This does not need to be a complex or difficult licence, but rather a simple right to use for the sole purpose of responding to the RFP.

The provision of material by the potential service providers to the customer as part of the bidding process can be slightly more interesting.

The customer will need to ensure in its RFP document that it is granted some form of right to use the material provided to it, as a minimum, for the purposes of assessing the bids submitted to it, although the customer might like to consider extrapolating the licence so that it can use intellectual property in material even if the bidder is not ultimately selected as the service provider on the project. For example, if the service provider suggests in the bid an alteration to the customer's existing processes, the customer might like to be able to use that suggestion even if it does not want to appoint the service provider to provide the outsourced services. The customer should therefore make clear in the licence rights in the RFP documents that it can use whatever is provided there as part of the bid process for these wider purposes.

6. Outsourcing contract provisions

The IP provisions within the agreement tend to fall into three broad categories:

- what each party brings to the deal for use within the term of the agreement;
- newly created intellectual property; and
- material that belongs to a party prior to the commencement date of the agreement or that is generated other than in the course of providing the services.

6.1 Licences to the customer's material

In many outsourcing deals the customer will need to provide something to the service provider for it to use in the performance of its services. This might be something associated with the outsourcing itself, such as existing process guides or certain software, or it could be the material that the service provider will need to process as part of producing the services and the outputs of the services.

The first step is to understand what the customer is supposed to be providing, and to enable the service provider to use it. This will form part of the negotiation between the parties – for example, will the customer be providing software that forms part of the 'system' (see definition in section 6.2 below) or is it the service provider's responsibility? There will be cost and practical implications for the party responsible for providing this, and so this ought to be considered as soon as possible in the process to ensure that both parties are clear on the respective expectations and their responsibilities.

Whatever the outcome, the customer will do well to state expressly – perhaps in a customer's responsibilities schedule – the software and the other material that it has responsibility to provide, so as to create a clear statement of its retained obligations, enabling it to get a clear picture of both what it will need to do on an on-going basis after the outsourcing has started, and of the cost of running the deal.

Assuming that the customer is to be obliged to provide certain material, it will need to ensure that it has the appropriate rights to pass these materials to the service provider. If the customer owns the intellectual property in the material, this will of course be a less taxing issue. If the material is itself licensed to the customer, the customer ought then to conduct an appropriate level of due diligence on the existing arrangements to ensure that it can pass the material to the service provider, without fear of breaching the terms of the third-party licences to which it is subject. This can be a time-consuming and laborious task, even if all the agreements are readily accessible; if they are not, then it can be more complex to piece together the arrangements and to approach the third party for appropriate permission (which itself can generate distracting discussion as to whether the provision to the service provider is permissible and the basis on which it should occur – often in return for further fees. Establishing any licence agreement on the basis that an outsourcing might occur is therefore good practice so as to avoid this situation).

The licence terms on which the customer makes available the material will then need to be set out in the agreement, which would need to be reflective of the terms that the customer is entitled to grant under the terms of its agreements with the relevant third-party owners of the material.

6.2 Licences to the service provider's material

One of the key reasons for appointing an outsourced service provider is to access its skills and expertise to improve the function and/or services being outsourced. This implies a need to leverage these skills both during and after the term of the agreement (as it would be perverse to have a temporary improvement to services and then not be able to enjoy those improvements at the end of the outsourcing contract).

The customer should therefore ensure that it is able to use what it wants, while the service provider will want to ensure that this use is regulated so that the value of what it is bringing to the table is properly controlled and recognised. The service provider's chief concern in this regard will be that the customer should no longer benefit from the service provider's intellectual property once that latter is no longer engaged in providing the services and receiving any payment.

There is therefore a usual demarcation between what the customer is entitled to use during the term of the outsourcing contract and what the customer can use after the term. This in turn tends to lead to a split between use of the outputs of the services (the deliverables) and the other material that the service provider uses in the course of performing the services.

For deliverables, please see section 6.6 below. For other material, usually consisting of some form of 'system' or 'platform', the first question is: will the customer need to use this during the term of the contract – that is, is use of that system part of the delivery of the services, as opposed to some form of back-office system that the service provider uses but which the customer does not need in the course of receiving the services? This will be an important question for the parties as it drives the extent to which the service provider needs to ensure that it has the appropriate rights to license the constituent elements of the system to its customers.

Assuming that there is something that the customer ought to be able to use, the following issues need to be addressed:

- What is that 'something' and what is it going to be called in the agreement?
- What is the scope of the usage right?
- Who is entitled to use it?
- How long can it be used for?

This 'something' is often referred to as a 'system of similar' to indicate that there is a form of underlying technology that the service provider is making available to the customer – for example, an accounting system in a finance and accounting deal or a claims management system in an insurance business processing deal. Whatever it is called, the key is that its description is adequate to ensure that the customer can do what it wants, and that the service provider does not give too much away.

6.3 Usage rights

In describing the usage rights, the system will be made up of various elements and various descriptions of IP rights, each of which subsist within the system itself. The descriptions of individual classes of IP rights (eg, copyright, design rights, even topography rights on microprocessor chips) is irrelevant in terms of describing the use of the system. Essentially, the customer needs a right to use the system in connection with its receipt, and to get the benefit of the services. Making references to classes of intellectual property in this regard is an unnecessary complication.

To be clear, use does not necessarily imply rights to interface or integrate other software and neither does it imply the right to make any changes to the systems. If these rights are required, they need to be carefully articulated in the agreement. Furthermore, the level of usage rights that are granted (either by way of contract or statutory law) might vary depending on the regime of IP laws applicable to the respective outsourcing transaction. This should be evaluated carefully before agreeing on a specific choice of law.

6.4 Use entitlement

Alongside the customer, various other parties may be believed to need to use the system. Whether these are relevant will depend on the nature of the services, and the basis on which the service provider's system (and other material) will be made available.

The customer and its affiliates are relevant users of the system. Other potential users are the customer's own customers and the customer's own suppliers of goods and services.

Clients and potential clients of the customer might need to use the system if what is being provided forms part of the customer's offering to its own clients. Often this might not be the case at the outset of any deal, but it is important to look into the future on outsourcing deals given their likely length. Missing them out in a situation where the customer needs its own clients and potential clients to use the system could be a costly mistake if the terms of the licence then need to be renegotiated.

Use by other suppliers is the most sensitive class of 'additional' user. The service provider's system is likely to be one of the principal reasons for choosing that particular service provider, over and above others. The system possibly contains market differentiating software and functionality. It could be what is sometimes referred to as the service provider's 'crown jewels' or 'lifeblood'. The service provider is then unlikely to be willing to allow its competitors to have access to and explore the system. As with the confidential material of the service provider, discussed above, the customer faces the challenge of trying to achieve a joined-up and interactive supply chain, while balancing the service provider's valid concerns.

6.5 Use length

One clearly important issue will be how long the customer is entitled to use this system. Often the drafting will end the licence at the end of the outsourcing contract term which, on its face, makes sense as this is when the customer and the service provider are no longer in a relationship, and therefore the service provider can justifiably withdraw use of the system. Customers need to watch out for two issues here. First, is the term defined to cover the termination assistance period, so as to ensure that it can transition over to the new service provider or back in house? Second, even after transitioning the services, does the customer need access to any historic data that might be left behind on the system and that would require a limited look-up right simply to retrieve?

For further detail on whether the customer should have the right to acquire any element of the service provider's system or equipment, see the chapter on exit.

6.6. Services deliverables or outputs

In the course of providing the services, the supplier will likely generate some outputs. In simplistic services agreements, the customer will lay claim to ownership of the intellectual property in these outputs on the basis that it paid for them and should own what it has paid for.

In outsourcing transactions, however, the analysis of outputs needs to delve a little deeper.

During the existence of an agreement between the service provider and the customer over a number of years, various outputs will be generated both behind the scenes and as delivered to and/or provided to the customer.

Most obviously, the actual outputs will be the outputs of the services. This includes reports, process guides and potentially some software – depending on the nature and scope of the services. The customer will want to ensure that it can use these outputs without being exposed to claims of IP infringement or of being under-licensed, and that it can use these after the term so as to avoid being locked-in with the service provider just so it can benefit from the services provided and deliverables generated during the course of earlier contracts. In this respect, the customer is unlikely to be in a position to control the use of a document deliverable and so is likely to want to argue that the scope of use that it is granted in respect of the deliverables is 'as good as ownership', including therefore the right to use, copy and modify the deliverables.

On its face, this seems straightforward enough, except when one considers that the deliverable could quite possibly contain at least two and maybe three classes of intellectual property:

- the service provider's pre-existing IP, which is usually described as the intellectual property or the element of the deliverable that existed before the term of the agreement or that was produced other than in connection with the performance of the agreement. This quite probably forms part of the service provider's toolkit in terms of what it brings to the deal and which it would look to retain and reuse on various projects;
- the newly created intellectual property – the element of the deliverable that

has been generated in the course of proving the services; and
- any third-party intellectual property incorporated into the deliverables.

The trouble with this analysis is that it is theoretical. Deliverables do not come with neat labels stating what is the service provider's pre-existing intellectual property and what is new intellectual property. As such, it will be crucial to appreciate that the terms applicable to individual elements will drive the usage rights of the whole – the lowest scope of use will effectively determine the use of the whole deliverable because the most restrictive use is the most one can do with a deliverable.

For this reason, many customers will argue that their view of the potential distinct classes of a deliverable's intellectual property is that they all ought to be treated the same, and as if the customer owned all the deliverables.

Assuming that there is an element of the intellectual property in the deliverable that is assigned to the customer, there will still, or at least could, be some pre-existing intellectual property in them as well. One cannot take the risk that the deliverables do not and never will contain pre-existing intellectual property as if there is no licence to this element and the deliverables contain pre-existing intellectual property, the customer will not be licensed.

A car analogy can be helpful here. Imagine that you commission someone to design a car for you. If the shape of the car were new, you would expect to own the intellectual property in the design so that you were the only one with that shape. As owner, you can dispose of it as you see fit. But the engine in the car might not have been specifically designed for you; in fact, it comes from a third-party engine manufacturer and the designer has tweaked it a little to fit in with your design – so the engine is both third-party intellectual property and service provider's pre-existing intellectual property. You do not own the intellectual property in the engine, therefore, and you would be restricted from copying the engine so as to become an engine manufacturer. This is fine as you do not intend to become a car manufacturer, you just want a workable car. However, you would need the right to mend the engine, maybe to tune it a little and let others do this for you. Then imagine that two years on you decide to get a motorbike, but to do so you need to sell the car. You obviously need to sell the whole car, even though you do not own the intellectual property in the engine, as a car without an engine is of little value. You would therefore see the whole as an indivisible unit called 'the car', even though the individual components of the car belong, from an IP perspective, to different people. You own the shell and the design of the shell; you can dispose of this as you want. But the engine is technically only licensed to you, you do not own the intellectual property in it. The rights that you should have been granted then in respect of the constituent elements need to be as good as ownership to enable you to maintain the engine while you own it, modify the engine to be able to improve its performance, sublicense these rights to let a skilled mechanic perform these tasks for you and the right to sell (or assign) the engine so you can sell the whole.

In terms of the newly created intellectual property, the question is: who should own this? The following discussion refers to common law countries which maintain a completely different copyright law system from civil law countries (where in fact copyright cannot be transferred to another party, but can only be subject to exclusive or non-exclusive usage rights, the former being effectively comparable to the ownership of intellectual property).

As indicated above, many customers take the view that they paid for it and so should own it (or in civil law countries should obtain an exclusive usage right in it). The service provider will otherwise argue that it has brought the benefit of many years of skill and experience, including its pre-existing intellectual property, which the customer is benefiting from, and that it should therefore own the newly created intellectual property so that it can continue to grow as a business and to provide the best possible service to its customers.

The question that the customer really ought to be asking itself is: what extra benefit do I get from owning this intellectual property that I do not get from a licence on the terms described above? There may be some competitive advantage from owning the intellectual property; some corporate policy may require to own it; some particular commercial advantage may be attached to the intellectual property. In answering this question, one point worth reflecting upon relates to the quality of certain IP rights. The principal IP right that subsists in a deliverable is copyright. Copyright protects the direct copying of the protected works. What it does not do is protect the underlying concept; it protects the manifestation of that concept. Thus, owning the intellectual property does not absolutely protect any competitive advantage; what it does is slow down the rate at which a competitor will (potentially) have access to the relevant object since the service provider (or another service provider) will need to recreate the object in a fresh, different way without reference to the copyrighted work.

Accordingly, depending on the nature of the deliverable and the scope of difficulty in reproducing the relative deliverable, ownership of the intellectual property might not be all it is thought to be. The customer needs to concentrate not just on IP ownership as the proper protection of its business in the course of the outsourcing agreement; it must think more laterally in terms of confidentiality provisions, non-competition, protection on staff, hiring rights and so forth – topics that are covered elsewhere in this book.

Therefore, the licence rights in respect of the elements of the deliverables not owned by the customer take on a much greater significance than the ownership of the intellectual property itself.

6.7 Third-party intellectual property

Third-party intellectual property is material that the service provider does not own, but that it has licensed to use in the course of providing the services.

A service provider will often seek to separate the licensing treatment of its own intellectual property from that of third parties on the basis that it itself uses the third-party intellectual property and/or material according to specific licensing terms, and is not therefore free to grant whatever rights the customer wants in respect of it. The service provider may well then seek to assert that the customer's use of any third-party intellectual property made available to the customer – whether in the system or in the deliverables – is subject to the terms of the relevant third-party licence.

The issues for the customer in this regard are that:

- the third-party terms may well be unknown to it;
- the third-party terms may contain unacceptable restrictions on its ability to use the system or deliverables that would affect its intended ability to use the systems and the deliverables and so cut across the terms relating to the use of systems and deliverables; and
- the licence may impose a liability regime on the customer that it does not want to accept.

Accordingly, the solution will often be that the third-party intellectual property ought to be treated as if it was indivisible from the service provider's own intellectual property and so that the licence terms applicable to the service provider's intellectual property are applied. It would therefore be the service provider's risk as to what terms applied, on the basis that it is the service provider's choice to include the relevant intellectual property in the deliverables. Alternatively, the customer could agree to specific third-party terms, so long as it agreed to the terms prior to the inclusion of the third-party material in the deliverables. If the parties cannot agree, it would remain the service provider's responsibility to obtain necessary licence rights to enable the customer to use the deliverables on the basis more generally described in the agreement.

6.8 Open-source software

One potentially complicating factor can be the use by the service provider of open-source software. Open-source software is often of particular concern to customers by virtue of the actual or perceived contamination risk – that is, that if open-source software is somehow combined with other intellectual property, the other intellectual property effectively becomes open source, and so potentially creates some form of obligation on the customer to open up and release all the intellectual property in its environment and within the deliverables for use by anyone.

As such, restrictions on the service provider's use of open-source software in the systems (at least insofar as it interfaces with the customer's environment) and in the deliverables themselves often apply.

Such restrictions – at least from a customer's perspective – then circumvent two issues: first, the basis on which the open-source software is licensed to the customer and, second, the perceived contamination impact over the use of the open-source software.

6.9 Know-how

As indicated above, part of the benefit that the service provider brings to the deal is its experience and expertise learnt from other arrangements. To be able to use such experience and expertise, suppliers will usually seek to ensure that there is a preservation of, and an ability to use elsewhere, know-how acquired in the course of providing the services.

Know-how is not an IP right *per se*, but it can be described as the practical skill and knowledge learnt from experience of undertaking and performing relevant tasks.

It is the learning of the best and most efficient ways of doing something that improve the service provider's offering, make the services cheaper to perform and so improve both the service provider's pricing and profitability.

Because know-how is not an IP right, it runs the risk of taking on a different, almost mystical, quality, of being an intangible right that coexists with traditional IP rights. To some extent, this is accurate, but the protection of IP rights ought to take precedence over and above the ability to reuse skills, so as to preserve the sanctity of the IP rights provisions.

Likewise, it will be important for the customer to maintain the protection of the confidential information that it has fought hard over, in line with the confidentiality provisions described in section 3. The customer would not want its procedures to find their way in the customer's know-how, with an associated ability to reuse that know-how, if those processes and procedure are considered confidential and potentiality competitively advantageous.

In these respects, the sensible approach is to allow for the ability to use know-how so long as such reuse does not constitute a breach of the IP and confidentiality provisions.

The ability to use know-how is probably something that the customer ought to consider carefully, on the basis that the customer may well want to exploit its own learning so as to reduce the amount of the functions that it outsources, to improve its own ways of working generally and otherwise maintain the benefits of what has been delivered to it during the contract term.

7. Customer data

As indicated above, the customer's data may well be the most important asset within the customer's business. Whether it is the customer's client list, its trade secrets, its own client's banking details or some other fundamental facet of its ability to perform, the ownership, protection and viability of the customer data will be paramount concerns in any outsourcing arrangement. For the purposes of this section, we assume that customer data will be treated as customer confidential information and so concentrate on the different perspectives as to the value of such data.

On most deals, by contrast, the service provider will be oblivious to the actual content of the data as it will appear as a collection of 1s and 0s, with no intrinsic value.

This dichotomy is important and relevant to the consideration of the risk profile applicable to the protection and then the remediation of any customer data. As one can predict, the customer will come at the problem clearly of the view that the data has considerable inherent value, and its inability to use any of it will have a materially detrimental impact on its business; the service provider will adopt a more phlegmatic approach since it cannot understand what any data is and, thus, can neither profile the risk nor absorb the potential liability.

The primary issue is ownership and preservation of title in the customer data. The customer will want a clear statement of its ownership of the rights in the data and a statement that the service provider will assign any IP rights in the data to the customer.

Also relevant to the issue of the intellectual property in the customer data relates to the ownership of database rights in the structuring and presentation of the data. Database rights subsist. Database rights allow their holder to continue to manipulate the structured database after the agreement has come to a close.

Again, this legal evaluation might change under a civil copyright law regime where IP rights in data can exist only in certain circumstances. Typically, such rights can exist only in databases and their particular composition rather than in the data itself.

7.1 Use of customer data

On the basis that the customer data is of significant commercial value, one would expect the customer to seek to impose stringent restrictions on the use that the service provider can make of that data.

Customer data will often be a specifically identified subset of the customer's confidential information and so would benefit from the provisions in relation to confidentiality. However, on the basis that the confidentiality provisions also include some permitted uses, the customer will need to verify whether it is appropriate for the customer data to be subject to the same rights for the service provider to use it. Usually, there will be a clear statement that the service provider may use the customer data only to the extent strictly necessary to provide the services and for no other purposes.

7.2 Access to customer data

The customer will want assurance that it can, whenever it needs to, access and gain a copy of the customer data. This might actually be a legal requirement if the outsourcing is structured as a commissioned data processing where the customer has to remain in full control of the outsourced data (see below).

Accordingly, outsourcing agreements often contain provisions requiring the service provider to deliver up the customer data within a finite period of time whenever requested by the customer. The service provider may be concerned by the costs involved in continually having to provide copies of the data, and this can be resolved via the inclusion of a 'reasonableness' clause or agreement as to the payment of certain costs in certain circumstances.

The customer may also like to include rights to access the service provider's premises and systems in order to obtain the data in the event that the service provider will not deliver up the customer data.

Lastly, customers often want to include provisions that prohibit the service provider from imposing liens over, or mortgaging the customer data so as to avoid any possibility that the customer is unable to gain unfettered access to the customer data as and when it wants.

7.3 Loss and destruction of customer data

Ultimate responsibility for loss or destruction of data will be determined by whether the service provider is hosting the data or not. If the service provider is providing hosting services, for example, then the presumption probably ought to be that the service provider has overall responsibility for the protection of the customer data against loss and security, and that the service provider is responsible for any loss or default unless the customer can be shown to have caused it (ie, the service provider is responsible for ensuring that no third parties do or do not do things that lose or destruct the data even if the third parties are not part of the service provider's supply chain). If the service provider is not hosting the data or is not providing services that affect the security of the data, then the likelihood is that the service provider is responsible to the extent that the loss or destruction arose from its act or omission.

Either way, it is important to establish a 'fix first, argue later' approach so that the customer data is recovered or reconstituted if it is ever lost, with the commercial consequences of such recovery/reconstitution dealt with as a separate issue.

8. Data protection

In most outsourcing transactions the service provider will be required to handle some degree of personal data on behalf of the customer. On some transactions, especially those relating to business processing, the amount of personal data to be managed and dealt with can be significant.

Data protection legislation varies from jurisdiction to jurisdiction, although approaches are increasingly similar.

At a very basic level in the European Union, for example, the data protection legislation is clear that where processing is to be performed by a third party, the data controller and the data processor must enter into a contract that:

- is in writing;
- states that the processing can take place only on the instructions of the data controller; and
- requires the processor to comply with relevant security measures.

Similar restrictions exist in other data protection regimes outside the European Union.

In an outsourcing context, therefore, there is no option but to include detailed data protection provisions in the outsourcing agreement. Depending on the respective way of adoption of the EU Data Protection Directive 95/46/EC into national laws there might be specific requirements to be met in different EU member states.

This chapter is not intended to be a review or critique of the various data protection legislation worldwide, but rather a consideration of the practical issues resulting from the handling of personal data in outsourcing transactions, and how these issues can be addressed. Accordingly, readers should look to a text specifically on data protection for guidance on the applicable laws. However, when we use terms such as 'personal data', 'data controller', 'data processor' and 'process', we do so in the context of how those terms are defined in the EU Data Protection Directive (95/46/EC).

8.1 Do the provisions need to be reciprocal?

Very often, the data protection provisions will be presented so that they apply to the service provider only, and impose obligations on the service provider only.

The rationale for this is that, historically, the data protection legislation imposes obligations on the data controller, and requires the data controller to ensure that the data processors process the data in ways that are consistent with the data protection legislation.

On the basis that the flow of data is usually one way, from customer to service provider, it is the customer that needs to ensure that the service provider adheres to the data protection legislation and, therefore, the customer that has to impose the obligations on the service provider.

Unless, of course, the service provider is passing to the customer a lot of its own personal data (which is unlikely), there accordingly seems to be little reason for the provisions to be reciprocal.

One caveat to this is where the service provider is also the data controller (see section 8.2 below).

8.2 Who is the data controller?

As indicated above, the data protection requires the data controller to ensure that certain standards are adhered to, and that the data is processed only in certain ways and for certain purposes.

The data controller is, essentially, the person that determines the manner and purposes for which the data is processed; this will be, in most outsourcing situations, the customer. The customer is using the service provider to supply services to it, and as part of this requires the service provider to process the personal data. The customer makes the assessment to appoint the service provider and decides to outsource the services/functions, including the associated processing of the data. Therefore, the customer determines the manner and purposes for which the data is processed.

Most suppliers are content with this position because they do not wish to take on the responsibility of a data controller under the legislation.

Some customers will like to be clear, however, that they are the data controller so as to maintain the clear demarcation of directional responsibility – that is, only they can determine the manner and purposes for which the personal data may be processed.

8.3 Purposes for which the data may be processed

The outsourcing agreement provisions will commonly include a clear statement that the data may be processed only for the purposes determined and notified by the customer to the service provider. This ought to be non-contentious.

The counter-point to this is that the service provider will often then look for a confirmation from the customer that the customer has the necessary consents to enable the service provider to process the data in accordance with the terms of the agreement. The service provider will want some form of mechanism to seek recovery from the customer in the event that a data subject that had not authorised processing later brings a claim against the service provider (as well as probably, the customer). The customer would need to be comfortable therefore that it has obtained all necessary consents to enable the service provider to process the personal data, especially in respect of sensitive personal data.

8.4 Responsibility for the technological and organisational measures

One of the core provisions imposed on data controllers, which in turn is passed down to suppliers in their role of data processors, is to implement appropriate technological and organisational methods to protect the personal data against accidental and unlawful destruction, accidental loss, alteration, unauthorised disclosure or access and any other non-permitted processing.

Most outsourcing contacts simply pass this form of words (encompassed in the seventh data protection principle) down to the service provider, for the service provider to take whatever steps would be required to achieve this objective.

There can, however, be some debate as to whose responsibility it is to determine the measures, considering the potential interpretations of what is required to meet this standard.

Suppliers will often argue that their obligation will be met if they comply with a set of security requirements set out in the agreement, or if they adhere to the customer's own security policy or another security policy agreed between the parties. This is consistent, suppliers would say, with the fact that it is the customer's primary responsibility as data controller to meet the requirements of this data protection principle, and that the customer therefore needs to make the determination. Any discretion left to the service provider is an inappropriate abdication of responsibility and, moreover, the service provider cannot define for the customer – in respect of the customer's personal data – what is and what is not 'appropriate'.

By contrast, customers will argue that the obligation should not be deemed satisfied by reference to the security requirements or similar in the agreement, because these requirements do not delve deep enough into the service provider's organisation to be able to ensure that the entirety of the service provider's organisation is maintaining and adhering to appropriate standards. The customer will argue that it has no ability to see behind the curtain of the service provider's organisation in order to determine – exhaustively – the security requirements. The service provider must therefore assume the responsibility for determining whether what it does behind the curtain is appropriate.

8.5 Overseas data transfers

Generally, transfers of personal data outside the European Economic Area (EEA) are forbidden unless the data controller is allowed to transfer the data and the state in which the transfer takes place offers an adequate level of data protection. At the time of writing, only a few non-EEA countries have been designated by the EEA as affording an appropriate level of protection – and even to those countries, specific conditions can apply.

Accordingly, outsourcing agreements usually include a prohibition on the transfer of data outside of the EEA without the customer's prior written consent, and an associated requirement for the service provider to enter into a data transfer agreement (usually on the EU model terms) where requested by the customer so as to facilitate a transfer outside the EEA.

Within the confines of an outsourcing arrangement, this itself generates a series of questions that need to be considered:

- Is personal data being transferred anyway?
- What constitutes a transfer?
- Who are the right parties to the data transfer agreement?

(a) *Is personal data being transferred anyway?*

Very often the transfer of personal data will be straightforward; in case of an overseas business process outsourcing operation that processes HR-related services, there will quite clearly be a transfer of personal data overseas to enable the service provider to supply the services from that location.

But what if the services were IT-managed services with third-line support desk in a non-EEA country? Does the provision to those overseas operations of the support ticket with the identity of the user constitute a transfer of personal data?

What if the overseas operations of an IT service provider should not, but could, gain access to the personal data via remote means? There is no simple answer. It will be necessary to consider carefully what data is to be transferred and the basis of that transfer, and then assess that in light of the prevailing legislation in the location in which the data controller is established in order to understand the degree to which data transfer agreements are required. In practical terms, most customers will put in place data transfer agreements in the event of any potential transfers.

(b) *What constitutes a transfer?*

Any processing of personal data overseas constitutes a transfer; this includes simply remote access of data even if that data neither 'relocates' to that overseas country nor ends up residing on servers located in that country.

(c) *Who are the right parties to the data transfer agreement?*

The data transfer agreement needs to be entered into between the data controller and the data processor that will receive and process the data in the relevant country.

These entities could be different from the parties that enter into the outsourcing agreement, depending on who the data controller is of the relevant data and the identity of the recipient. This therefore needs to be carefully reviewed so as to ensure that the right parties are entering into the data transfer agreement, especially so that the data protection legislation is complied with.

8.6 Assistance with requests for data subject access and regulatory requirements

From time to time, data subjects make enquiries of the data controllers and make subject access requests. It is part of the data controllers' responsibility to be able to respond to such requests, as well as being able to provide good customer service.

Accordingly, the customer will need to include in the outsourcing agreement clear provisions for the service provider to forward on to the customer any requests for subject access so the customer can comply with these in a consistent manner across its organisation, and for the service provider to provide assistance and information with regards to responding to any subject access request.

Likewise, customers will often seek to ensure that any queries from regulators are passed directly to the customer and are not handled unilaterally by the service provider.

Many suppliers will seek to impose parameters around the extent of the support that it provides, because it could be time intensive and/or result in them incurring costs that they would not ordinarily have, as part of the services. As such, it is normal to strike a balance between the provision of the assistance and the information that is, to some extent, an absolute requirement considering that it ties to the customer's legal obligations, and the costs of doing so.

Liability and indemnities

Anne Friedman
John McKinlay

1. Limitation of liability

1.1 Introduction

Outsourcing agreements frequently include a provision that limits one or both of the parties' liability exposure with respect to claims and damages that arise in connection with the agreement. These provisions often address the treatment of indirect and consequential damages (where those principles are relevant to the law that governs the contract), as well as provide for a maximum monetary limit for which a party can be liable with respect to claims for direct damages.

1.2 General principles

As a general legal principle, there is no inherent restriction to the amount of damages recoverable following a breach of contract. Under both English and US law, for example, general formulas and rules are used to determine the types of damage that can be recovered with respect to a breach of contract claim (eg, punitive damages are generally not recoverable for breach of contract), but there are not restrictions on the amount of money that can be recovered within the permissible categories. Another general principle of most laws pertaining to major outsource-related jurisdictions (including the United States, United Kingdom and Europe) is that parties to a contract may include provisions relating to damages that will override otherwise applicable contract principles (and the same principle and approach apply to many other legal systems that frequently govern outsourcing contracts, including English law and the laws of most of the countries on the European mainland). As such, parties to contracts have developed the concept of a 'limitation of liability' clause through which the parties can mutually agree to exclude or include expressly certain types of damage that the parties have the rights to recover in the event of certain types of breach. Such clauses are standard (although not ubiquitous) in most outsourcing agreements. Limitation of liability clauses allow the parties to predict their liability exposure better in the event of certain types of contract breach.

There is no set of requirements that a limitation of liability clause must include so long as it is otherwise enforceable, as discussed below. Depending on the complexity of the outsourcing arrangement, these limitation of liability clauses can be relatively simple or incredibly complex. The key points with respect to drafting such clauses are addressed later in the chapter, but at a high level, common elements found in these clauses in outsourcing agreements include:

- maximum amount of money that is recoverable for claims of direct damages for each party or 'liability cap';
- waiver of either or both parties' right to recover consequential, indirect, punitive and other forms of what do not qualify as direct damages or are to be excluded in any event;
- types of claim that are excepted from the maximum amount of recoverable direct damages and/or from the prohibition of indirect damages; and
- types of damage that the parties agree shall qualify as recoverable direct damages under any circumstance – that is, deemed direct losses).

Limitation of liability clauses are generally enforceable under general contract law so long as the parties have fairly negotiated the provision, the language of the provision clearly sets forth the scope of the limitation, and the limitation is not unconscionable or against public policy (although this can be subject to nuances under some local laws, the analysis of which sits outside the scope of this book).

From a practical standpoint, limitation of liability clauses are frequently some of the most negotiated (and often most difficult to finalise) parts of an outsourcing contract. Parties to contracts usually want to confirm that the other contract provisions that dictate a party's risk, such as indemnities, warranties and service levels, are fully agreed prior to finalising the limitation of liability language.

1.3 Drafting issues

Drafting an effective limitation of liability clause is a very detail-oriented, precise exercise. Not only must the parties draft the language so that it is enforceable in accordance with the above paragraph, but the parties must also clearly articulate their positions regarding what types and amounts of damage are recoverable for claims that arise under the agreement. For example, a party expecting that consequential damages are not recoverable would not want to allow for recovery of such damages if they are recoverable under the exceptions language that appears in another section of the liability clause.

This section details points that authors of such clauses should consider when writing the agreement to buttress the chances that the clause is both enforceable and accurately reflects the agreement of the parties with respect to liability exposure.

(a) Drafting tips to evidence enforceability of the clause

Although these provisions are typically enforceable, there are drafting and lawyering tactics that authors can utilise to evidence that the clauses meet the enforceability standard, including placing the language in a conspicuous location with bold or other stand-out font, retain the various iterations of the language in order to demonstrate that the clause was fairly negotiated and ultimately reflects the intent of the parties, and itemise and clearly draft the language so that the intent of the original parties is understood by any reader.

(b) Liability cap on direct damages

The parties may elect to use many methods and calculations to determine the amount of the liability cap, and they should review a number of considerations prior to finalising the calculation. Below is an annotated sample of liability cap language (numbers in square brackets refer to commentary further below):

Cap On Liability for Direct Damages. Except as otherwise expressly provided in section TBD (exclusions from limitations on liability), the aggregate cumulative monetary liability [1] of either party [2] for any and all direct damages for any and all claims, events or occurrences arising under or relating to the agreement, notwithstanding the form in which any such action is brought, whether in contract, tort or otherwise, shall be limited to an amount equal to the greater of: (a) [$___________]dollars; and (b) the sum of all amounts, including charges, paid and payable to supplier during the [TBD] month period immediately preceding the claim, event or occurrence giving rise to the direct damages, or if such claim, event or occurrence occurs in the first [TBD] months of the term,) multiplied by the amounts, including charges, paid and payable to supplier during the [TBD] month of the claim, event or occurrence giving rise to the direct damages (the "direct damages cap").

[1] The language above contemplates that the "aggregate cumulative monetary liability" is the calculation that should apply, meaning that the monetary liability amount set forth later in the paragraph is the maximum amount of direct damages that will apply during the entire term for all claims not excepted otherwise. There can be variations on this approach depending on the parties' preference, which may be guided by factors including the term length, the amounts contemplated, the quality of the parties' relationship, etc. For example, the parties can choose to have the liability cap re-set during the term after a certain amount of time has passed (ie, start over). Such a cap might then be applied to all causes of action arising in a set 12-month period, for example. An alternative approach would be a cap set on a per-claim basis – that is, which will apply to each individual claim or set of connected claims.

None of these formulations are inherently right or wrong, or necessarily better or worse for either customer or service provider; much will depend on the proposed size of the cap/limits of liability themselves. For example, a service provider might be happy to suffer the relative uncertainty of a per-claim cap if it is set at a low amount, in preference to a much larger aggregate cap set over the term of the entire outsource agreement (on the basis that the service provider may well conclude that it would be highly unlikely – albeit not impossible – that it would suffer multiple claims and yet still continue the outsource relationship).

Another key consideration related to this language is whether the outsourcing agreement in question includes a series of statements of work that operate under a master agreement, or whether there is a single scope of work for the arrangement. If there are a series of statements of work, each of which has its own set of charges, the calculation of the liability cap could vary enormously if the liability cap applies to the master level. For example, if an outsourcing agreement has two separate statements of work, each of which charges $1 million per year and an aggregate contract liability cap is in place, a breach of only one of the statements of work would result in a cap of $2 million. If the parties' intent is instead that each statement of work should be subject to an individual liability cap of $1 million for a breach, the language in the limitation of liability clause must be drafted to reflect that intent.

[2] The language above states that each party is subject to the liability cap equally, which is the most common approach; however, parties can agree that it applies differently to each party, or that different amounts apply to different parties (eg, a lower cap is often set in favour of the customer).

[3] This language determines how to calculate the monetary amount of the limitation. Note that this is a sample and a number of variations can apply. The points below offer considerations that parties should make when constructing the formula:

- The formula above states that the limitation will be the greater of two possible amounts, which is a somewhat complex formula. The parties can instead agree that there be only one approach to calculating the amount (eg, insert a set monetary amount, such as $1 million, or use an approach described in the last bullet below rather than use the greater of the two). The method chosen by the parties is truly variable from one engagement to another, although the most common model is to apply a percentage-based multiple to the service provider's annual charges.
- This section contemplates that there will be a pre-set liquidated amount for the liability cap. Parties often reach this amount based on their anticipated value of the contract.
- Whether a party includes this 'paid or payable' language is important because it describes whether the calculation of the cap will include all amounts that the customer has paid the supplier, or whether the calculation should include all invoiced and otherwise unpaid amounts. What constitutes 'being payable' may then need further explanation (eg, does it mean invoiced but as yet imposed, or also cover work in progress even if an invoice has not been raised yet?)
- Using a set number of months' charges to determine the liability cap is the most common formula in outsourcing agreements. Depending on the type of relationship, the range of the number of months involved is anywhere from 12 months of charges to 24 months of charges.
- This type of language is frequently included to address the question of how to calculate the amount of the applicable liability cap if the initial period of the number of months of charges has not yet occurred. This is an area where the parties often offer varying solutions for the calculation.

Additional points to consider: Any number of issues can arise during the course of a negotiation that affect the rules regarding the calculation of the liability cap. In addition to those addressed in the sample language above, parties may wish to consider certain additional points when drafting a limitation of liability clause, including:

- Should all charges be included in the calculation or should some types, such as pass-through expenses, be excluded? How should the parties treat any service credits account by reason of service level failures with respect to the calculation?

- What are the consequences for the parties in the event that the liability cap is in danger of being (or has been) reached? Are there notice obligations? Would a party have a termination right in such case?
- Given the nature of the relationship, should more than one liability cap exist? For example, should there be a separate cap for claims brought by the end customers of an outsourcing customer? Or if the parties cannot agree as to whether certain types of claim should be excluded from the cap, can the parties agree on a separate cap for those types of claim? In complex outsourcing arrangements, this is an area where parties frequently craft very creative solutions and approaches.

(c) ***No liability for indirect damages***

The language below represents a common approach used to express the parties' intent that indirect damages be not recoverable by either party except under specific circumstances:

Limitation on Non-Direct Damages. Except as otherwise expressly provided in section [xx](exclusions from limitations on liability), neither party shall be liable for consequential, incidental, indirect, special, exemplary or punitive damages, or for any lost profits, lost sales or loss of business, regardless of the form of the action or the theory of recovery, even if advised of the possibility of such damages and regardless of the form in which any action is brought.

Not all legal systems have the same understanding of what constitutes direct/indirect damage; the language used will accordingly need to be adapted in light of the contract's share of governing law.

(d) ***Exclusions from limitations on liability***

Below is sample language that can be used as an introduction to the claims that will be excluded from both the liability cap and the limitation on indirect damages:

The Direct Damages Cap for direct damages liability and the limitation on non-direct damages in section [xx] shall not apply to:

[list of losses then to be set out]

The types of claim frequently excepted from either or both the liability cap and the limitation on indirect damages (ie, so as to then be claimable on an unlimited basis) include but are not limited to:

- claims for fraud, wilful misconduct and (in civil law jurisdictions, at least) gross negligence of a party;
- claims for personal injury, death or damage to tangible personal and real property;
- indemnification claims;
- confidentiality;
- data protection;
- compliance with laws;
- infringement;

- the service provider's abandonment or wrongful termination of the agreement; and
- fines and other governmental penalties.

Note, however, that parties draft this language as required to reflect the agreement of the parties. For example, the claims that are excepted from the liability cap for the customer may be different than those excepted for the service provider. Furthermore, the parties may agree that certain types of claim should be excepted from the liability cap, but such claims should be included in the limitation on non-direct damages. This differs widely from contract to contract, and is completely deal dependent.

(e) ***Acknowledged/deemed direct damages***

The parties can agree at the time of contracting to deem certain types of damage as direct in order to avoid any disagreement regarding the categorisation of such damages later in the term of the agreement. There has been a noticeable trend in recent times towards the inclusion of any such provisions, and for the list of such deemed direct losses to become ever longer. Standard language that parties can use is: "The following shall be considered non-exhaustive direct and recoverable Losses, and neither Party shall assert that they are indirect, incidental, collateral, consequential, exemplary or special damages."

The above language is followed by a list of the damages that the parties agree will be direct damages. The list can include a variety of items, including but not limited to certain administrative costs, costs related to data breaches, costs related to equipment, property, and data loss or destruction, workaround costs and replacement services. Customers in particular will also seek to include expressly all damages related to indemnification claims as direct damages (so as to avoid any potential legal debates as to whether an indemnity would allow recovery of contract damages – a legal issue not entirely clear in any event).

(f) ***Other excluded loss***

The contract may also stipulate other heads of loss that will not be claimable in any event. Typical candidates for inclusion in such a list from a service provider perspective might include loss of goodwill/reputation, loss of anticipated savings, loss of profit/revenue, or loss or corruption of data (at least to the extent due to the customer's failure to adhere to reasonable data back up procedures).

Some of these exclusions are well established in the outsourcing market. However, different service providers may take different approaches, depending on the nature of the services, the size of the deal and their competitive posture in the overall procurement process.

1.4 Conclusion

The summary provided in this chapter sets forth the basic principles with respect to limitation of liability clauses and is meant to introduce the complexities that can arise with respect to these provisions, particularly in the context of outsourcing engagements. A key point for any drafter to keep in mind at all times is that this clause often has a complex relationship with the other parts of the agreement, and the drafter needs to draft and negotiate this clause with precision and care.

2. Indemnities

2.1 Introduction

An indemnity in a contract is a commitment by one party to take responsibility for losses that the other party has suffered. Indemnities provide a way of recovering losses that is different from the normal route of claiming damages for breach of contract.

However, while the rules applying to indemnities differ from those governing breach of contract claims, the exact way in which they differ varies from jurisdiction to jurisdiction. Consequently, the use of indemnities in contracts also varies.

The purpose of this section is to consider the underlying principles of an indemnity, and then how they operate.

2.2 General principles

The starting point in considering indemnities is to understand that they are intended to compensate one party when a pre-agreed set of circumstances occurs. Indemnities are used to provide a simpler and more straightforward method of recovery than proving breach of contract. In their ideal form, if an event has occurred and loss has been suffered, then the suffering party is entitled to recover the amount lost in the same way that it would recover a debt. Things are rarely this straightforward, though.Where it is difficult to quantify the loss in advance, not all of the perceived advantages of indemnities may be available, as shall be discussed later in this chapter.

There is no restriction as to the type of claim that is suitable for an indemnity, but typical examples include:

- events occurring in relation to IP rights;
- events relating to information used or accessed under the contract, such as confidentiality, data protection and information security;
- identified breaches of legislation such as health and welfare legislation and anti-bribery;
- preventing third parties to the contract from taking certain action (eg, no claims from subcontractors or subsidiaries against the other contract party);
- certain deliberate acts such as fraud and serious misconduct;
- in Europe, claims relating to the Acquired Rights Directive; and
- in the United States, for any breach of contract claim, to allow recovery of attorney's costs that would not otherwise be chargeable.

As regards a common theme (other than in respect of the last example, which is US specific), indemnities are typically used for losses that do not arise in what might be said to be the normal course of the contract. In other words, it is unusual to see an indemnity applying to a breach of the core provisions of the contract such as failure to deliver to specification, breach of service levels, delay etc. If faced with an indemnity for such matters, it is usually possible to argue that it is being used too broadly, and that indemnities should instead be reserved for distinct or special categories of losses.

Whether or not there needs to have been any fault on behalf of the indemnifying party depends on the drafting of the indemnity. For example, the occurrence of an event alone may be sufficient to trigger the indemnity, such as where a service provider's subsidiary sues the customer, irrespective of the reason for this. By contrast, indemnities may be drafted to apply only where the event has been caused or contributed to by the indemnifying party, such as where a lack of appropriate security controls has led to information being accessed improperly.

Indeed, there is no reason why an indemnity cannot apply even where the beneficiary is at fault or in breach of contract in some way. For example, it is common in certain contracts for the recipient of a confidential report to agree to indemnify the author of the report should it come into the public domain and the author is sued as a result of the contents of the report. This indemnity can still apply even if the reason for the author being sued is a defamatory comment in the report. It is, however, good practice to be explicit if an indemnity is intended to apply even in the event of fault or negligence on the part of the indemnified party, to avoid any uncertainty should the wording be challenged in court.

2.3 Drafting issues

The effect created by an indemnity is highly influenced by the way in which the relevant provisions are drafted. In order to illustrate this, let us look at a sample clause and the issues that arise (the numbers in square brackets refer to commentary further below):

1.1 The Service Provider will indemnify Customer [1] against all amounts payable under any final judgment, verdict, court order or settlement [2] to the extent resulting from any third party claim arising from any breach of its intellectual property rights arising from use of the Deliverables in the place of supply of the Deliverables [3], provided that [4]:

(a) the Customer notifies the Service Provider within 7 days of the claim;

(b) the Customer gives the Service Provider control over the conduct of the claim [5]; and

(c) the Customer provides such assistance as the Service Provider requires in relation to the claim [6].

1.2 The indemnity set out above is the Customer's sole remedy in respect of any claim that the Deliverables breach any intellectual property rights. [7]

[1] Identification of the beneficiaries of the indemnity

It is not necessarily the case that the indemnity should apply only to the other party to the contract.

For example, it is important to consider whether the indemnity should also apply to other group companies of the parties, such as those that may have the benefit of an outsourcing system or that may have access to confidential information shared under the contract. Even if it is inappropriate to extend to the whole group, there may be circumstances that justify extending the indemnity to specific group companies – for example, those companies that process personal data in certain jurisdictions. There may even be a case for extending the indemnity to all group companies other than certain identified entities – for example, excluding entities in jurisdictions where the intellectual property is not licensed for use.

As well as group companies, it is appropriate to consider whether the indemnity should be extended to third parties. For example, a business process outsourcing may have an interface accessed by end-user customers, who arguably should also benefit from the indemnity. Another example would be for an Acquired Rights Directive indemnity to extend to successor service providers in respect of any liability that they may incur as a result of staff transferring to them.

The indemnifying party's position will generally wish to limit the indemnity so far as possible to apply only to the other party to the contract, and will argue that it is inappropriate for any third party to benefit directly from the indemnity. Whether this is correct will be a matter of negotiation in the circumstances, bearing in mind that if the indemnity is given only to the other party to the contract, that party will have to consider how to deal with any claims made against it by third parties in respect of the event giving rise to the loss.

[2] Types of loss covered

The grantor of the indemnity will want to ensure that, before being forced to pay out, its liability has been conclusively established. By contrast, the beneficiary will not necessarily want to wait until the end of what may be a very long and drawn-out process before seeing its losses compensated. The wording in this example states that amounts are due only after a final judgment, whereas often the drafting is such that as soon as any amount is awarded, the indemnity applies.

In addition, the wording of this clause could operate to exclude internal costs unless awarded by a court or included in a settlement. This could result in a significant loss for the beneficiary if it has incurred high internal costs in analysing or dealing with a claim. It is common for indemnities to include specific reference to recovery of internal costs, which in many cases would be much more likely to be incurred than any court-awarded sum.

[3] Extent of the indemnity

In the example, the necessary event to bring the indemnity into operation is "any third party claim arising from any breach of its intellectual property rights arising from use of the Deliverables".

It is vitally important to pay careful attention to this aspect of the clause. If there are circumstances that fall outside this wording, then the indemnity will not apply. Therefore, there is no such thing as a standard indemnity. In this example, the indemnity is stated to apply only to third-party claims. This type of wording may limit the indemnity to apply only to situations where a third party has actively made a claim, as opposed to any proactive settlements that the beneficiary of the indemnity may be keen to make. Also, the claim relates to use of 'deliverables'. Where defined terms such as this are used, it is vital to check that these cover all the relevant IP rights – including IP rights used in background materials that the customer uses.

The indemnity in this instance is also limited by geography to the place of supply. This sort of limitation is common in relation to certain IP-related indemnities. Whether this is justified will depend on a number of factors, not least the intended use of the IP rights. In any event, care should be taken to consider potential changes in plans or circumstances over time, which may render such limitations unworkable or unreasonable.

[4] Provisos to the operation of the indemnity

One of the most important points to check is whether the operation of the indemnity is subject to any provisos (as is the case in this example). The whole benefit of the indemnity will be lost if the provisos are not strictly adhered to. It is easy to see how the result could be disproportionate if the indemnifying party has suffered no actual detriment.

For example, it is common for the indemnified party to be required to give the indemnifying party prompt notice of the claim in question. This is to ensure that effective steps can be taken to minimise the exposure, whether by the indemnifying party remedying the situation or by engaging early with the claimant. However, if the indemnity ceases to apply entirely unless notification is given within a set period of time, this may be unreasonable. An alternative would be for the indemnity not to apply to any additional costs arising from late notification, rather than preventing the indemnified party from relying on the indemnity at all.

[5] Control over the claim

In certain jurisdictions, using an indemnity gives more discretion to the beneficiary of the indemnity to decide how best to deal with the claim than would be the case in a standard breach of contract claim. However, for the indemnifying party there is the practical concern that it could be left financially exposed if it does not seek to exercise some control over the way that the claim is handled.

For example, if a claim is made under an IP warranty that deliverables breach third-party IP rights, then the party making the claim against the other must mitigate its loss. This may mean, for example, that it ceases using the deliverable rather than seeking to negotiate for a licence from the third-party rights holder, if the loss from ceasing to use the deliverables would be less than the cost of the licence. However, if the same situation were covered by an indemnity, it may well be open to the indemnified party to obtain a licence even if this is not the cheapest option.

To avoid this situation, the indemnifying party generally seeks control over any claim, and restricts the indemnified party from making any admissions to avoid in effect writing a blank cheque.

This point is rarely controversial, but difficulties can arise where the nature of the claim means that it has (or could potentially have) a high profile. In such circumstances, the indemnified party may be more sensitive about the indemnifying party running the claim entirely on its own due to reputational risk, and may look to have some oversight or retained right over the way that the claim is handled.

Lastly, certain obligations often apply to the indemnifying party regarding the way that the claim is handled. Most commonly, contracts specify that it must take over the claim within a reasonable period of time, failing which the indemnified party can control the claim itself and still rely on the indemnity. It may also be the case that the indemnifying party has to grant security for costs in return for being able to control the matter. This is more controversial and tends to be used where there are concerns regarding whether the resources of the indemnifying party will be sufficient should the claim against the indemnified party succeed.

[6] Assistance by the indemnified party

It is normal for the indemnified party to agree to provide assistance in the running of the claim. In one sense this may be essential given that the claim will generally remain in the name of the indemnified party, and therefore its periodic help will be required. More generally, the indemnified party will have detailed knowledge of the circumstances that underpin the claim to which the indemnity relates, and the indemnifying party will wish to have access to this information. However, the indemnified party should expect to have its reasonable costs in providing this assistance covered, something that is missing from the clause included in the example.

[7] Whether the indemnity is the sole remedy

In this example, the indemnity is stated to be the sole remedy. Three issues arise from this.

First, is it appropriate to exclude any other remedies under the contract (eg, the right to terminate the contract for material breach)? Depending on the nature of the matter being indemnified, financial compensation may well be sufficient. However, for some indemnities (eg, for claims arising under anti-bribery/corruption law), the indemnified party will want to retain all its other rights under the contract.

Second, if the indemnified party is willing to concede that the indemnity is to be the sole remedy, it should ensure that this relates only to claims covered by the indemnity. In the example given, the indemnity is the sole remedy for all IP claims relating to the deliverables, which goes wider than the indemnity itself. If this wording were accepted, certain claims under the contract that could arise (eg, those outside the jurisdiction where the deliverables were supplied) would have no effective remedy at all.

As a final point, there is always the risk that an indemnity has not been drafted as intended, or is for some reason held to be ineffective or unenforceable. In such case, a sole remedy clause would exclude the basic right to sue for damages that might otherwise apply. For this reason if no other, the indemnified party will generally resist this clause on the basis that it is unreasonable to be left without any right to compensation for loss.

2.4 Recovery of losses

When it comes to the crucial question of what losses are recoverable under an indemnity clause, a number of issues arise that relate to how indemnities operate in practice. These are considered below.

(a) ***How much is recoverable?***

This depends on the drafting of the clause in question. It is possible that this question is very easy to answer. For example, an indemnity that allows one party to recover the amount of any regulatory fine (eg, under data protection legislation) would simply result in an action to recover the amount as a debt if it were not paid. By contrast, if the indemnity is for the amount of expenses incurred in defending a third-party IP rights claim, the parties may need to spend considerable time agreeing or litigating over the correct amount of expenses that relate to the claim in question.

(b) ***Are amounts payable under indemnities calculated differently from amounts payable under breach of contract claims?***

Certain jurisdictions treat indemnities differently in this regard.

For example, under English law, certain (although by no means all) case law suggests that the normal rules that apply to breach of contract regarding mitigation of loss and remoteness of damage do not apply in the same way to indemnity claims. In practice, what does this mean?

If a party does not have to mitigate its loss, this means that it does not need to find the cheapest solution to the problem. Whether this allows the indemnified party to do nothing to mitigate the loss suffered is less clear. It is probably the case that the indemnified party can look at a range of reasonable options and choose the one that best fits it, and still rely on the indemnity.

As regards the second point, if this is indeed the case this means that the indemnifying party cannot argue that the amounts claimed as being caused by the event covered by the indemnity were too far removed from the event itself. However, it is unlikely that this extends as far as is often thought. In practice, courts are likely to ensure that the amount must be reasonable in the circumstances to prevent one party from making entirely extravagant claims under the indemnity.

In any event, where the desire is to have indemnities treated differently from breach of contract claims, it is sensible to draft the indemnity to apply to certain facts, rather than drafting it to apply to a breach of a provision of the contract. In other words, an IP rights indemnity should be stated to apply in circumstances when an IP infringement claim is made, rather than applying where there is a breach of warranty in respect of IP rights.

(c) ***Do the financial limits of liability apply to indemnity claims?***

The simple answer is that the typical limitation of liability clause will apply to indemnities (at least in the absence of clear contract language to the contrary). The second consideration that then arises is whether it makes sense to have an indemnity limited by the caps on liability under the contract.

For some indemnities, the answer is no. For example, where a service provider agrees to indemnify a client for any claims made by the service provider's subcontractor, then it makes no sense for that indemnity to be limited, since it is intended to operate as a total block on such claims. Contrast this with an indemnity for breach of data protection requirements. There is no real difference in principle between an indemnity of this nature and a normal claim for breach of contract and, therefore, it is more justifiable to apply a cap, even if this is a higher cap than for standard breaches of contract.

What is market practice in this regard? Irrespective of the theory, some will argue that all indemnities should be uncapped, and others would hold that (with the exception of IP rights) all should be capped. In the United Kingdon, market practice is almost always for IP rights indemnities to be uncapped, common for confidentiality and Transfer of Undertakings (Protection of Employment) (known as TUPE) indemnities to be uncapped, and for the remainder to be decided by the bargaining strength of the parties.

Human resources and Acquired Rights Directive/ Transfer of Undertakings (Protection of Employment)

Kai Bodenstedt
Tom Kerr-Williams

1. Introduction

People are a key element of any outsourcing arrangement. Yet, and perhaps surprisingly, they are often overlooked when a customer and service provider are locked in commercial discussions. Service levels, credits, charges and other crucial aspects of an outsourcing agreement are obviously vital; often deals can stand or fall on whether agreement can be reached in relation to them. What is sometimes forgotten, however, is that outsourcing is a people business. Indeed, in the majority of cases, the savings that will be generated, or the benefits obtained, by outsourcing services relate to the number, skills or location of the people that will perform those services.

The people-related cost of an outsourcing can also be significant. Often redundancies will be involved as a workforce is reshaped. The costs of any reorganisation need to be included in the commercials of any deal. Whether costs associated with workforce reshaping are borne by the customer, the service provider or a combination of the two will be important. If not carefully thought through and contracted for, people costs can present a nasty sting in the tail for a service provider when time comes to exit from a contract.

Cost is not the only reason why good sense dictates that people issues are managed carefully and from an early stage. The quality of a service may be significantly affected by the ability of a service provider to complete knowledge transfer from the customer's incumbent workforce and by whether particular specialist skills can be effectively retained. The need for specialist knowledge and skills can vary significantly from one outsourcing deal to the next, and a sensible view of this needs to be taken when planning for any change of provider, outsourcing or insourcing. This is particularly the case in complex outsourcing projects that require highly specialised skill sets across a large number of employees in order to provide the outsourced services seamlessly, and the service provider may not have that luxury on day one from among its incumbent workforce. Hiring from the open market may prove to be difficult, especially in times where there is a high demand for qualified IT engineers. In these circumstances the customer's employees may be essential to make the service viable from the outset.

This chapter considers the way in which people issues can be managed, the movement of employees from customer to service provider (or from one service provider to another) and the ways in which a customer can seek to protect the service that it is contracting for by exercising controls during the life of the contract.

2. People – scoping the service

At the start of any process that will lead to an outsourcing, whether that be a re-tendering exercise or an insourcing, a sensible customer will ask itself what it wants to achieve from the process from a people perspective. Any number of outcomes is possible, but each is likely to be helped by careful consideration of the answers to the following questions in advance:

- Is the service people critical? This will more usually be the case, for example, where a service such as on-site desktop support or bespoke application development is being outsourced, than where the in-scope service is more generic, such as cloud-based hosting or business process administration.
- Is the service provider likely to need any of the people currently performing the service, or can it source required personnel from its own workforce or the open market more cost effectively?
- What would be required on exit – would a replacement service provider need people to effect a smooth transfer of the services?
- Are the services location specific or can they be performed remotely from either the same country or another country?
- If redundancies are needed as the workforce is reshaped, is the customer happy for those to be made by the service provider, or does the customer want to control any dismissals?

Once the best people solution is known, then (and, ideally, only then) can the structure of the transaction be considered from a transfer and control perspective.

3. People transfer

The customer now will ideally have an idea of whether it needs (or wants) people to transfer to the service provider (or on to the replacement service provider) as part of the transaction. The next key question is: what mechanisms are available to deliver the solution that the customer is looking for?

Just pausing for a moment; this is the best order in which to approach the people issues inherent to any sourcing deal. Too often, the customer will seek pricing from potential service providers without giving sufficient thought to the people aspects of the deal. If it does so, the customer risks difficult discussions further down the line as the down-selected service provider begins adding additional cost into the contract to cover any potential people transfer-related liability.

3.1 No automatic transfer

In many countries, an outsourcing transaction will simply involve the dismissal of employees by the customer and the potential re-hire of any number of those same employees according to the service provider's requirements. This is the case in the

United States and across most other countries outside Europe. The answer to the above questions will still be relevant to solution design in such countries. If the customer is obliged to pay costly severance to employees who are dismissed, that may affect the commercial viability of the deal unless the customer can convince those employees to forego severance in return for a job with the new service provider. This can be complex in some countries. In Japan, for example (another country with no automatic transfer provisions), employees often have considerable loyalty to their original employer and dismissals are notoriously hard to implement. If particular employees are key to the service being outsourced, considerable investment may be necessary to persuade these key employees to move with the services.

Knowledge transfer and retention will be an important consideration in many deals. In a country with a buoyant labour market and no legal method for moving employees other than offering them a new job, the price to be paid for someone with skills or knowledge that are key to the service could be significant. Careful thought will be needed in those countries regarding how the solution can be designed to account for these issues. In some cases, an approach involving secondment of employees from the customer and/or carving out of certain services from the outsourcing agreement may be required.

3.2 Automatic transfer

In a number of countries, including across the Europe Union, legislation provides protection for employees in the event of a business sale or outsourcing. The application of that protection is not universal and so careful thought needs to be given to whether and how it is likely to apply, and whether an outsourcing solution can be designed to give the desired result from an automatic transfer perspective. Some other form of automatic transfer provisions exist in other countries outside Europe. In Singapore, for example, the extent of the protection will depend upon the seniority of the employee. Non-managerial and non-executive employees may transfer, whereas those more senior are unlikely to.

The key piece of legislation relevant in the European Union to the people aspects of an outsourcing transaction is the EU Acquired Rights Directive (77/187/EC, subsequently revised and consolidated in Directive 2001/23/EC). Although the concept of the automatic transfer of employment under the directive is an EU-wide concept, it has been interpreted and applied differently across member states. Unusually, the United Kingdom is much more protective of employee rights in this regard than many of its neighbours. Other countries, such as Germany, have taken a less liberal approach to the question of whether an automatic transfer is likely to occur.

By way of example, German directive-implementing legislation would be triggered only if the business (or a part of it) is transferred to a third party. The term 'business' has a wide scope and includes tangible assets and/or intangible assets. In businesses that rely mostly on manpower in order to be functional (eg, cleaning services) the implementing legislation would be triggered if the service provider hired a (substantial) part of the workforce from the customer. In other cases where the business is defined by its assets (eg, a factory cafeteria), a transfer of the substantial part of these assets is required (ie, the kitchen equipment) in order to trigger the implementing legislation.

By contrast, in the United Kingdom the directive's principles are implemented by the Transfer of Undertakings (Protection of Employment) Regulations 2006. These regulations are almost universally known as 'TUPE' and any transfer to which they apply is termed a 'TUPE transfer'. The term 'TUPE transfer' has now become a relatively international term for a transfer of people consistent with the principles of the Acquired Rights Directive. We will use the phrase here to cover all such directive-related transfers.

TUPE applies to a 'relevant transfer', which in the United Kingdom at least includes both of the following:

- a transfer of a business, undertaking or part of a business or undertaking where there is a transfer of an economic entity that retains its identity (Regulation 3(1)(a) of TUPE). We will call such transfers 'traditional TUPE transfers' to the extent relevant, but they are not the main focus of this chapter; and
- an outsourcing, re-tendering or insourcing of activities that remain fundamentally or essentially the same (Regulations 3(1)(b) and 3[1] of TUPE). This type of transfer is commonly known as a 'service provision change'.

The main impact of an outsourcing transaction triggering a TUPE transfer is that the contracts of employment of all those employees assigned to the activities that are transferring will move automatically by operation of law. The move is a purely legal one, with the new employer (the transferee) stepping into the shoes of the old employer (the transferor) as though the individual had always been so employed. With the exception of certain pensions liabilities (referred to in more detail below), all of the rights and liabilities connected with the employment relationship with the transferor move to the transferee. This includes historic employee claims, grievances and any latent claims that neither employee nor employer were aware of at the time of transfer – for example, underpayment of wages or equal pay liabilities. This can be something of a shock to non-EU parties unfamiliar with TUPE, which find it difficult to grasp why they should be liable for defaults on the part of a previous employer.

The other significant impact is that the existence of a TUPE transfer triggers important obligations upon both the transferor and the transferee to inform and consult with representatives of any employees affected by the transfer. Two key considerations arise in relation to this obligation to inform and consult. First, the timing of any consultation process may need to be built into a transition plan. Second, failure to inform and consult properly can give rise to significant liabilities. By way of example, in the United Kingdom the maximum award for failure to inform and consult is 13 weeks' pay per employee. In other countries, such as Belgium and France, the failure can give rise to criminal fines. Such liabilities will therefore need to be the subject of appropriate indemnification in any outsourcing agreement where TUPE is considered.

4. The $1 million question: does the directive/TUPE apply?

One of the facets of TUPE that is both a benefit and a frustration is that it is almost impossible to say with certainty in any given scenario whether TUPE will apply. There is no independent way of determining the answer to this question. Taking the United Kingdom as an example, the only way for a definitive view to be obtained is for an affected employee to bring a claim in the local labour tribunal. Employers cannot bring such a claim and although friendly employees could in theory be encouraged to do so to clarify the position, this never happens and would in any event have a very significant impact upon deal timing. The question is therefore one for the parties to any outsourcing contract to give their best guess. Set out below are some relevant factors to be considered, before we go on to look at how the existence of a TUPE transfer can facilitate or hinder the outsourcing process.

Another key factor to consider in an outsourcing transaction involving multiple countries is that TUPE may be triggered in some countries, but not in others. Much will depend upon the way the individual member state has implemented the Acquired Rights Directive, or outside the Europe Union the equivalent legislation, and the case law that has developed in any given country since implementation. As a rule of thumb, however, a TUPE transfer is much more likely in the United Kingdom than in France, which sits at the other end of the spectrum, with Germany somewhere in the middle.

The traditional TUPE transfer test is one that is broadly consistent with the way in which the directive has been implemented across much of Europe; countries such as South Africa have adopted a similar test of whether a business has been transferred 'as a going concern'. In large part, the traditional TUPE transfer is designed to protect employees where the assets of a business are sold and in circumstances where without it, employees would lose their jobs without any real protection, even though the work that they were doing before the transfer is continuing. The traditional TUPE transfer test is not one that sits easily with the concept of an outsourcing transaction. A key principle of the traditional test is that for TUPE to apply, there generally needs to be an identifiable stable economic entity that has retained its identity through the transfer to another organisation. The test can therefore apply to the outsourcing of an entire business division that is separately organised, with its own separate profit and loss, and assets. It is much less likely to apply to the outsourcing of a service currently performed in-house. For example, one would not expect the traditional TUPE transfer test (or, indeed, the similar test in South Africa noted above) to apply easily where application development for a major bank was being outsourced when it had previously been dealt with in-house as only a small part of the functions of an in-house IT team. All cases will, however, depend on their particular facts.

It was with this in mind that the UK government decided to go further than the Acquired Rights Directive when it implemented changes to TUPE in 2006. Those changes introduced the service provision change test, described above, and were designed to remove uncertainty and, at least in theory, to make it much more likely that TUPE would apply in an outsourcing scenario.

In a straightforward outsourcing of an in-house function, where transformation of the service will take place after the services have moved to the service provider, TUPE is very likely to apply in the United Kingdom, the key question being whether the 'activities' being carried out before and after the outsourcing are fundamentally the same. Clearly, they will be where a 'lift and shift' approach is taken, with the service provider then tasked with implementing changes to the service. Less clear is the position where changes to the services are effected immediately after the outsourcing has taken place. Examples of this grey area include an immediate transition to a cloud-based environment, or a re-tendering process where the customer decides to change the nature of the services that it is procuring to fit revised business requirements better.

Such an approach may be very common, particularly in the IT sector. A customer tied to a particular service for the duration of a contract may well consider redefining its requirements in any request-for-proposal process. Some services may no longer be required, and others may be procured differently in the light of technological developments. In a recent UK case, the courts were prepared to find that a re-tendering process that involved the customer dispensing of a requirement for services that amounted to 15% of the whole package under its first contract meant that there was no automatic transfer between the old service provider and the replacement service provider.

Another key principle underpinning any TUPE transfer is that it has to be possible to identify which employees move to which new employer. Technically speaking, whether TUPE is capable of applying to a particular scenario is a preliminary question (is there a 'relevant transfer'?), followed by a separate exercise to determine which employees will be caught by the transfer when it takes place. The key question is whether the employees are assigned to the undertaking or the organised grouping of persons who will transfer. This can be difficult to determine in practice.

Take the example of an employee who is working in a shared services centre. The service centre has three clients, and the employee is employed to work across all three clients performing application development work for each. He does not have a client-specific job title and is simply employed in the service centre to service whatever client requirements exist at any given time. That employee is very unlikely to transfer, even in the United Kingdom. The practical effect for the service centre operator might be that unless it has built redundancy costs into its charging model in some way, or else obtained an indemnity from a particular client for any redundancies triggered when work is withdrawn, it will be on the hook for dismissal-related costs. Contrast this with a service centre where the work is shared, but employees are organised into client teams. An employee has the job title 'Client A, application developer'. He might work from time to time on things for clients B and C, but most of his time (certainly over 65%) is spent working for client A. He is likely to transfer if client A moves its work in a way likely to trigger a potential TUPE transfer, bearing in mind the principles discussed above.

This can have a particular impact in the case of multi-sourcing transactions. If a customer moves work from a single service provider to a model where different services are procured from separate specialist providers (eg, move to a multi-source model), it may be difficult to ascertain which employees are assigned to which element of the services. Some may be – for example, if the original provider has separate teams working on separate services. But where there is a breaking-up of services and the service provider does not separate out its work in the way now proposed by the customer, this may defeat the application of TUPE and create a potential headache for the outgoing service provider.

5. Pre-transfer workforce reshaping

If the customer and the service provider are in a position to cooperate to achieve the most desired outcome from a people transfer perspective, steps may be taken to re-design the workforce pre-transfer so that the correct people move. This is most likely to be possible in a first-generation outsourcing, where the customer and service provider are able to work closely together. Where a re-tendering is taking place, the customer may have a more restricted view of how the workforce is structured. Ideally, the customer will have in place provisions in the outsourcing agreement that not only provide it with appropriate visibility, but also prevent the shape of the workforce being changed by the service provider in the run-up to exit. Such provisions, discussed in more detail below, are often described as 'lemon dropping and cherry picking' clauses. These prevent a service provider from loading the contract with poor performers or those expensive to dismiss in the run-up to exit, while also preventing it from enticing away the best performers to other client work.

Workforce reshaping before a transfer can make it more or less likely that particular groups of employees are assigned (and, therefore, likely to transfer), but care needs to be taken. For example, German employment law, which is highly regulated, may make it quite difficult to provide for a clean transfer in these circumstances. First, the reassignment of employees to different parts of the business needs to comply with the terms and conditions of the respective employment contracts. Second, in businesses where a works council is established, the reassignment of employees may trigger consultation obligations towards the works council. These consultation obligations alone are mostly a formality, but could make consulting with the works council about the outsourcing as such (to the extent that this is required) more difficult. Additionally, German case law may interpret such reassignment to parts of the business as a circumvention of mandatory employee protection laws that would have the consequence that all employees (ie, also those employees that were not supposed to transfer and assigned to a different part of the business) in fact transfer to the service provider. In order to mitigate these risks, it is quite common that a list of employees who are supposed to transfer is attached to the outsourcing agreement. The parties then typically agree on some form of contractual remedy for the customer if additional employees transfer to the service provider. These provisions are discussed below.

A different and more complex way to control the workforce that transfers to the service provider in some countries is to identify a certain skill set (education, work experience) that may be allocated to the outsourced services. This is typically done when several complex IT services are outsourced. Ideally, the customer would agree with its works council (or similar applicable body) on a collective agreement which provides that only employees with the required skill set may work on the respective IT service. If such collective agreement is in place and the customer then outsources IT services to a service provider, the employees that transfer from the customer to the service provider will be defined by the collective agreement. This would avoid some of the risks outlined above, in particular those of assigning employees to other parts of the business. However, the difficulty will be to allocate skill sets to the respective IT service that are so clearly defined that there can be no ambiguity as to which employees hold these skill sets. Any sensible service provider will still look for warranties and indemnities that give it protection if the customer has failed to conclude a collective agreement that is sufficiently certain.

6. Is it worth having the argument?

As noted at the start of this chapter, the uncertainty of application of the Acquired Rights Directive and TUPE offer both benefits and downsides. It means that either party can argue for one interpretation over another, but it also means that either party can argue for an interpretation that does not suit the other party. This can be a challenge for replacement service providers in particular and some careful thought is needed before a bullish position is adopted in negotiations.

Replacement service providers may be tempted to structure a new service in a way that defeats the application of either TUPE or the directive. That would enable the service to be taken over clean of any employee-related costs. Whether this will suit an individual customer will, however, depend on the extent to which it has already indemnified the current service provider for redundancy costs upon exit. If it has, then the costs may be greater if TUPE does not apply than if it does.

It will also depend upon the extent of any control that the customer has over the approach to be taken by the outgoing service provider. If the commercial relationship has become strained and there is insufficient indemnity protection, then the outgoing service provider may tell its employees that TUPE will apply and that they should then engage with the replacement service provider regarding what will happen to their jobs. The replacement service provider may then have a large number of disgruntled people knocking on its door on or before the first day of the contract. It may be indemnified by the customer for any associated costs (this indemnity should certainly be sought), but that will not protect it from the time, inconvenience and potential reputational damage of having to deal with those employees who have been caught in the middle.

The converse position may also arise. The replacement service provider may need employees (both in terms of a need for local headcount and by a reason of subject-matter knowledge), but unless the customer has in place contractual restrictions upon it doing so, the incumbent service provider may seek to entice away from the customer highly skilled or business-critical employees before the transfer takes place. In some countries, the employees would have the right to object to the transfer with the consequence that their employment stays with the transferor (as is the case in Germany) or comes to an end automatically absent another job offer from the transferor (as is the case in the United Kingdom). The right to object varies across those EU jurisdictions that have implemented the Acquired Rights Directive – the Netherlands, Spain and Italy are all examples of countries where employees do not have any clear right to object to the transfer of their employment if TUPE is triggered. If the employees object, then there is little that can practically be done to guarantee their movement from one service provider to another, other than offer jobs that are commercially more attractive than their current terms and conditions.

Ideally, therefore, an agreed position will be reached between the customer, the original service provider and the replacement service provider. This will enable the process to run more smoothly and ensure that people liabilities do not escalate.

7. Drafting to deal with Acquired Rights Directive/TUPE risk

7.1 General drafting issues

A well-drafted contract will not be overly dependent upon the application of TUPE at either commencement or exit. It will likely give a best guess between the parties as to whether TUPE applies, but will then seek to assign liabilities in a sensible commercial way regardless of the TUPE position. The following are key elements of a good HR schedule:

- a split of liabilities, with a transferor taking responsibility up to the point of service cut-over and the transferee after that point. Responsibilities that are carved up by these provisions will include employment costs, liabilities created by failure to comply with TUPE and responsibility for legacy employee claims and issues. Care should be taken to ensure that the time when the claim is made does not undermine the indemnity – if the claim is made after the transfer but relates to the period before the transfer, it should be the responsibility of the transferor;
- provision for employees who are not part of the proposed solution, but who allege transfer. These are often called 'woodwork' employees – that is, employees who have later come out of the woodwork – or 'wrong pockets' employees. These provisions will normally allow the party to whom the employees are alleging transfer a period to dismiss and coverage for dismissals. In some cases, the transferee – instead of wanting to dismiss – will prefer the option of employing the individuals and passing the cost through to the transferor (or the customer). Such true-up provisions are less common, but can be useful where the original service is effectively a black box with the customer having limited ability to determine whether anyone is likely to transfer to a replacement service provider and, if so, who;
- information provisions that enable the customer to obtain a sensible idea of the shape of the service provider's workforce prior to exit. These provisions are often agreed in addition to standard business-as-usual reporting obligations imposed upon a service provider; and
- commercial provisions dealing with liability for costs associated with workforce reshaping at commencement of the contract, during the life of the contract and upon exit. The drafting of these provisions and the question of who bears liability for redundancy costs and to what extent is a commercial question. The customer may wish the service provider to take the workforce 'as is' with a brief to reshape to fit the service provider's target operating model during the first year of the contract. If so, then the customer is likely to be asked to bear the direct costs associated with that reshaping, usually in

the form of an indemnity for redundancy costs. Alternatively, the customer may agree to deliver to the service provider only those employees that it needs. This can often be the case if the customer is fairly paternalistic and wants to deal with any transfer-related redundancies itself. Any subsequent service provider driven reshaping is then more likely to be at the cost of the service provider.

7.2 Pensions

Pensions have special treatment under TUPE. The general principle is that the occupational pensions liability does not transfer from one party to another. EU case law has, however, created a key exception to this. It is important to be aware of, and to draft for, the liability because it can be significant. Liabilities under a pension scheme that do not amount to old age, invalidity or survivors' benefits are not prevented from transferring. The most common such liabilities are those related to enhanced pension provision upon either redundancy or early retirement. That provision must be funded by the current employer, but as the assets sitting in the old employer's pension scheme (and that would be used to fund the liabilities) do not transfer, this can create a painful headache (and high cost) for the new employer. Due diligence can help to find out whether such liabilities exist, and appropriate warranty and indemnity protection can then assist with closing the otherwise significant gap.

8. Information and consultation

An information and consultation process is required in EU member states where a relevant transfer will take place. This process can vary in length and complexity, but needs to be factored into any deal time line. In the United Kingdom, for example, there is no set timeframe but consultation must take place sufficiently in advance of the transfer for there to be a genuine dialogue undertaken with a view to reaching agreement. In Germany, employees have a minimum period of one month to object to a transfer and so the consultation period must start at least one month before the transfer is due to take place. Consultation must be with appropriate employee representatives and this can also vary from country to country. Thus, in the United Kingdom the representatives must either be from a recognised trade union or else elected/mandated for the purpose, while in Germany, France and the Netherlands consultation will ordinarily be with the appropriate works council.

9. Controlling the outsourced workforce

Since the quality of the outsourced services and the way those services are rendered to a large extent depends on the employees used by the service provider, the customer will often try to exercise control over the workforce that is rendering the outsourced services. Commonly, this is done by including control provisions in the outsourcing agreement that apply during its term.

The service provider, by contrast, has to deliver the services in a way that corresponds to the service levels set out in the outsourcing agreement. Often, the outsourcing agreement provides for quality benchmarks and the failure to meet these benchmarks will in most cases have a negative financial impact upon the service provider. Therefore, the service provider needs to have a skilled and competent workforce in place from day one of the outsourcing agreement regardless of any provisions in the agreement that seek to control this.

This section looks at typical control clauses implemented in outsourcing agreements to enable the customer to control the workforce used by the service provider during the term of the outsourcing agreement.

The ability to include contractual provisions that allow the customer to control the activities of the workforce during the term of the outsourcing agreement exists regardless of whether the workforce transferred automatically (under the Acquired Rights Directive or similar). The outsourcing contract between the parties can be crafted to provide for a broad range of options allowing the customer a degree of control. The main tools in this respect are:

- specific quality requirements;
- the ability to remove underperforming employees;
- involvement in recruitment and vetting of employees; and
- notification and information rights of the customer.

There are different approaches on how to implement such controls:

- A contract may contain only a few broad clauses with generic language. From the service provider's point of view, this would have the advantage of giving the service provider a great amount of flexibility. From the customer's point of view, however, it has the disadvantage of limiting the control that can be exercised since it lacks clear guidelines on how the services should be rendered; or
- The outsourcing agreement may provide for exhaustive and detailed clauses and impose penalties/reduction in fees on the service provider if these clauses are violated. Again, from the customer's point of view such language would increase the level of control and, thereby, provides greater assurances in respect of maintaining the quality of the services at the desired level. From the service provider's point of view, however, detailed quality and reporting requirements and corresponding warranties are probably less favourable since it increases the pressure to provide the required quality throughout the term of the agreement. The service provider will therefore probably agree to such control clauses only if this is reflected in pricing.

Typically, a balance is reached between detailed and specific language on certain elements and broad and rather vague clauses on other issues.

9.1 Examples of quality requirements

Details of quality requirements will depend on the services that are being outsourced. However, some areas typically have a significant impact on the core business or reputation of the customer and, therefore, are of special importance. Any shortfalls and deficiencies can have an immediate and significant impact on the business. Accordingly, it can be necessary to set certain standards within the outsourcing agreement. To this end, typical HR-related quality requirements are the following:

- To avoid personnel shortage and allow business growth in the future, the service provider needs to have enough employees to render services effectively. Although this might go without saying, it is common to include a contractual clause that requires the service provider to allow for an adequate number of employees and maintain an adequate resource pool. For some business-critical services, the service provider may also be asked to commit contractually to putting in place and sharing with the customer a detailed succession plan for key employees.
- The quality of the services rendered by the service provider depends on the qualification of its employees. It is also relatively common to oblige the service provider to offer adequate training for the employees and set out vetting procedures that guarantee to maintain a certain standard. Provisions can in some cases set out in detail the key qualifications that are necessary to perform the duties to ensure that there is no room for misunderstanding.
- Often the contract will also address the recruitment of new employees, in particular setting out requirements or at least guidelines for the recruitment process. A recruiting clause could include a minimum number of trainees, requirements concerning the profile and skill level (eg, language, experience and qualification), as well as vetting procedures for the term of the outsourcing agreement. In some cases, the customer will wish to have some level of involvement in the recruitment process, though this can often be contentious.
- In the area of production, it is of paramount importance to secure the quality of the actual product. It will therefore be necessary to define production techniques, quality assurance measures and equipment maintenance. Provisions concerning both capacities and production time should also be considered in order to avoid production shortfalls. Clear thresholds should be implemented.
- The contract should explicitly contain a compliance clause under which the service provider warrants to comply with legal standards. This is crucial as in some countries the customer can be held liable for breaches of employment law committed by the service provider. It is in the interests of the customer to seek protection from this additional liability.
- Obligations to comply with certification standards that are applicable to the outsourced services (particularly relevant to the outsourcing of IT services) should also be added. A violation by the service provider could put the customer at risk of losing its certification.
- In cases where the service provider has access to sensitive data, it is advisable to set out rules that guarantee the confidentiality of such data. This concerns data that relates to both the business and the employees.
- Commonly, the customer will want the right to direct the service provider to remove employees that it considers not to be up to the job. This is often a heavily negotiated provision. Service providers are generally reluctant to allow the customer complete discretion to require removal without good

reason, but aware that in practice if a customer will not work with a particular employee, that person will need to be replaced sooner or later.

9.2 Examples of notification and information rights

Notification and information rights of the customer are important safeguards in relation to the above quality requirements. Usually, only the service provider has access to figures, statistics and information concerning its business. Some of this information will be needed to ensure that the service provider will be able to fulfil all the requirements effectively. Therefore, an outsourcing agreement will often contain notification and information rights. With the information provided, it is possible to assess the quality of the service provider's workforce and determine whether there is a need for intervention. Examples include:

- turnover rate;
- information regarding key employees who have served notice, or to whom notice has been served;
- succession plans for key employees; and
- information regarding long-term sickness absences/maternity leaves/etc.

The service provider will often also be asked to report any compliance violations immediately. This is particularly the case where there are liabilities that sit with the customer.

Termination and step-in rights

Sharon Rowe
Anthony Willis

1. Introduction

'Termination of a contract' is the process of bringing the contract to an end before it expires. Termination can occur unilaterally or by the consent of both parties to the contract.

Termination rights are used very infrequently in major outsourcing contracts: bringing such major engagements to a premature end is a big decision, and not one taken lightly. Even if a party feels that it has a right to terminate, the commercial and practical consequences can be significant (and may not be adequately recompensed by any financial compensation available under the outsourcing contract). However, in those rare circumstances in which outsourcing contracts need to be terminated, the existence of clear and effective termination rights, and equally clear consequences stemming from their exercise, is critical to minimising the risk to the terminating party of claims of repudiation of contract and claims for damages by the other party.

This chapter provides an overview of the main ways in which outsourcing contracts are terminated, focusing in particular on termination for default (ie, breach). It also offers guidance on the content of termination provisions, how to go about terminating a contract, and ways to minimise the risk of claims of repudiation of contract when terminating a contract.

This chapter also discusses step-in rights, which allow the customer to assume responsibility for service provision for a limited period. Customers can use these rights to address service provider default, generally in circumstances in which they do not wish to terminate the contract; these rights are frequently misunderstood in the context of outsourcing contract negotiations.

2. Termination

2.1 When can a party terminate a contract?

A contract should specify the circumstances in which either party can terminate it. Outsourcing contracts commonly permit termination in the following circumstances:

- for default (or breach) by the other party;
- for convenience; and
- for 'neutral' causes (ie, triggers for termination that could apply even if neither party is at fault *per se*).

Parties to a contract may also agree to terminate the contract by consent, even if this is not expressly stated in the contract.

Additional rights to terminate a contract for material (or repudiatory) breaches may also exist under common law (eg, in the United Kingdom and Australia). These common law rights may apply in addition to the rights that are expressly included in the contract, unless the contract provisions expressly exclude them. Careful consideration will need to be given to the potential application of such rights (or similar rights as may otherwise be implied at law, depending on the relevant governing law of the contract).

Each of these circumstances is discussed in more detail below.

(a) Termination for default (or breach)

The right for one party to terminate a contract if the other party has breached an obligation is referred to as a 'termination for breach' or 'termination for default' right.

In major outsourcing contracts, it is standard for the customer to be able to terminate the contract for specified significant (often defined as 'material') breaches by the service provider, such as a significant delay in commencing performance of the services or a persistent failure to meet minimum service levels. What is 'material' or 'significant' will usually be a question of fact for a court to determine, and will ordinarily be judged in the context of the overall project. Put simplistically, the longer the outsourcing engagement is (both regarding scope and duration), the more serious the breach would need to be in order to justify termination.

This creates a considerable element of doubt/uncertainty for the customer (because if the customer terminates on the basis of a breach by the service provider ultimately found by a court not to be material, then it may well end up having to pay damages to the service provider – see section 2.6 below). Accordingly, many outsourcing contracts seek to remove the element of doubt by pre-defining levels or types of breach that will trigger the termination right (eg, breaches of particular clauses such as those regarding IT security or, more often, failures of service levels beyond set thresholds), often referred to as 'minimum service levels'.

Major outsourcing contracts may also include a right for the service provider to terminate the contract for a default by the customer, although this is usually limited to a breach of the payment obligations. This may seem unfair on the service provider, but the customer will argue that it would be more seriously affected by contract termination, and that the service provider will ordinarily be able to be financially compensated for any default by the customer. Service providers may, in any event, seek to retain further termination rights for limited categories of material breach of their IP or confidentiality rights, especially if they are also willing to provide lengthy termination assistance and additional service periods, even if the right of termination is exercised.

Generally, two types of termination for default provision are used in outsourcing contracts: those that permit immediate termination for serious breaches of the contract which cannot be remedied, and those that permit termination for less serious breaches which were capable of being remedied but were not remedied during a specified period after the breaching party received notice to remedy the breach (typically 30 days).

If a provision permits immediate termination for trivial breaches, it may be 'read down' or not enforced by the courts. Similarly, if the terminating party has discretion to allow a period of time for the other party to remedy a default but without specifying what the period will be, a court may imply an obligation that the period must be 'reasonable'. Depending upon the governing law of the contract, an obligation for the terminating party to 'act in good faith' may give rise to the same 'reasonable notice' requirement.

Accordingly, best practice is to ensure the following:

- Only a breach of a condition (ie, a critical term) of the contract can give rise to immediate termination rights. Such terms should ideally then be identified up front.
- For less serious breaches, the period given by the terminating party to the other party to remedy the breach is reasonable (ie, it is practicable for the breaching party to remedy the breach in that period). A period of 30 days is commonly specified in outsourcing contracts, but shorter periods are also seen, depending on the nature of the outsourced services and the potential effects of any default on the customer's business.

Including these requirements will minimise the risk of disputes between the parties over the exercise of their rights for termination for default.

Circumstances in which immediate termination for breach is available commonly include:

- insolvency (or similar) of the service provider;
- failure to provide any services for a specified period (whether by reason of *force majeure* or in the event of the service provider abandoning or repudiating its obligations to provide the services);
- if the service provider loses a permit or licence that is necessary to provide the services;
- material breaches that are not capable of remedy;
- repeated breaches of a single, critical obligation (eg, a requirement to meet a service level that is critical to the customer's business, and to a particularly significant degree – see section 2.1 (a)); and
- exhausting the amount of any financial security or liability cap following one or more claims against the service provider under the agreement.

Circumstances permitting termination for breach only after the terminating party has given the breaching party the opportunity to remedy the breach commonly include:

- failure to provide a particular service described in the services schedule;
- failure to comply with a law or policy;
- failure to meet a particular service level;
- failure to complete a particular transition or transformation related task; and
- other breaches that are capable of being remedied.

When can a right to terminate for default be lost? Parties to a contract need to be aware that if the other party breaches the contract in a way that gives rise to a right to terminate and the terminating party does not exercise that right, or acts in a way that is inconsistent with that right, then the terminating party may lose its rights to terminate in respect of that breach. This is because the terminating party may have 'affirmed' the contract through its actions and therefore waived its rights to terminate in that instance. Accordingly, a party with a right to terminate a contract for default must either act promptly in enforcing its rights or expressly reserve its rights in communications with the other party (which can be done only for a limited period). This is especially problematic in the context of outsourcing projects where, owing to their size and complexity, the contracting parties tend not to rush to exercise termination rights as soon as these arise, preferring in the first place to try to work through their problems in the hope that things will get better. Clearly, this should be done with care and with the benefit of strategic legal advice (if only in the background).

(b) Termination for convenience

In many outsourcing contracts, the termination provisions will include the right for the customer to terminate the contract 'at will' or 'for convenience' (ie, simply by giving written notice to the service provider), usually on the basis that the customer pays compensation to the service provider. This permits the customer to exit the contract if, for example, a change in its structure or functions means that the services are no longer required, or if the underlying financial rationale for the outsourcing deal no longer represents value for money.

It is theoretically possible for a service provider also to have a right to terminate for convenience, but such rights are very uncommon, to the point of being almost unheard of.

Best practice in respect of the drafting of termination for convenience provisions includes setting out the particular categories of costs and expenses that the service provider may claim if the contract is terminated. These commonly include the costs of licence fees and leases for premises used only for the provision of the services, and the costs of making staff redundant. However, a provision generally requires the service provider to mitigate its losses resulting from the termination and to claim only 'unavoidable' costs from the customer. The customer may, as an alternative, seek to avoid uncertainty by seeking the service provider's agreement to a simple pre-set termination fee that will be payable if the termination for convenience right is exercised (usually on the basis that the size of such fee decreases over time, as the service provider derives more revenue/recovers its sunk costs from payment of the charges).

If a contract includes a right for the customer to terminate for convenience, then it is generally also a requirement of the contract that the service provider includes equivalent rights in all its subcontracts so that there is a limit on the costs that the customer must pay.

The inclusion of a termination for convenience provision increases the risk to a service provider in entering the contract and, therefore, the service provider may increase its charge to offset that risk. Put simply, a five-year contract will generally be more profitable to the service provider than a three-year contract; however, if a five-year contract contains a right for the customer to terminate for convenience at no charge from year 3 onwards, then the service provider may treat the whole deal as providing guaranteed revenue for only three years, and to price accordingly. The customer should consider this when deciding whether a termination for convenience right is required. The setting/calculation of the termination fee itself will also be a topic of much negotiation, particularly regarding whether the service provider should be able to recover any element of 'foregone profit' from the remainder of the envisaged term after the termination date, as applied to just its actual costs of exit and unrecovered elements of the amortised costs.

In practice, termination for convenience provisions are rarely exercised. Aside from the payment of any termination-related fee, there is also the cost and disruption of a change in service provision to consider. Even if a customer wants to terminate for convenience, best practice is for it to seek to negotiate with the service provider to terminate the contract by consent, conditional upon an agreed amount of compensation being paid by the customer (which should ideally then be lower than the normal termination-related fee). Alternatively, the customer may find that its new service provider is willing to bear some or even all of such costs in order to win the work for the customer. This will all obviously depend on the commercial dynamics of the project in question.

(c) Common law rights to terminate for breach

In common law jurisdictions, the right to terminate also exists at common law, even if express termination rights are not included in the contract itself.

The right to terminate a contract for breach at common law arises only in respect of repudiatory (or similar) breaches – for example, if there has been a breach of an essential term, such as a failure to provide any services or a failure to pay for any services, or if the conduct of a party to the contract is such that it demonstrates that it has no intention of complying with its obligations under the contract. This may occur if a service provider has fundamentally misjudged the financial basis for a particular project and discovers that trying to continue with it – perhaps over several more years – will result in substantial financial losses.

The express termination for default provisions in outsourcing contracts tend to permit the wronged party to terminate the contract in more cases than common law termination rights and, therefore, common law termination rights rarely add anything to the express rights in the contract and are accordingly very infrequently used.

In common law jurisdictions, however, the termination provision should make it clear whether the contract preserves common law termination rights, or whether those rights are excluded. Sometimes customers seek to exclude or limit common law termination rights so that if the customer fails to perform its own obligations, damages are payable but termination rights are unavailable to the service provider. Whether any such limitation or exclusion would be wholly effective will depend upon the particular contract and its governing law, as well as the circumstances of the particular case.

(d) *Termination by consent*

The parties to a contract are also able to terminate the contract by consent – that is, if they both agree to do so. This is the case regardless of whether or not the contract expressly permits termination by consent, as it is always open for the parties to a contract to agree something different or in addition to what is contained in the text of the contract.

In such cases, the parties generally enter into a new written agreement that states when the original contract will be terminated and what consequences follow. For example, this may arise if the outsourcing project has not worked out as planned for either party, but where there is no clear-cut cause or the causes are in dispute and the parties decide that they would rather negotiate the terms of their parting than end up in a formal dispute resolution process.

An alternative to termination by consent is to amend the existing contract so that it expires earlier than previously agreed, although this will not be appropriate in all circumstances.

(e) *Neutral termination rights*

An outsourcing agreement may also contain a range of termination triggers that are exercisable when neither party is at fault as such (usually, but not exclusively, in favour of the customer).

Examples of such termination triggers include:

- insolvency – for example, if either party is wound up, goes into administration or otherwise becomes unable to pay its debts. Customers may object to allowing any service provider the right to terminate the contract if the customer is still paying its bills while in administration (eg, when they are working their way through their financial problems). Customers may also insist on including a termination right that is exercisable at some point short of the service provider's actual insolvency (on the basis that if the service provider becomes insolvent, it will be unable to fulfil its obligations regarding the provision of termination assistance, etc);
- *force majeure* – for instance, if it becomes impossible to provide (or receive) all or a significant part of the services for an extended period of time;
- change of control – usually a right that exists in favour of the customer only. The argument goes that the customer has selected a particular service provider on the basis of its culture and ethos, and so should be entitled to exit if the control of the service provider changes (which may create a risk of the approach/mindset of the service provider changing thereafter). This can be contentious, particularly with stock exchange-listed service providers that can say, with some justification, that they have no control over who may seek to acquire their shares in future, and also that a change of control should not of itself allow for termination if the services are otherwise still being provided in accordance with the contract terms. Potential compromises may be to allow for payment of at least part of the relevant termination for convenience fee and/or to restrict the right of termination to changes of control involving a narrower subset of entities (eg, competitors of the

customer, specified entities or suppliers that the customer has engaged in material litigation in recent years); and

- change in law or regulation – for instance, if the provision of a particular service on an outsourced basis goes contrary to any law or regulation.

2.2 What is the process for terminating a contract?

It is common for termination provisions in outsourcing contracts to set out a process to be followed if a terminating party wishes to exercise a right of termination. In exercising its rights, a terminating party must strictly follow the process described in the clause. If the provision is not strictly followed, the other party may challenge the exercise of the right and a court may find that the termination was a 'repudiation' of the contract by the terminating party. (Repudiation is discussed further below.) The process for terminating a contract that is set out in the termination provision should be as simple and clear as possible to minimise this risk.

A terminating party is generally required by the contract to issue a notice to the other party as part of the process of termination. Even in circumstances in which the contract does not state that a notice is required, issuing a notice is the most practical method of terminating the contract, as it will be the clearest and most transparent method. This minimises the risk of confusion and disputes.

Most outsourcing contracts do not specify that any particular words need to be used in the notice terminating a contract. However, each notice should clearly state that the contract is terminated and the date on which the termination takes effect. It is also good practice to state the basis on which the contract is terminated (ie, "pursuant to clause [x] of the contract for a breach of clause [y] of the contract by the service provider") and what the other party must do (eg, deliver up confidential material, remove service provider items from the customer's premises, etc).

If a party breaches the contract and the contract requires that the party be given the opportunity to remedy a breach, the terminating party must issue two notices. The first notice must identify the breach and require the other party to remedy it within a specified period (either as set out in the contract, or a reasonable period of time). The second notice must record the fact that the other party has not complied with the first notice and terminate the contract on that basis.

If a party breaches the contract and the contract permits the other party to terminate the contract immediately for that breach, the terminating party needs to issue only one notice, which identifies the breach and terminates the contract.

Termination notices should also, as best practice, expressly reserve all the terminating party's rights under the contract or otherwise in law or equity, so as to permit the terminating party to claim damages for any breach.

2.3 Termination in whole or part

Outsourcing contracts often specify that termination (whether for default or convenience) may occur in respect of whole or part of the contract. In addition, if the parties to a contract agree to terminate the contract by consent, they may also agree to terminate it in whole or in part.

'Termination in part' typically involves removing some of the products or services being provided. In practice, this can be quite complicated, as it can have knock-on effects on service levels, pricing (especially bundled or volume-discount pricing) and reporting, and can ultimately make it uneconomic for the service provider to perform the remaining elements of the contract. For example, the service provider may have provided discounted pricing on the basis of providing all the products and services set out in the contract, and obtaining an economy of scale in respect of its overhead and back-office functions.

Given this, if a customer decides to terminate a contract in part for a default or for convenience, it can result in a dispute with the service provider as to how to give effect to such a change. Of course, if the termination in part is to remove a discrete product or service that has discrete pricing and service levels, then disputes are less likely to arise.

Accordingly, prior to exercising any rights to terminate part of the contract for either default or convenience, the customer should take into consideration the risk of disputes or legal challenge. Preferably, the service provider should be asked to comment on the changes proposed to be made to the contract to give effect to the partial termination prior to them being implemented, to minimise the risk of disputes.

If the parties agree by consent to terminate the contract in part, then all the details and the consequential changes required to the contract can be agreed in writing in advance. If this is done, it will minimise the risk of disputes.

If terminating in part, best practice is for the parties to prepare a new version of the contract with marked-up changes. This will assist in ensuring that all the consequential amendments required to the contract have been included, and that it is clear what has changed as a result of the termination in part (and what has not changed).

2.4 Rights and obligations that apply on termination

The obligations of parties under outsourcing contracts can be interdependent and technically complex. There can also be numerous subcontractors and third parties involved in the provision of the services, which can make termination complicated. Given this, all outsourcing contracts should preferably include a provision that sets out the rights and obligations that apply following termination. The same rights would also apply upon expiry. Such a provision may include the following obligations:

- to deliver up documents, software, hardware and other equipment;
- to return material comprising the other party's confidential information to that party, or else to destroy it;
- to update and comply with the transition-out plan (if there is one);
- for the service provider to transfer equipment or premises leases (to the extent that the leases are used only for the contract);
- to assist in the transition of service from the current service provider to the customer or a replacement service provider nominated by the customer, including providing 'knowledge transfer' to incoming personnel;
- to novate subcontracts to the customer or replacement service provider;

- possibly, for the service provider to transfer its personnel (whether by operation of law, or potentially via some form of consensual contract process involving the individual personnel); and
- to preserve and possibly to extend IP rights (eg, if an extension to the customer's sub-licensing rights is required to enable the customer to pass those rights to a replacement service provider).

The contract should also provide that certain obligations (eg, obligations regarding confidential information) extend beyond the term of the contract notwithstanding its termination (or expiry), and that termination is without prejudice to the rights of the parties arising prior to termination. This preserves the rights of:

- the terminating party to claim damages for breach of contract from the other party in instances in which the other party was in breach of the contract; and
- the other party to claim compensation from the terminating party in instances in which the terminating party exercised rights to terminate the contract for convenience.

2.5 Transition-out plans

Given the complexity of major outsourcing contracts, best practice is to have a transition-out plan (or similar) that sets out exactly what the parties will do upon termination or expiry. The plan should address all the issues that are likely to arise on termination or expiry, such as the need to transfer equipment, software, subcontracts and personnel, as listed in the provision described above relating to rights and obligations that apply on termination. The level of detail in the plan should encompass, for example, whether particular software licences can be novated or whether the customer or replacement service provider will need to purchase new licences.

Sometimes, an outsourcing contract provides that the transition-out plan will be developed at a later date "to be agreed", or that the plan was required to be provided by the commencement date, but the obligation was neither met nor enforced. It is often too late to develop a transition-out plan after a termination notice has been issued, as at that point the service provider has the least incentive to perform its obligations fully and the most incentive to minimise its resourcing and costs. Accordingly, customers should ensure that the transition-out plan is in place and ready to be implemented if a termination notice is issued. See in this regard the chapter on due diligence and transition, and the chapter on renegotiations, retenders and termination assistance.

2.6 Repudiation

If a terminating party is exercising a unilateral right to terminate a contract under a termination provision (eg, termination for default or convenience), it must take great care to exercise that right strictly in accordance with the terms of the contract.

A failure to do so can result in a court finding that the terminating party has itself repudiated the contract. 'Repudiation' means that the terminating party has acted in a way that indicates that it is neither ready nor willing to perform its obligations under the contract (ie, it has acted inconsistently with the contract, as if to deny that the contract is in effect). If a terminating party is found to have repudiated a contract, the other party may have a right to terminate and may also be entitled to damages, whether or not it exercises the right to terminate.

Repudiation can occur in a range of circumstances including if a terminating party issues a termination notice when it does not have the right to do so. For example, a terminating party cannot generally exercise a right to terminate a contract for default if the other party's breach has not yet occurred. This is the case even if the breach is imminent and if terminating in expectation of the breach would assist in mitigating the losses suffered by the terminating party. The terminating party must generally wait for the breach to occur before issuing the notice.

2.7 Key issues when drafting termination provisions

Even if never exercised, a well-drafted termination provision can be a strong incentive for proper performance of the contract.

The following are some key issues to remember when drafting termination provisions:

- The termination provision should reflect the particular contract and key risks under that contract. Customers, in particular, should not assume that standard termination provisions will be sufficient – the contract may have particularly critical milestones or service levels that should give rise to immediate termination rights.
- If the provision allows for immediate termination for particular events, the events must be critical to that contract, otherwise the rights may be unenforceable in some jurisdictions. In any case, including onerous termination rights may provoke the service provider into adding further contingency into its pricing, resulting in the customer paying for protection that it does not need.
- The termination provision should be simple and clear, and include a well-defined process for terminating the contract. This minimises the risk of disputes and claims of repudiation of contract if the provision is exercised.
- For major outsourcing contracts, the termination provision (or another clause) should require the parties to implement a transition-out plan upon termination, which must be agreed at least in outline form at the point of contract signature.

2.8 Key issues when exercising termination rights

The following are some key issues to remember when exercising termination rights:

- The terminating party must strictly follow the process set out in the contract.
- The terminating party should issue a written notice of termination.
- The notice of termination:
  - must meet the notice requirements under the contract;
  - must clearly convey to a reasonable person in the position of the recipient that the contract is being terminated; and
  - should expressly reserve the terminating party's other rights at law or in equity, as discussed above.

In addition, if the termination is in response to a breach of contract, the following will apply:

- If the contract requires that the other party be given an opportunity to remedy a breach prior to termination, then the period must be reasonable.
- The terminating party must exercise its rights in a timely manner or it risks being deemed to affirm the contract and/or waive its rights to terminate in respect of that breach.

2.9 Use of termination rights for leverage

One of the most frequent uses of a right of termination is to give the terminating party the leverage to renegotiate the contract on more favourable terms, in return for not exercising its right to terminate. This is understandable and can be very effective, but needs to be undertaken with the benefit of careful legal advice in order to avoid crossing the line inadvertently while seeking to effect a termination, and also to avoid leading to accidental waivers of the termination rights.

3. Step-in rights

3.1 What are step-in rights?

Step-in rights in outsourcing contracts enable the customer or its nominee to take over service provision in certain, specified circumstances – generally (albeit not exclusively), upon the serious default of the service provider.

3.2 What are the features of effective step-in rights provisions?

From a customer's perspective, a step-in rights provision should:

- set out the circumstances in which the customer can exercise its step-in rights (ie, the trigger events) (discussed further below);
- provide that whether a trigger event has occurred is determined by the opinion (or 'reasonable opinion') of the customer (ie, it is a subjective rather than objective test);
- provide the ability for the customer to perform the services itself or to engage a replacement service provider to perform those services (even a competitor of the original service provider) using, as applicable, the original service provider's systems, processes, equipment, personnel and premises;
- require the service provider to provide assistance to the customer and its nominee in performing the services (at no additional cost);
- enable the customer to elect whether the step-in rights will be exercised in respect of all or part of the services;
- require the service provider to pay:
  - the customer's (reasonable) additional costs in performing the services if the customer is performing the services; or
  - for the replacement service provider if a replacement service provider is performing the services, and other (reasonable) expenses incurred by the customer in exercising the step-in rights;
- suspend the service provider's obligations to perform the services while the

step-in rights are exercised, and also expressly suspend its right to be paid for the services;

- provide that the customer's rights to other remedies arising from the breach remain unaffected (eg, termination rights);
    - if necessary, include additional or increased access rights, IP rights and rights in confidential information to ensure that the customer can perform the services or engage a replacement service provider; and
    - address how step-in comes to an end (usually when the customer is satisfied that the trigger event no longer applies) and what consequences follow.

The acceptability of such provisions to the service provider will depend on a range of factors, including, in particular, the nature of the services, the customer's business and whether the service provider will receive compensation if the step-in rights are exercised. For example, in some jurisdictions the public sector and financial services sector are subject to regulatory requirements that come close to mandating the inclusion of step-in rights and, therefore, service providers are likely to accept their inclusion in contracts with customers in these sectors. However, a service provider will most likely require financial compensation if step-in rights apply in circumstances that are not associated with any default by the service provider, regardless of the sector in which the customer operates.

3.3 What are the trigger events?

The trigger events (when the step-in rights may be exercised) must be set out in the provision itself and vary between contracts. However, they are generally circumstances of serious delay or other serious default by the service provider (ie, a breach of contract that would permit the customer to terminate the contract), or in the event of a serious disruption caused by a *force majeure* event that is not otherwise dealt with by either party's disaster recovery/business continuity planning.

The following are examples of circumstances that may be included in a provision as trigger events:

In the reasonable opinion of the Customer:

- *there has been a substantial breach or non-performance of the contract by the Service Provider which substantially prevents, hinders, degrades or delays the performance of any:*
    - *critical aspect of the services; or*
    - *critical function of the Customer, for more than 48 consecutive hours;*
- *the Service Provider purports to terminate the contract other than in accordance with its legal rights, or otherwise repudiates or abandons the contract; or*
- *an insolvency event occurs in respect of the Service Provider.*

3.4 When are step-in rights exercised?

Step-in rights in outsourcing contracts are generally exercised only if all of the following circumstances occur:

- The service provider is in material breach of the contract.

- The customer is unwilling to terminate the contract for default (eg, due to the relationship of the parties or the particular circumstances of the breach).
- The contract is for business-critical services.
- The customer is confident that the service provider will still be able to resume service provision at a later date.

The reasons why step-in rights are rarely exercised are discussed below.

3.5 How are step-in rights exercised?

The process for exercising step-in rights should be clearly set out in the contract. Customers must strictly follow the process described in the contract when exercising step-in rights to minimise the risk of claims by the service provider that the rights were not properly exercised. A failure by a customer to exercise step-in rights strictly in accordance with the contract could be a repudiation of contract and, if so, the customer may be liable to the contractor for damages. Repudiation is discussed in section 2 above.

Generally, the step-in rights provision requires the customer to issue a notice to the service provider to exercise the rights when the customer is satisfied that a trigger event has occurred. The provision may or may not require the customer to provide reasons in the notice. However, even if the customer is not required by the provision to provide reasons, the customer should, in any event:

- exercise the step-in rights only strictly in accordance with the contract;
- maintain evidence of its reasons for believing that it has properly exercised the step-in rights, in case the service provider challenges the exercise of the rights; and
- consider consulting with the service provider prior to exercising step-in rights. While this strategy presents a risk that the service provider may seek a court injunction to prevent the exercise of the rights, it may also (depending upon the governing law of the contract) place an obligation on the service provider to raise any legal impediment to the exercise of the step-in rights (eg, identifying that the customer's IP rights under the contract are inadequate to step-in). If no such impediment is raised, then the customer may have greater confidence that the service provider will not seek to challenge, or may be prevented by the operation of law from challenging, the customer's right to exercise step-in rights in those circumstances.

Once step-in rights have been exercised, it is important for the customer to keep the original service provider informed as to what the customer or any replacement service provider is doing. This provides the original service provider with the opportunity to object or to raise issues or concerns in a timely manner, and to facilitate the original service provider resuming performance of the services at a later date.

If the service provider does not raise any issues or concerns, then it is more difficult for it to argue at any later stage that the step-in rights were exceeded, or that the replacement service provider has taken an action that will make it more difficult or expensive for the service provider to resume the performance of the services.

It is also important for both parties to keep communication channels open, so that the customer knows when it is likely that the trigger event will cease (ie, when the service provider can restart the provision of the services). Once the trigger event has ceased, then the contract generally requires the customer to issue a notice to the service provider to resume provision of the services.

3.6 What are the advantages of exercising step-in rights?

Step-in rights enable a customer to exercise a degree of 'self help' to ensure continuity of service, in order to address a service provider's serious non-performance or defective performance of a contract without the customer having to terminate the contract. Frequently, a cause of interruption in service will be temporary and/or capable of being rectified, and the customer may therefore be reluctant to exercise the 'H-bomb' option of contract termination, especially if the service provider has otherwise been performing to an acceptable (or even good) standard.

3.7 What are the disadvantages of/impediments to exercising step-in rights?

While many major outsourcing contracts include step-in rights, they are rarely exercised – even in situations in which the service provider is in material breach of contract. This is because they result in the customer assuming the responsibility for service provision or finding a replacement service provider. With these responsibilities comes considerable risk.

It often transpires that a customer that is considering using its step-in rights is in no position to assume provision of the services itself, whether because of lack of technical skills and resources, or a lack of willingness to incur the risk of service failure. Therefore, before exercising step-in rights, the customer must almost always be able to identify and engage a suitable replacement service provider to provide the services, albeit on a temporary basis. This can be difficult to do in a hurry, particularly as another supplier may not want to assume responsibility for what may well be a major, high-risk project that is already in serious trouble.

Another impediment to exercising step-in rights can often be found in IP or confidential information provisions. The customer must ensure that it has sufficient IP rights and rights in confidential information to enable it to sub-license its rights to the nominated replacement service provider. In some cases, and particularly if the customer has inadequate IP rights, it is impossible or impracticable to exercise the step-in rights at all. Similarly, service providers will sometimes place limits on the content of access that they can be compelled to provide to their materials, premises, personnel and systems. For example, a step-in rights clause may state that the customer is not permitted to use systems or premises that are also used by the service provider for the provision of services to the service provider's other clients.

In order to exercise step-in rights, a customer must also be satisfied that given time, the service provider will be in a position to resume provision of the services. This will be the case only if the trigger event was an isolated or short-term incident. If the service provider is either unwilling or incapable of performing the contract, then step-in rights are unlikely to be useful. Exercising step-in rights in such circumstances may just complicate contract administration (and damages calculation) and increases the customer's liability and risk. In these circumstances, it may be preferable to exercise termination rights instead.

One of the main problems with step-in rights becomes apparent only once the trigger event has ceased and the original service provider is required to resume provision of the services from a nominated replacement service provider. At this stage, the original service provider may blame the replacement service provider that was engaged during the step-in period if a problem occurs in the provision of services (eg, a failure to meet service levels or a need to change the technical requirements), and vice versa – that is, the original service provider may claim that the problem is the fault of the work performed by the replacement service provider, while the replacement service provider may claim that it is the fault of the systems or processes of the original service provider. Such a dispute may be difficult to resolve. Contractual provisions can be used to minimise this risk (including provisions requiring the original service provider to cooperate with the replacement service provider); however, no provision will remove this risk entirely.

Given the above disadvantages and impediments, step-in rights should be exercised only:

- as a last resort;
- when necessary for a customer to maintain business-critical functions;
- when it is either impractical or impossible to terminate the contract for service provider default and to engage another service provider; and
- when it will be possible for the service provider to resume provision of the services.

Before considering exercising step-in rights, a customer should:

- undertake a comprehensive risk assessment. What is the cost/benefit analysis of exercising step-in rights compared to terminating for default or taking other actions? The customer must consider the risk of disputes in exercising the rights and disputes as to which party is responsible for issues arising during the step-in period if the service provider later resumes service provision;
- ensure that it is satisfied that the service provider can resolve the trigger event and, if it is resolved, has the ability and willingness to provide the services;
- unless it can provide the services itself, identify a replacement service provider and ensure that the replacement service provider will be able and willing to perform the role (noting that sometimes the original service provider will have defaulted because it is technically impossible to provide the services);
- identify the IP rights and rights in confidential information required to exercise the step-in rights and ensure that the customer has those rights (and can pass them on to a replacement service provider through sub-licences, if needed); and
- anticipate, and budget for, a significant additional management effort and resourcing requirement (the costs of which may not all be recoverable).

3.8 When should step-in rights provisions be included in a contract?

Step-in rights provisions are not necessarily appropriate for every outsourcing contract. They are generally used for major outsourcing contracts and contracts relating to business-critical functions. If an outsourcing contract is for an off-the-shelf solution that could easily be substituted and for basic services that other service providers could easily provide, it is highly unlikely that step-in rights would be exercised and, accordingly, might not be required. In such cases, the inclusion of such a provision may unnecessarily inflate the contract price (as the service provider builds risk into its pricing).

However, for customers in major outsourcing contracts, including a step-in rights provision provides a strong incentive for a service provider to focus on meeting its obligations under the contract because its exercise will result in:

- embarrassment;
- substantive administrative effort;
- loss of revenue;
- liability for costs;
- most likely, providing a foothold for a competitor to assist the customer as a replacement service provider; and
- increased access to the service provider's facilities, personnel, premises, equipment and other resources and/or intellectual property by the customer or its replacement service provider.

A step-in rights provision is only one type of provision that provides a performance incentive to the service provider. As it should be exercised with extreme caution and as a last resort, for the reasons described above, it is unlikely to be the most important of such provisions.

Assets and third-party contracts

Gareth Stokes

1. A tale of two transfers

1.1 Introduction

The introduction to this book considers the similarities between outsourcing contracts and business transfer arrangements, characterising outsourcing as two business transfers. From the customer's perspective, this would constitute one outbound transfer at the start and one inbound transfer upon termination or expiration, with a period of services provision in the interim.

Business transfer arrangements in the context of corporate mergers and acquisitions (M&A) work involve a great deal of effort. A rough outline of the activities involved would include:

- identifying the in-scope assets of all types (physical assets, contracts, intangible assets such as intellectual property, employees, premises, etc);
- checking the ownership/contract position in relation to each such asset;
- dealing with the buyer's due diligence enquiries;
- carefully setting the scope of any warranty or indemnity protection to deal with any potential risks and issues; and
- dealing with the transfer formalities applicable to each such asset.

Key differences exist between an asset transfer in a purely corporate M&A context and one in an outsourcing context. In the M&A arena, there is generally no expectation of an ongoing relationship between buyer and seller after the transfer, whereas in the outsourcing arena, there clearly is. That significantly affects the risk profile and incentives on each side. The corporate M&A seller wishes to obtain the best price for the lowest continuing risk (in terms of warranty coverage), whereas the outsourcing customer cares less about asset transfer value, but is extremely interested in ensuring that the service provider has everything necessary to provide the services required during the contract term.

The same basic process should be followed in each case, and we list common issues to be addressed below.

1.2 Common issues

(a) *Due diligence*

In this context we describe due diligence on the customer's asset and contract estate only. (See the relevant chapter for more details of due diligence as part of the procurement process.) The customer will need to undertake an internal due diligence process before the outsourcing to determine which assets and contracts the outsourcing will affect.

(b) ***Identifying and checking in-scope assets/contracts***

As part of the due diligence, all assets and contracts that may be affected by the outsourcing need to be identified and the status checked. A good starting point for this identification exercise is to look at the function to be outsourced and the staff who provide that function in whole or part – regardless of whether such staff might be in scope to transfer to another employer as part of the outsourcing process (see the chapter on human resources for more detail on staff and staff transfer issues).

Based on the day-to-day activities of such staff, it is then possible to identify the equipment that they use in the course of their activities – whether ordinary office equipment, laptops, specialist machines or otherwise.

For example, consider a bank outsourcing the handling and clearing of cheques. In that case, the staff will cover a range of individual actions within the cheque-processing function. This will encompass everything from couriers collecting cheques deposited in branches to staff operating the processing lines for scanning the paper cheques – taking in fraud detection specialists and IT specialists compiling batch files along the way. The assets for that business process therefore potentially extend from the in-branch collection to the cheque processing lines (paper handling and scanning equipment), as well as the various elements of IT equipment used in connection with the service.

Similarly, the contracts most relevant to the function to be outsourced and the day-to-day activities of the affected personnel can be identified. Staying with our example, these might include contracts with third-party couriers, software licences for the specialist cheque-processing software, and maintenance and support agreements relating to the hardware and software.

Having looked at the assets and contracts directly relevant to the staff carrying out the relevant functions to be outsourced, you now need to consider the wider context. Inevitably, those staff will also benefit from a whole series of assets and contracts more widely available within the customer enterprise operations. In our cheque-processing example, those are likely to include everything from facilities-related assets and contracts (office equipment, cleaning contracts, catering, etc) to the bank's standard IT systems, personnel, accounting functions, software licences and maintenance arrangements.

There is no easy way to shortcut what is generally a laborious forensic exercise in establishing exactly which assets and contracts have a bearing on the function to be outsourced.

(c) ***Does the customer need or want to transfer?***

Once all of the potentially relevant assets and contracts have been identified, the next question is to determine – in each case – whether the asset or contract needs to be transferred and whether the customer wants to transfer it to the appointed service provider.

In general, the question of whether a contract or asset needs to be transferred will depend upon factors such as whether:

- the asset or contract is specific to the service, or of wider application within the customer's organisation; and
- it is something that can be easily replaced with a commodity product or service generally available in the market, or whether it would be difficult for the service provider to secure a suitable alternative (whether because of cost, specific customisations to the asset or contract secured by the customer, the fact that the asset is out of production or the contract is no longer offered by the vendor).

In other cases the customer may want to transfer the asset or contract. This might be because it is not useful to the customer's business outside of the services that are being outsourced, or it is seen as bearing cost or being associated with liability issues (eg, maintenance liabilities) that the customer wishes to rid itself of as part of the wider outsourcing. In cases where the asset or contract carries some form of liability (whether one that has already crystallised or a potential liability that may crystallise in future), the service provider is likely to account for that liability or risk within its pricing, whether as a general uplift, a specific risk premium or otherwise. Therefore, the customer should investigate exactly what cost or risk premium the service provider has attached to the asset transfer to check that it is not overpaying for the relevant liability in some other form.

Where an asset or contract need not be transferred, and the customer does not want to transfer it, then the customer will retain the asset or contract. In those cases it is likely that the service provider may still need to use the asset or benefit from the contract from time to time. Where the customer retains the asset or contract, then it will need to establish the extent to which third parties, including the service provider, have a right to use or benefit from the retained assets and contracts.

(d) Right to transfer/right to use

Where assets and contracts have been selected for transfer to the service provider, the obvious next question is whether that transfer is dependent upon permission from a third party.

In relation to physical assets, if the customer owns the asset outright (ie, there are no finance payments outstanding, etc), and the asset does not form part of any security, then the customer can feel confident that it is entitled to transfer the asset to a third party. However, where there are finance arrangements, or the asset forms part of a specific security arrangement for a debt (as opposed to a floating charge over a general class of assets), then consent to the transfer may need to be sought from the relevant finance provider or creditor.

Contracts need to be considered both in terms of the benefit of the contract (ie, the right to enjoy the services or licences provided) and the burden of the contract (the obligation to pay, and various other obligations relating to the use of the services or licensed material, together with boilerplate obligations including confidentiality provisions).

In some jurisdictions, it is possible to transfer the benefit of a contract separately to the burden. Taking English law as an example, if a contract exists between A and B and is silent on the matter of assignment, then B could assign the contract to C without involving A, but that assignment would transfer only the benefit of the contract to C. The burden (ie, the obligations under the contract, including as to payment) would remain with B, and if any of B's obligations were not performed, then A would have a right of action against B and not C. Of course in this example, if the contract explicitly restricts assignment by B, then B could not assign to C without first seeking consent or a waiver from A.

Typically, in order for the burden of a contract to be transferred to a third party, both the original contract parties and the third party will need to be involved. Continuing the example above, for B to transfer both the benefit and burden of its contract with A to C, then a tripartite novation would be required, which in summary sees:

- B agree to remain responsible for its obligations under the contract prior to the date that the novation occurs;
- C agree to assume responsibility for B's former obligations under the contract from the date that the novation occurs for the remainder of the term; and
- A agree to release B from future obligations under the contract from the date that the novation occurs and accept C in B's place.

Even in jurisdictions that allow for the burden of a contract to be transferred without a formal tripartite novation, it is still generally better to enter into a novation agreement. A formal tripartite document will evidence the understanding and intention of the parties, putting the question of lingering post-transfer responsibilities beyond doubt.

In many cases a service provider will not need to have a contract formally assigned or novated to it. Instead, it will simply be taking advantage of the customer's existing contract in the context of providing services to the customer (and not for the service provider's own use or that of its other clients) in exactly the same manner as the customer's own staff did before the outsourcing. In fact, where there has been a transfer of the customer's staff to the service provider as part of the outsourcing, it is fairly likely that it will even be the same individuals interacting with the relevant third-party contractor.

In these cases, the customer is more interested in ensuring that the service provider has the right to use the contract as if it were a member of the customer's staff. Many organisations pre-emptively include rights for service providers to use the third-party vendor's services as a matter of course in their contracts in the expectation that outsourcers may need to use the relevant contract.

Where inclusion of appropriate usage rights in the contract has not occurred, then there may be a risk that the relevant third-party vendor would consider any use of the services or licensed materials by a service provider to be a breach of the relevant contract – and the risk is definitely greater where software or other intellectual property has been licensed. This is one of the types of breach that major software platform vendors are keen to pick up via audits, increasing the risk further.

To solve the problem, the customer ought to seek appropriate usage rights or consents from the third-party vendors before any use by the service provider occurs. Ideally, this would be done before the customer enters into the main outsourcing contract with the service provider to avoid creating commitments from the customer to the service provider that the customer may not be able to fulfil. However, if time scales do not allow for that, and there is a window between the contract signature date and the date that the service provider commences provision of the services, appropriate consents can be sought in that window.

(e) *Rights to be secured in new contracts*

As we cover in more detail below, the customer is likely to want to have any contracts that are novated to the service provider at the outset of the arrangements transferred back to the customer on exit – or transferred on to a replacement service provider if someone else is appointed to provide the services at that time.

The contracts to be novated back or onward upon exit will not just be those that were transferred to the service provider upon entry. Some of those contracts novated on entry will likely have expired, and may or may not have been replaced – depending on the transformational aspects of the outsourcing. Conversely, the service provider may have entered into new subcontracts specifically to support the outsourcing that would need to form part of the bundle of exit/transferring contracts.

Wherever the service provider is entering into new contracts (eg, to renew or replace those novated to it on entry) or entering into entirely new subcontracts, it needs to have that eventual exit transfer in mind. The service provider should be securing at the time of negotiating and executing such contracts that the relevant third party explicitly provides prior consent to a novation back to the customer or onward to a replacement service provider on exit, and the customer would be well advised to ensure that an obligation for the service provider to secure such rights in its subcontracts is included in the main outsourcing agreement.

(f) *Formalities of transfer*

Depending on the legal requirements in the relevant jurisdiction, different asset types, contracts and IP rights may require different legal formalities when they are transferred. In order for the assignment, novation or other form of transfer to be effective, it is essential that the proper formalities be followed.

Depending on jurisdiction, issues to consider include the following:

- Does the transfer need to be in writing? Is a simple agreement sufficient, or does a special type of document (eg, a deed) need to be used?
- Is notice sufficient, or does the counterparty's consent or agreement need to be similarly recorded in writing? Is the arrangement one between two parties, or is a third party's involvement needed?
- Do the documents need to be independently witnessed, signed under oath in front of an authorised person, or notarised in some form? Do they need to be stamped or sealed when executed – especially if executed by a company?
- Do the documents need to be lodged with any legal authority? Is the consent

of any court, regulator or authority required?
- Do any registers need to be updated to record the transfer of ownership or an interest in any rights?
- Are there any minimum time periods, waiting periods or other legally imposed time limits that would affect the transfer? Have these been allowed for within the transition plans on entry and exit? Whether legally imposed or not, do certain authorities that may need to be involved have long waiting times before they are likely to deal with the matter?

2. Assets

2.1 Outbound asset transfer(s)

Once the outbound assets have been identified (see section 1.2 (b) above), and have been determined as being in scope for a transfer to the service provider rather than simply being used by the service provider (see sections 1.2 (c) and 1.2 (d) above), then other practicalities remain to be settled.

Commonly, any assets to be transferred from the customer to the service provider will be transferred on the service commencement date. The obvious underlying logic for this is that from that date, the service provider is the party that needs to own and use the relevant assets in order to provide the services. That said, where there is a staggered transition of services to the service provider, it then follows that the transfer of assets may need to be staggered to match the same schedule.

Rarely, there will be other reasons for the transfer of particular assets to occur to a different timetable to service commencement – for example, where a given asset needs to be retained by the customer to complete a particular year-end activity for which the customer will remain responsible in the first year after service commencement. Therefore, it is worth considering whether a simple transfer of all assets on the service commencement date is necessarily the correct approach.

Assets transferred to the service provider on entry tend to be transferred at no substantial cost in consideration for the other obligations in the contract, or occasionally for a nominal payment (£1, €1, $1 or a similar small sum in the currency used in the contract). In some deals (but these tend to be the exception), the customer might wish the service provider to 'buy' the assets at net book value for other financial structuring reasons (after all, the service provider will simply charge the cost back to the customer via some other means in the charging mechanism). Where this happens, the customer tends to use the service provider almost as a source of finance, and can expect this to be reflected in higher termination charges to account for the recovery of the sums paid for the assets in the event of early termination of the contract without the service provider being at fault.

2.2 Risk, title, insurance

As with any transfer of physical assets (whether in an outsourcing context, a business sale or a simple goods sale arrangement), legal ownership, or 'title', in the asset may transfer at a different time to the transfer of responsibility, or 'risk', in the asset. This separation of risk and title is particularly relevant where the assets need to be moved to a different site, or where control of the underlying premises at which the asset is located is also transferring.

The question of which party bears the risk in particular assets is important because it has a direct bearing on which party ought to be insuring them. It can also have a knock-on impact in determining the responsibility for service failures. It could certainly be argued that it is unfair for a service provider to be held responsible for service failures where the reason for those failures is that assets which are critical to its ability to deliver and which were based in the customer's premises have been destroyed by the deliberate or negligent actions of the customer.

To illustrate the issue, consider the situation where ownership in standard desktop computers used by staff involved in providing a service transfer to the service provider on the service commencement date, but the staff and computers remain located in premises owned and controlled by the customer. Then compare that with a situation where expensive specialist processing equipment vital to the service is to be moved from the customer's premises to new premises used by the service provider as a delivery centre. In both cases, the title to the assets (the computers on the one hand and the specialist equipment on the other) might transfer on the service commencement date.

However, in the former case, the service provider could argue that at least some of the risk in the desktop computers remains with the customer as they remain within its premises. If the premises burn down due to reasons outside the control of the service provider, should the service provider have to replace them, or is that a matter which the customer's insurance should cover? And while the service provider ought to have a business continuity and disaster recovery plan to allow it to carry on providing services in some form notwithstanding the destruction of those computers, if there is a degradation in service quality while the service provider buys new computers and sets them up properly, should the service provider be able to claim some relief from liability?

In the latter example, where assets are being moved, it is easy to see that the service provider bears complete responsibility – and all risk – once the assets are installed in its site. But the process of dismantling, transporting and reassembling the processing equipment might be far from straightforward, and the question of who should bear the risk at each stage will vary depending upon who is undertaking the activity (or arranging for it to be undertaken by third-party removals experts). If the disassembly is carried out by the customer's staff in preparation for transport, and they damage the equipment during disassembly, then – regardless of whether title may already have transferred to the service provider or not – it seems logical that risk should remain with the customer for such disassembly and damage that might be caused during disassembly.

The difficulty with the transfer of risk when goods are being transported is that it is often difficult to determine exactly when damage occurs and, therefore, whose risk it is. Damage done (inadvertently) during disassembly by the customer might not be discovered until the processing equipment is reassembled and found not to function properly. In that case, how can the service provider prove that the damage was done by the customer at the disassembly stage? Because these arguments are rarely clear cut, it is often best to agree an arbitrary risk-share during a particular period (in this example that could be the period from the start of disassembly through transportation until fully reassembled and tested) to avoid any need to determine forensically the cause of damage. Both parties are then equally incentivised to ensure that damage does not occur (as they will both bear some cost if it does occur) and it reflects the fact that both parties bear an equal interest in successful transfer and physical relocation of the asset. After all, it is vital to the successful delivery of services in future and, therefore, the service provider's ability to get paid.

All of the same issues then apply in reverse when assets are transferred back to the customer by the service provider on exit, so it may help the customer to have a more reasonable view of what to expect from the service provider on entry when it appreciates that it will have the same responsibilities upon exit.

2.3 Maintenance, refresh and new asset purchases during the term

It is an unfortunate reality that entropy must always increase – and there is no contracting out of the laws of physics. Even when treated properly and maintained to a high standard, assets will wear out or, in relation to technology products in particular, become obsolete even if they still function.

During the multi-year term of a typical outsourcing arrangement, assets will need to be replaced and refreshed. The schedule of replacement will often be determined by an asset refresh plan, which in turn is linked to the way that the value of the assets is depreciated over time in the owner's accounts, with different asset types being depreciated over different time periods in accordance with their expected useful life. IT assets are typically regarded as having a shorter shelf life, and may be depreciated over three or five years. Other assets may have a longer expected useful life, and be depreciated over proportionately longer periods. Cutting across this will be the need to replace any asset that is broken or damaged, regardless of age (see comments on which party ought to bear the risk in the assets in section 2.2 above).

In addition to the replacement or 'refresh' of assets that are transferred to the service provider by the customer, it is likely that the service provider will need to procure additional assets that it will then dedicate to the provision of services to the customer. These specifically purchased and dedicated assets then become part of the pool of assets upon which the provision of services is dependent, and as such any replacement or refresh policies should apply equally to these newly procured assets.

Where any asset is to be replaced, the service provider needs to ensure that the replacement, if not a like-for-like replacement, is at least equally capable in terms of quality, features, functionality, etc. Any newly procured asset that is not replacing an existing asset would need to meet the necessary requirements for that asset.

Maintenance and serving requirements will vary depending on the nature of the asset. In some cases, little or no regular servicing or maintenance will be required, and the asset will simply be covered by a 'support' arrangement of some kind (see section 3.2 below). Other assets will require regular servicing and maintenance, and indeed certain aspects of support arrangements may be invalidated if those servicing and maintenance obligations are not observed. The service provider will need to be made aware of any such requirements (or given a proper opportunity to discover them via the due diligence process – see section 1.2 (a) above and the chapter on procurement, negotiation and delivery process) and should then be obliged to comply with them in relation to the assets.

Generally, the service provider should be required to comply with the customer's pre-existing policies in relation to replacement and refresh of assets. However, the customer's requirements can have a significant cost impact. There is a big difference between an obligation to replace an asset once it is fully depreciated and has reached the end of its expected life, and an obligation to replace broken assets only, which can result in still-functioning assets remaining in use for longer. The latter policy might offer a short-term benefit by reducing the cost of purchasing replacement assets, but can increase support and maintenance costs in the long term as the asset estate becomes fragmented and increasingly diverse, with older assets remaining in the mix for long periods.

The customer will wish to retain strategic control over how and when assets are replaced and refreshed. This is not confined to simply requiring the service provider to comply with the customer's replacement and refresh policy, however. Certain assets – and this is perhaps particularly the case for IT assets – are very unlikely to be replaced on a like-for-like basis due to the rapidly changing availability of products in the particular market. In those cases, the choice of replacement products can have long-lasting strategic implications for the future architecture of the customer's systems and processes. Therefore, the customer should also reserve to itself strategic and architectural decision making about the future direction of the service, and the service provider's decisions when selecting new or replacement assets should be aligned with such strategy.

2.4 Finance and costs

Any decisions regarding how asset purchases (whether new or replacement assets) are financed will need to be viewed in the context of the wider conversation between service provider and customer as to the overall charging structure. One way or another, the cost of asset purchases and refreshment of the asset estate will be a cost that the service provider will be looking to recover within the overall charges.

In broad strokes, the assets can either be paid for transparently by the customer on the basis of the actual costs to the service provider (with or without additional margin, depending upon what additional installation or commissioning activities might be required), or the service provider can seek to blend the asset costs into its other charges to be recovered over time.

Where the customer is to be charged for the assets on the basis of their cost to the service provider, then the matter is relatively straightforward. The customer is likely to then want matters to be as near to 'open book' as possible, to ensure that it has clarity as to the costs as they are incurred, along with a clear view as to which of the assets are likely to be refreshed in future.

Where the asset refresh costs are built into the other charges, then the service provider inevitably takes a risk that future charges may not fully compensate for the capital investment in purchasing the asset. This may result in the addition of a risk premium to pricing to accommodate the fact. However, provided that the structure of the exit transfer (see section 2.6 below) is done on a fair basis with a predictable price being paid by the customer for the assets that will be transferred to it upon exit, the service provider should have no reason to seek to add an element to any termination charges to account for the value of assets transferring upon exit.

Depending on the customer's accounting practices, where a given asset is used by the service provider exclusively or very nearly exclusively in providing services to the customer (see section 2.5 below), then the customer might still have to recognise the value of the asset and its depreciation within the customer's own accounts. This need for the customer to recognise the asset in its accounts can apply even where legal title in the assets is held by the service provider. In such circumstances, much of the expected accounting benefits of transferring assets to a service provider as part of an outsourcing may be negated, and can drive the customer toward preferring to retain title and refresh responsibility, with the service provider having a right to use the assets, and possibly an obligation to undertake procurement, commissioning and installation associated with refresh as part of the services.

2.5 Exclusive/non-exclusive use

Typically, where the customer is transferring assets to the service provider, or paying for new or refreshed assets to be purchased in order to support service provision, the customer will wish to ensure that the assets are used exclusively to provide services to it, and not to the service provider's other clients. If the relevant assets are used entirely on the customer's own premises, or on the service provider's premises but within a dedicated facility, exclusivity of use tends not to be a problem. It is only where a shared delivery centre is to be used that the question becomes more complicated.

In such circumstances, if the relevant asset will benefit the service provider and its other clients, then clearly the full cost of such asset should not be passed on to the customer. Instead, the relevant asset costs become part of the service provider's general overhead, and some proportion then is taken into account within the charges payable by the customer for the services.

The quid pro quo, where the customer is not meeting the full cost of the asset and it is not used exclusively to deliver services to the customer, is that the asset will generally not form part of the pool of assets that the customer can require are transferred to it or onward to another replacement service provider on exit.

While having assets exclusively used in the provision of services might provide comfort to the customer (in terms of asset availability, system integrity and resilience and data security, among other benefits), potential downsides exist. Section 2.4 above touches upon possible accounting issues that exclusive use can cause. It can also mean that the customer is paying for a system and set of assets designed to cope with peak usage, resulting in some portion of the estate of assets sitting unused for the majority of the time. As a result, having shared capacity available to cope with peaks – with appropriate security protections in place – can offer significant cost advantages in some cases.

2.6 (Re)transfer on exit

Having transferred the assets to the service provider on entry, and with the service provider having then purchased additional and replacement assets, the customer will wish to ensure that it has the right to have relevant assets transferred to it or onward to a replacement service provider on exit in order to ensure service continuity. The customer will generally wish to ensure that it has a right to require the transfer, but is not obliged to undertake it. While the service provider tends to accept this position, if an asset or collection of assets is so specific to the service that the service provider would not be able to reuse or resell the asset on exit, it may occasionally be reasonable to specify that the customer must take such asset upon exit.

In most cases, though, the best way to think of the issue is as the customer having a 'right to buy' certain assets on exit. The two challenges tend to be deciding which assets are within scope of the customer's right to buy, and what the price should be.

(a) Which assets are in scope for transfer?

In general, the greater the extent to which an asset has been used wholly or mainly for the purposes of providing a service to the customer, the easier it is to see why such asset should be the subject of the customer's 'right to buy'. Exclusive or near-exclusive assets will readily fall into this category.

The challenge comes when some aspect of the service has been provided using substantially shared facilities and assets. In those cases, the customer and service provider may wish to agree on a notional percentage to determine whether an asset is in scope for possible purchase. The service provider will want to ensure that the bar is set higher than a simple majority of use to avoid the customer buying assets that are genuinely important to its delivery to its other clients. A notional figure tends to be set at around 75% of the total use of the asset of the 12 months preceding exit, with assets that meet such test then being within scope of the customer's right to buy.

(b) Deciding the price to be paid for the assets

The customer will obviously not wish to pay twice for an asset, and this principle tends to inform asset-pricing discussions on exit. Where it has already met substantially all of the cost of the asset at the time that it was purchased (or if the cost of the asset was factored into the service charges, as were then paid over the contract term on an amortised basis), then the customer can reasonably expect that such asset will be transferred to it upon exit without an additional charge. This tends to be the case where the customer has been paying for assets on an open-book basis (see section 2.4 above).

Where the customer has not met the entire cost of the asset already, the service provider will expect to be paid for the asset. There are various methods that can be used to determine the price payable at that point. Service providers will tend to argue that a fair market value should be paid, in the hope that the asset might still arguably have a market value that is greater than its depreciated value in the service provider's accounts, allowing recovery of a greater sum. Customers, by contrast, will be more concerned with avoiding having to pay twice. The asset's net book value tends therefore to be the customer's preferred value in such circumstances.

Where customers and service providers are at loggerheads over the proper value to attribute to an asset for 'right to buy' purposes upon exit, then relying on expert determination is often the most straightforward solution. Asking a jointly appointed independent expert to decide the correct price that the customer should pay (rather than the asset's 'value', which is a different question) avoids either party forcing its opinion on the other.

3. Third-party contracts

3.1 Manage, novate or a bit of both?

Once the relevant contracts have been identified (see section 1.2 (b) above), then the customer (with input from the service provider where appropriate) should decide whether the contract is to be novated to the service provider, or whether the service provider will simply need a right to use the services or licences provided under the contract. In the latter case, the service provider will often take on *de facto* management obligations in respect of the contract.

The question is not necessarily straightforward for every contract. In general, a contract under which relatively simpler services (eg, support services) are being provided that will be entirely subsumed within the outsourced services, and the customer has no direct need to use for other purposes, is one where it makes sense to novate the contract to the service provider. Conversely, a contract in which the customer has a need to maintain an ongoing relationship with the third-party vendor for other reasons (eg, a software licence that relates to software which is also used in other parts of the customer's business) is a good example of one the customer will want to retain, but then extend to cover the service provider's use.

In many cases a single contract might cover both the licensing and support elements. What should the customer do in such cases? It wants to retain the licence, but has no direct need for the support element that will become part of the service provider's responsibilities. In that case, the customer can partially novate and amend the relevant contract, such that the licence remains with the customer and is extended to allow the service provider the necessary usage rights, but the support element is completely transferred to the service provider.

3.2 Costs – ongoing and cost to transfer

Where a contract has been novated, it has become a subcontract and should be treated accordingly, with the service provider bearing the costs as it would for any other subcontract. Any retained contract remains with the customer, and the customer remains directly responsible for the payment of fees under that contract, even where the service provider might manage the day-to-day receipt of services from such vendor.

In some cases, third-party vendors will see any request to novate or extend usage rights as a revenue-generating opportunity. The customer may find that it is able to push back successfully against any request for additional fees from a vendor on the strength of the wider relationship, particularly where there really is no practical impact upon the vendor and no net increase in the number of licensed users. All too often the vendor will successfully claim additional costs in relation to a transfer. If these have not been anticipated and allowed for within a service provider's charges, then the service provider tends to legitimately expect the customer to bear that cost.

Similarly, where the service provider has not otherwise been given an opportunity to discover the quantum of charges attributable to a contract that is in scope for novation (whether via due diligence or otherwise), and has not therefore allowed for such charges within its overall pricing, the service provider will need to be allowed an opportunity to revise its pricing as soon as such contract charges become known. The easiest and most obvious mechanism within the contract to achieve this is the change control mechanism, which also affords the customer an opportunity to examine the service provider's proposed uplift in its pricing before it becomes effective.

3.3 Liabilities and relief events

As stated above, once a contract has been novated, it can be treated to all intents and purposes as a subcontract. Just as the customer can legitimately expect the service provider to be liable for the acts and omissions of its other subcontractors, the service provider should bear that same risk in relation to the novated contracts from the point of novation.

Where the customer retains a contract, then the customer's claim, in the event that such third party's breach or negligence causes issues under its outsourcing contract with the service provider, would be against the third-party vendor rather than the service provider. The service provider should be entitled to claim relief in such circumstances if the breach or negligence by the third-party vendor has a knock-on effect upon the service provider's ability to provide the services to the required standard – although as a condition of granting such relief the customer should require that the service provider:

- notify the customer of the relevant third-party vendor's failure;
- notify the customer of the likely knock-on impact (limiting the relief claimed to directly caused impacts); and
- use reasonable endeavours to mitigate the effects and or implement work-arounds.

The notification of the third-party vendor's failure and management of the response is particularly important where the retained contract is one which the service provider is charged with managing as part of the services.

3.4 Service levels and credits – the chess clock/double-dipping challenge

A subtle twist on the above liability question applies when considering the service level regime. The service provider might argue that its ability to meet certain of the required service levels is dependent upon a third-party vendor responding within a given timeframe. This typically occurs in an IT outsourcing context, where second or third-line support requests in respect of a particular software package might need to be passed to the relevant software vendor.

Therefore, from the service provider's perspective it could look like a service level that measures both the service provider's activity and that of a third-party vendor is asking the service provider to take a risk that the service provider has no control over – especially if the customer retains the relevant third-party vendor contract. The service provider might therefore suggest that the parties apply a principle where any calculation for service level based on response time includes only the time when the service provider is undertaking activity, while time taken by third parties to respond is excluded from the calculation. This approach is often described using a chess clock metaphor, with the time ticking while the service provider is thinking and making its move, but the clock stops while the problem is over with the third-party vendor.

However, if the customer used end-to-end response time data in setting the expected service level that it has asked for in the contract, then applying this 'chess clock' approach results in a false measure. For example, assume that the customer has data demonstrating that, for a given collection of software, any incidents of a particular severity were, on average, dealt with by way of an implemented work-around within 120 minutes of being reported. In that case the 120-minute work-around time has been calculated including the time taken by third parties in responding to support requests and providing their own inputs to the final work-around. If the service provider is allowed to apply a 'chess clock' principle to exclude each support request to a third party, and that time then does not count toward the 120-minute service level, that could have the effect of significantly extending the real end-to-end response time that the customer receives.

In that case a chess clock approach without reducing the related service level to allow for it amounts to a form of double-dipping by the service provider – getting relief for something that was already accounted for when the original service level was set. This can be dealt with in two ways.

The least complicated approach is to keep the service level as is and have no chess clock. This can be justified by pointing out to the service provider that if the reason that it misses a service level is because the third-party vendor fails to respond in a timely fashion, to a degree that amounts to a breach of the vendor's contract with the customer, then the service provider can claim relief via the mechanism described in section 3.3 (b) above – the argument from the customer's perspective then being that all cases where the service provider fails the service level and the third-party vendor is not in breach must therefore be the service provider's fault.

Alternatively, the service level mechanism can be adjusted to accommodate a chess clock principle, but all the service levels then need to be recut (based on another analysis of the underlying data) to work out the relevant timings not counting any time that the customer was waiting on a third party. Depending on the service level, this can result in a dramatic reduction – the 120-minute average in our above example could then be slashed to under 20 minutes for software estates with lots of external second- and third-line support providers. It also means that the monitoring of service level performance needs to be more sophisticated, with not just reporting and work-around implementation times monitored and used to calculate the service level performance, but every handover point to and from any third-party vendor noted and the timings calculated accordingly. If a given issue requires two different vendors to be contacted, that takes the timings and measures from being based on two data points (incident report and work-around implementation) to six (adding in outbound and inbound handovers to and from the two vendors). This is a real issue for customers, as it adds considerably to the overhead involved in auditing accurate measuring of performance by the service provider.

3.5 The third-party vendor relationship

Depending on the contract and the vendor, the decision of whether to novate the contract or retain it may be driven more by the customer's desire to maintain a commercial relationship with the relevant vendor, or leverage the service provider's relationship with that vendor, than specific service-related considerations.

Particularly with larger software vendors with multiple software products, if the customer uses other products from that vendor in other parts of its business, then it may see an advantage in retaining the contracts. This could be driven purely from an overall relationship perspective, or more concrete commercial concerns such as volume discount pricing that would be lost (whether affecting the outsourced function, or the other parts of the customer's business that use that vendor's other products) if some of the contracts were novated to a service provider. In such circumstances, the vendor will generally also want to maintain a good overall relationship with the customer, which the vendor sees as a valued client. This can be to the customer's advantage if it then needs to approach the vendor to extend usage rights to the service provider without wishing to pay a fee for the privilege.

In other cases, the service provider may have a far better relationship with the relevant vendor than the customer has. Even for relatively large enterprise customers, the volume of licences and support services that a major global IT service provider or systems integrator might purchase from major vendors will dwarf those that the customer purchases. This will often mean that those service providers can get better deals (based on its global purchase volumes across all its client accounts) than the customer could ever hope to get. Where this is the case, it will clearly make commercial sense for the customer to look to benefit from those arrangements.

3.6 New contracts, replacement contracts and retransfer on exit

Just as with assets (see section 2.3 above), in addition to the third-party contracts novated to the service provider upon entry the service provider will probably enter into some new subcontracts that are specific to the services to be provided.

Again, the customer will require that any contracts that were novated to the service provider on entry (to the extent still in force), together with any new contracts that are specific to the services, should be capable of novation to the customer on exit. As before, the customer will want to have the option to require novation rather than be compelled to do so, and similar principles to those discussed in relation to assets (section 2.6) will apply.

Ideally, in order to ensure that this is the case:

- the novation agreements between customer, service provider and third-party vendor that novate the contracts to the service provider on entry should

include provisions permitting the customer to reverse the novation again at its option on a future date – or nominate a replacement service provider as a new novatee; and
- any new subcontract that the service provider enters into should include provisions allowing it to be novated by notice to the relevant third-party vendor either to the customer or a replacement service provider nominated by the customer.

The relevant third-party vendors may or may not be happy to agree to such compulsory retransfer, or onward transfer, novation provisions in advance. If the third-party vendor will not make an absolute commitment to future novation at the customer's option, the next best option for the customer is to have the vendor agree to act reasonably in considering such a request in future. This increases the risk for both customer and service provider that contracts could become locked in with the service provider due to the third party not consenting to novation, and an assessment of that risk and its consequences will need to be made on a case-by-case basis.

While it is easy to see that the above retransfer/onward transfer wording should apply to any contracts novated to the service provider on entry, as those were historically contracts used exclusively for the customer's benefit, it is not so clear cut for new subcontracts. If the new subcontract is exclusively used for providing services to the customer, then it is easy to see why the customer ought to have a right to direct its novation upon exit from the main outsourcing arrangements with the service provider. For contracts used for the customer and the service provider's other clients, a similar challenge exists in determining whether the customer ought to be able to direct their transfer on exit. In practice, a solution very similar to that discussed above for assets (section 2.6) tends to work well, and can be used to determine the question.

Since services contracts tend to operate on the basis of periodic charges, there is usually less of a challenge in considering the exit transfer price of a contract. It is easy to apply a fair apportionment of the charges – where the service provider would be responsible for charges up to the novation date, and the customer or replacement service provider for charges from and after that date. Exceptionally, the service provider may have paid some up-front fee for a contract that is depreciated over a longer period (a licence fee being probably the most common example), and that upon the exit date may not have been depreciated to zero. Where that is the case, the service provider might want to be paid some amount for the remaining value in the contract. If this is the case, then the treatment described above for asset transfer pricing can be deployed.

Lastly, where the service provider is to enter into new subcontracts during the term in order to replace contracts novated to it by the customer that have subsequently expired, then similar strategic and architectural questions to those considered above in relation to assets might apply. In that circumstance the customer will wish to control any new subcontracting, and the principles described above in relation to new asset purchases would apply equally to new subcontracts.

4. Related issues

Several types of contract and asset tend to be treated differently to the general case described in this chapter so far. While similar high-level issues and commercial drivers to those discussed above may apply to the contracts or assets in question, in most jurisdictions a large number of additional legal requirements drives different treatments and behaviours.

4.1 Premises

While a lease or licence to occupy premises is certainly a contract, and land itself is an asset, the very different treatment of real estate assets and interests at law (with the principles applying in different jurisdictions varying considerably) mean that land and premises issues always need to be considered separately from other assets and contracts.

There are myriad issues associated with premises and land. These range from legalistic issues about the nature of different forms of legal interest that can be granted to more practical day-to-day issues such as responsibility for compliance with health and safety requirements by staff on site. If not handled properly, the consequences can be dire – it would be a disaster if the customer intended to allow the service provider a bare licence to access premises on a short-term basis, and accidentally ended up granting a lease over part of its premises entitling the service provider to claim long-term occupancy.

Wherever the customer is to allow the service provider rights either to attend its sites (eg, to carry out *ad hoc* maintenance) or to work 'permanently' on site during the term (based among the customer's other employees, or in a dedicated area), it is essential that proper advice is sought from real estate lawyers in the relevant jurisdiction. For multi-jurisdictional deals, it is not uncommon for very different access and occupancy rights to exist on a per-jurisdiction basis due to local legal differences.

4.2 Customer-owned/service provider-owned intellectual property

While IP rights are, in most jurisdictions, a form of asset (albeit intangible), they are treated very differently to the other assets. Third-party licences can sometimes form part of the contracts that may be transferred or retained, but for more information on IP rights in outsourced services contracts, see the chapter on confidentiality, intellectual property and data.

4.3 Employee transfers

Last but by no means least are the various employees connected with the services. The customer's and service provider's contracts with the employees who provide and receive the services are a form of contract, but in most parts of the world these employee contracts are treated very differently to typical commercial contracts.

In some cases the law applicable in the relevant jurisdiction will dictate that the contracts of employment of certain employees automatically transfer from customer to service provider on entry and then back again, or on to a replacement service provider, on exit. In other jurisdictions employees are not afforded this protection.

In either case, it would be dangerous to see those as contracts to which the principles outlined in this chapter could readily be applied – for more information about employee issues, see the chapter on human resources.

Governance, vendor management and dispute resolution

Peter Brook
Gregory Tulquois

1. Introduction

Once a contract has gone 'live', the parties have an ongoing relationship that the governance section of the agreement is designed to bring some order and structure to. This will be particularly useful if unexpected things happen or if things start to go wrong: a set of objective provisions can help to cool any potential disputes as the parties can follow the pre-defined processes.

It can be tempting to use an off-the-shelf or standard/precedent set of provisions, but they should ideally be crafted to reflect how the parties intend to work together. This can be harder than it seems, unless the parties are very experienced and have agreed on how their day-to-day relationship will work. There is no one-size-fits-all set of governance practices. Essentially, it is all about relationships, information and change.

Unfortunately, the governance provisions are rarely given the priority that they need, and they can be little more than an afterthought. The best route is for the negotiators to engage with the people who have been tasked with running the contract after it has been formed so as to develop a workable set of mechanisms.

2. Governance

2.1 Process

The governance provisions should cover a number of areas both during implementation and live operation of services. They should provide for meetings and reports at all stages of the project, including potential and actual future changes. They should include mechanisms that can be used to resolve any commercial, operational or technical issues that might arise as part of the project.

The type of governance provisions required, and the level of detail, can be influenced by a number of factors including the term, value and criticality of the agreement – more valuable and critical contracts are likely to require a closer working relationship (or at least reporting lines) with the service provider. However, and as raised above, the key is for them to be practical and realistic, and the parties should ensure that they fit into their respective existing governance structures and processes across their organisations.

For some projects, the governance framework will be fully developed and set out when the agreement is signed. Another approach is for the agreement to specify a procedure under which formal rules can be established. These rules are then commonly embodied in a code of practice that details the operational and management processes by which the services are delivered, but, as a document, it is non contractual. However, an 'agreement to agree' is not legally binding and if a formal and robust arrangement is required, the former approach is recommended as best practice.

Governance covers not one issue but a collection of many, often interlinked, issues. There is no common list of items that should be covered. We have considered some of the common areas below.

2.2 Relationship management

As in a marriage, communication can make or break a commercial relationship. It can allow problems to be identified and resolved early, and build an atmosphere of mutual trust and appreciation of the other's priorities. To make this as simple and effective as possible, the channels of communication should be defined and ideally tested before the contract commences.

Three key levels of communication are strategic, business and operational communication. Strategic communication is for senior management, which will often be less frequent but will help to resolve any of the material questions or difficulties relating to operation of the contract. Business communication is around the financial and commercial parts of the contract and will include issues such as payment, transfer of risk and general contract management. Lastly, operational communication is for technical and frontline staff – it is the most frequent and detailed.

The communication across these channels should be peer-to-peer; there should be clear routes for escalation of issues if things go wrong so that they can be resolved peacefully within the terms of the contract.

These levels of communication will often manifest themselves through nominated representatives, boards, steering groups or committees. These can relate to specific tasks (eg, transition, annual review, problem resolution) or general operation of the agreement (eg, project board). When preparing the provisions covering these bodies, the parties should consider:

- the remit/terms of reference of each body (what is it empowered to do, what areas does it consider?);
- how its members are selected, both initially and during the process for changing members;
- the frequency and locations of its meetings – each party will prefer to be on home territory, but the outcome may be either dictated by the strongest party in the initial negotiation or left to be agreed as the contract progresses;
- the process for setting agendas and keeping minutes – written records are always important as they can help in any disputes in the future;
- voting systems when decisions need to be made including minimum numbers of each party who should be present to pass any decision and what happens if no agreement can be reached (eg, will one party have a casting vote?); and
- the process for escalating differences to any higher body.

This chapter later considers the process for resolving formal disputes; throughout the relationship provisions, there should be clear links to the dispute procedure to enable a seemless consideration of disputes so that nothing can stop services from continuing on a day-to-day basis.

2.3 Records

Records will assist the parties with keeping track of decisions that are made, log outputs from the contract and generally help to operate smoothly, particularly where there is a change of personnel.

The change procedure is covered further below; from a records' perspective, copies of change requests and agreed changes should be kept so the parties are clear on what was agreed. Where the words of the contract itself are changed, then a conformed copy of the contract should be maintained so that the parties know exactly what the new contract says. Once the lawyers have left the scene, this can seem inconvenient, but failure to keep the contract up to date can and does result in expensive litigation. The parties should agree on how and where the 'single version of the truth' is kept to help to avoid disputes.

Records should be kept of the various communications referred to above, including minutes from any committee meetings, details of current members and timetable for future meetings.

While operation and maintenance manuals can be expensive to run, recording how the services are provided in such manuals may assist with the continuity of the services. These manuals can then be handed over to any new suppliers, although the current service provider may prefer to keep hold of what it sees as its crown jewels. A particular subset of manuals relates to exit (a manual for how exit will be conducted should be created early in the contract). Exit can come unexpectedly and sometimes the parties will not be on good terms, so it is in the interests of the customer to require the service provider to record what exactly will happen when the contract comes to an end – otherwise it can be disorganised and continuity of the service may be affected.

Lastly, there are day-to-day records relating to things such as certificates, licences, registrations or warranties obtained by the supplier in relation to the provision of the services or documents relating to the charges such as invoice and tax records.

In addition to agreeing what type of records should be kept, the parties should consider and agree on how, where, at whose cost and for how long the records should be kept, as well as the process for the other party accessing the records. None of it is very exciting, but in the biggest transactions there may be millions of individual records relating to the contract and how, where and how long they are kept for can represent a material cost for the parties.

2.4 Reporting

Linked to records is report, which tends to be a one-way process, usually from the service provider to the customer, whereby the former agrees to keep the latter up to date with specified information at agreed intervals. This may cover reports on progress, delay, tests, management information, insurances, security and *force majeure* events. The contract should consider the agreed format and processes for such reports, or should set a mechanism for this to be worked out at the start of the contract.

2.5 Change

Notwithstanding all the great effort at the start of the contract, change will almost inevitably occur and the parties should consider how it will be handled. Change may arise because of developments in the business of either party, outside influences such as changing laws or simply because one party may want something different or have a better way of doing something. Outsourcing contracts typically span several years, and so change would be better viewed as a certainty rather than a possibility.

The contract should include mechanisms for how changes are requested, agreed and recorded. This may vary according to whether they are strategic, business or operational, and the level of detail and formality may differ accordingly. The parties should also consider including an acceleration process for any critical matters.

A key issue will be to consider how much changes will cost (either specifically or a mechanism for calculating the cost), and this cost should be both the price of the end services and the cost of conducting the change mechanism itself. Suppliers often claim that customers can be prolific and random in requesting changes as they consider different options for changes to their business and this hidden cost, if not properly recovered, can result in the customer acting like a child in a sweet shop as it tests the art of the possible.

The right to reject or mandate changes will be important, and where there is exclusivity on either party, then it will be critical. A customer that has granted exclusive rights to a service provider will need to have the right to require changes to be made, or if the supplier cannot achieve the change then the customer should be released from the exclusivity commitment.

2.6 Key personnel

Key personnel may be on the periphery of governance, but can be important where the identity of the people supplying part of the service is important. If the contract was awarded through a competitive process, then the customer will want to ensure that the best people remain dedicated to its account. Accordingly, the customer may want to include key personnel provisions.

These provisions will usually name individuals as part of the delivery team and the supplier will be required to ensure that these individuals dedicate an agreed percentage of their time to the contract. The supplier is also usually required to obtain consent from the customer before changing a person in a key role (sometimes the other party will be able to vet persons nominated as potential replacements).

2.7 Conclusion

While governance seems mundane and is often seen as boilerplate in a contract, it is often critical to the success (or failure avoidance) of projects.

The parties should consider early on how they want to run the agreement to balance sharing of information with letting the supplier get on with its job. If they agree on the processes up front, then the contract can run itself; objective mechanisms can often get the parties through sticky moments when clear processes and systems take the heat out of potential disputes or give early warning of potential issues, allowing quick resolution before they become material.

3. Dispute resolution

3.1 Overview

Despite the best intentions of the parties, disputes can and do occur. At the start of the relationship, it can be difficult, while planning for success, to consider what would happen if things go wrong and the parties are unable to agree on how to resolve it. However, experience shows that it can be an important consideration and one that should be made carefully. If the parties get it right, then the provisions can help the parties to achieve a cost-effective resolution in a way that preserves their relationship. If they get it wrong, then it can be very expensive and time consuming.

The dispute resolution section in an outsourcing contract will describe the process that should be followed when a dispute arises. This may start with simple negotiation between the parties, moving on to involvement of third parties, whether voluntarily or forcefully, through mechanisms of last resort such as court proceedings.

Over a number of years the trend has been to avoid disputes going to court as it can be expensive for both parties, and the courts have pushed for parties to seek amicable solutions where possible. Accordingly, dispute procedures have changed substantially over a number of years and instead of providing for litigation or arbitration, they seek alternative methods for resolving disputes to maximise the prospects of resolution in a cost-effective manner. As outsourcing contracts become ever more high value and complex, the need for careful consideration of the various options available becomes even more important.

The dispute procedure will usually involve a tiered system that seeks to resolve disputes via increasingly complex and expensive mechanisms. The ultimate aim is dispute avoidance; accordingly, each tier's aim should be to avoid reaching the next stage for the sanity and finances of the parties.

Before considering how to decide which tiers to include in a particular dispute mechanism, we must set out the details of the potential tiers.

3.2 Basic negotiation

Many disputes are resolved by sensible negotiation between the parties. This will often happen without the parties giving any thought to the formal dispute resolution processes recorded in their agreement. Accordingly, this is the method most widely used. The agreement can help by specifying that negotiation should be held between increasingly senior counterparts in each party who are not directly involved in the project and, therefore, hopefully able to consider the dispute in a less impassioned and more commercial manner.

Negotiation is flexible and informal, and cost effective if it works. Nothing is guaranteed in this regard, though, and much will depend on what is at stake, and the attitudes and personalities of the key individuals on both sides.

Each party will ideally wish to stop the other from being able to refer, in any possible future formal legal proceedings, to oral or written communications that might have taken place as part of the negotiations. This means that, for English law-governed contracts and those of many other jurisdictions, commercial discussions that genuinely seek to resolve disputes or settle claims (whether in accordance with a formal dispute resolution procedure or otherwise) should be conducted on a 'without prejudice' basis. However, in some jurisdictions, such as Dubai, the local courts will not recognise this term and 'without prejudice' communications will not necessarily be protected from disclosure to local courts.

3.3 Mediation

Mediation is effectively enhanced negotiation where a neutral third party helps the party to explore options to resolve the dispute. The mediator works with the parties to reach a negotiated settlement through facilitation, but does not make a binding decision. The decisions will become binding if agreed and recorded in an agreement signed by all the parties.

The mediation itself will normally involve an initial all-party meeting and opening statements by the parties followed by private meetings, break-outs and further all-party meetings. Mediation can be cost effective and quick, and is often successful; of the processes involving third parties, it provides the most positive of outcomes as it avoids costly formal proceedings and often both preserves the relationship between the parties and enables the project in dispute to continue. However, if the parties have entrenched positions and no settlement is reached, then there will be wasted costs and delay.

3.4 Litigation

Litigation is the process of resolving disputes through the use of the formal court system and is what parties will use in the majority of cases where alternative resolution mechanisms have failed to bring about settlement. It is not voluntary, except in the sense that the claimant chooses to issue a claim in the first place. Once a case is started, it is not usually possible to withdraw without paying the other side's costs. The court will then impose a decision that will be binding on the parties, and the successful party may enforce that judgment.

The steps taken in litigation will vary from country to country; some countries are adversarial (eg, England, Australia and the United States), while others are inquisitorial, which involves a more cooperative approach (common in most European and Middle East jurisdictions).

Litigation can be a lengthy and expensive process; parties can try to avoid it, but it has the advantage of leading to a final and impartial decision that is binding on the parties.

3.5 Arbitration

Arbitration is the resolution of disputes through a formal and binding but private process led by one or more arbitrators. Arbitration is usually conducted according to the rules of a recognised arbitral institution such as the International Chamber of

Commerce, the London Court of International Arbitration, the American Arbitration Association or the UN International Trade Committee.

Arbitration can be popular in international outsourcing deals because international treaties can make cross-border enforcement easier than through litigation. Also, arbitration can be held in a neutral venue that may make it fairer and reduce 'home advantage'.

3.6 Expert determination

This involves the appointment of an independent third party who makes a final and (usually) binding determination. It tends to be used for resolving technical matters (eg, to determine whether software meets its specification). Despite being commonly provided for in outsourcing contracts, it is rarely used because it can be difficult to isolate the discrete point on which an expert is required to give a determination. For example, the issues behind whether particular software has met its specification may be numerous and include whether acceptance processes have been followed or whether both informal and formal variations made at the request of both parties are binding. Expert determination can also be unpopular due to lack of any formal process – for example, the expert is not required to give reasons for his decision and it can be hard to find good experts. Lastly, there is no convention for cross-border enforcement of expert decisions, so they are even more unpopular where an outsourcing has an international dimension.

3.7 Other forms of dispute resolution mechanisms

Other mechanisms include early neutral evaluation (where an independent third party issues a non-binding opinion on the likely outcome), mini-trial (presentation of each side's case to a panel comprising a mediator and senior executive from each side) and med-arb (a process combining mediation and arbitration). However, these mechanisms are rarely seen in outsourcing contracts.

3.8 Key factors when choosing which mechanism should apply

Outsourcing contracts will usually include at least two or three dispute resolution mechanisms to deal with disputes or particular types of dispute; it is vital that the contract clearly states how the different mechanisms will work and whether they can work concurrently or consecutively. Relevant factors in choosing the appropriate dispute resolution mechanisms for a particular outsourcing can include those outlined below.

(a) Claimant or defendant

Depending on the nature of the deal, it is sometimes possible to predict which party is more likely to initiate a dispute. If a party is more likely to be a claimant, it may wish, for example, to ensure that it chooses a process where it can easily enforce any judgment or award that it obtains. Similarly, a likely defending party might be happy to choose a process that would make enforcement trickier.

(b) ***Type of dispute***

The nature of the outsourcing may determine the extent to which the deal will be suited to a particular type or types of dispute resolution. For example, particular technical issues could be dealt with by expert determination, in which case resolution of these could be carved out in the contract from the form of dispute resolution deemed more appropriate for other issues.

(c) ***Multi-party disputes***

If any dispute arising is likely to involve parties other than the service provider and the customer (eg, other suppliers, subcontractors), then arbitration will be unsuitable – unless all relevant parties have agreed to this mechanism in each of the relevant contracts. By contrast, the courts generally have the power to join third parties to the core proceedings. Accordingly, if the contract has a number of associated contracts then court proceedings may be better so that the different matters can be heard together and consistent decisions can be made. If different venues hear different parts of the claim, then they may make inconsistent decisions and a party may find itself liable to its customer but have no remedy against its subcontractor, even though the latter was at fault. If one venue hears all the connected disputes, then this issue should be avoided.

Particular issues can arise in this regard in the context of multi-source engagements; in such cases, best practice for the customer will likely be to investigate/require a common dispute resolution process for all involved service providers, so that issues that might effect all of them can be resolved in a consistent and coherent way (and at reduced cost/administration for the customer). See further the chapter on multi-vendor projects.

(d) ***Private or confidential?***

If the parties wish the dispute to remain private, techniques such as arbitration or mediation will be attractive. On other occasions, the threat of publicity can be a powerful weapon and therefore litigation may be preferred.

(e) ***Injunctive relief***

There may be situations in an outsourcing contract where it would be beneficial to retain the ability to obtain emergency relief so as to preserve the status quo (eg, an injunction to prevent a party from ceasing to provide services). If a contract contains a clause referring disputes to litigation, then this ability will exist in any event.

(f) ***Enforceability***

Broadly speaking, arbitration awards are more easily enforceable in a wider range of jurisdictions than court judgments. Potential claimants should be particularly interested in the ease with which any judgment or award can be enforced against an opponent's assets and should therefore research the enforceability position in relation to any proposed litigation or arbitration clause.

3.9 Conclusion

Parties to outsourcing contracts should have a good working understanding of the various options available when negotiating contracts and dealing with disputes when they arise. No single dispute resolution process is entirely risk free or without disadvantages, and each dispute will have its own particular facts, issues and potential solutions. Dispute resolution is a key area of the parties' relationship in an outsourcing contract; it warrants a clear and suitable procedure to be set out in the contract from the outset.

4. Contract/vendor management

4.1 Introduction

The fundamental element of the success of outsourcing projects is its performance in accordance with its terms.

Once the agreement has been entered into, temptation can be great to archive it and let operational stakeholders within each of the customer and the service provider's organisations arrange performance without regard for the provisions of the contract. The parties, and more often the customer, tend to overlook the importance of careful contract management.

This could lead to services not being properly measured, assessed and more generally delivered, which is directly harmful to the customer, or to expanded, changed and more onerous services than agreed upon, which affects the service provider's profitability. This can be exacerbated by the large, complex and strategic nature of outsourcing projects, which therefore requires a great deal of active and precise management.

Managing the contract is accordingly an art form, different in its approach and tools from those needed for an effective initial negotiation.

Contract management requires addressing essential aspects structuring the methodical performance of management of the life of a project. The rest of this section addresses key processes that should be implemented and orchestrated through a robust governance process.

4.2 Contract awareness management

In particular in large transactions, the day-to-day management of the project will certainly involve individuals who were absent during the negotiation streams and may be frightened by this large and imposing contractual documentation.

It is therefore indispensable, through contract awareness enhancement, to bring stakeholders up to speed on the contents of the agreement in order to allow them to use this as a point of reference to manage performance and issues.

In order to achieve that, providing them with a copy of the contractual documentation is necessary but neither sufficient nor perfectly adequate. The full agreement or even a summary thereof will be lengthy, complex, using legal terms and including dense clauses: it will not give the team practical, immediately usable information.

The most efficient approach is to prepare a contract user guide, which will not only summarise the agreement, but also translate it into simple, practical terms (using, where needed, charts and diagrams), including frequently asked questions and answers, directions as to where particular topics are dealt with in the contract and explaining the main points to monitor and the tools that should be used.

The guide should focus on the following core themes, which are structuring for the management of the contract: services, service levels and service credits, incident and problem management, change procedure, responsibilities of the party for which the guide is prepared, governance, reporting and escalation, and charges, invoicing and payment.

Ideally, the guide should be accompanied by the provision of workshops to present its key aspects to its intended users.

4.3 Performance monitoring and issue management

Assessment of the service provider's performance is often based on a performance monitoring report submitted by the service provider to the customer. It is a fundamental document that will be reviewed in governance committees.

The parties must be familiarised with its content, and ensure that the report is comprehensive and matches the contents that were agreed upon. It is often recommended that the report include the following information, as illustrative examples:

- for each service level, the actual performance achieved over the calendar month over which the services were measured, and that achieved over the previous 12 calendar months;
- the level of each incident that occurred;
- which incidents remain outstanding and progress in resolving them;
- for any severity level 1 and severity level 2 incidents occurring in the most recent calendar month, the cause of the fault and any action taken to reduce the likelihood of recurrence;
- for any repeat failures, actions taken to resolve the underlying cause and prevent recurrence;
- the service credits to be applied indicating the incident(s) to which the service credits relate;
- a rolling total of the number of incidents that have occurred and the amount of service credits that have been incurred by the service provider over the previous 12 months; and
- relevant particulars of any aspects of the performance by the service provider that fail to meet the requirements of the agreement.

Issue management must be addressed either in respect of specific incidents affecting the performance of the services, or more generally in respect of any problem that may arise.

Incident logs should be implemented. It is recommended that the logs include as illustrative examples regarding incidents in the operational performance of the services:

- the unique record number assigned by the customer to the incident;
- the date and time that the incident is reported to and received at the helpdesk;
- the nature and location of the incident;

- the person making the report;
- the severity level assigned to the incident, as verified by the customer;
- an estimate (produced with all due care and diligence) of the number of authorised users that are affected by the incident (whether they are individual users or groups of users);
- the action intended to be taken or that has been taken to rectify the incident;
- details of any communication with the customer in connection with the incident;
- notes/comments regarding any mitigating circumstances with regard to the incident;
- the service provider's plans for remedying the incident and/or for preventing the incident from re-occurring, including details where applicable of the estimated time within which the incident will be remedied; and
- the reasons for any inability of the service provider to meet the service level so as to resolve the incident.

4.4 Change management

Because of their complexity and/or length, most outsourcing contracts require change and/or renegotiation in the course of their performance.

4.5 Change control

Contracts generally include a detailed mechanism governing proposals to change the terms of the contract or more generally to effect changes that affect the terms of the contract.

Many such changes require renegotiation of important elements of the contract or otherwise have a material impact on the balance of the transaction as entered into by the parties.

It is therefore important that the change-related documentation that the parties use when discussing and agreeing on changes cover all of the impacts upon the contract (and in particular all those as may relate to service levels, planning, price, liability, warranty periods or other provisions).

The change-related documentation (often called 'change control notes') must be negotiated and prepared with the close involvement notably of the customer, in order for the customer to track the impact of the change on the services and price, and avoid any unpleasant surprise in the form of a significant price increase or degradation of the service. Similarly, the service provider has a fundamental interest in ensuring that changes requested by the customer do not hinder the profitability of the transaction.

4.6 Contract consolidation

For large transactions or those that perform over several years, the parties often agree on a large number of changes over a period of years. This can be quite daunting and render the contract difficult to interpret or even to understand.

It may become necessary to restate/consolidate the contract – that is, to update it so as to reflect in a single consolidated form all of the changes made over the years.

This can be a large task, as many change control notes may, in part, reverse or further alter the effects of changes agreed on earlier in the contract term, and so various different layers of charges may need to be assessed.

5. Audit and benchmarking

Best practice of contract management requires, on the customer side, the implementation of contract audits to ascertain compliance with the terms of the agreement and of benchmarking exercises, the purpose of which is generally to verify whether the conditions of the contract for the customer are still approximately in line with what the market generally offers in a similar context – that is, ensuring that prices and services are still competitive.

5.1 Audit

Contract performance audit can be a very effective means of creating bargaining leverage for a customer during renegotiation. As with any large-scale outsourcing/managed services contract, it could be that the service provider has overlooked or omitted some of the more detailed/specific service-related requirements; the service provider will likely be keen to negotiate with the customer a transactional resolution of this omission in order to avoid either such an audit being conducted in the first place or being obliged to implement its findings, at significant potential cost.

5.2 Benchmarking

The benchmarking process involves a third-party benchmarker, from which the customer requests to compare the project in question against other similar services and to report as to the competitiveness of the terms and conditions of the project being reviewed.

The price (under similar services in a similar context) is usually the key element being benchmarked, but other aspects of the overall offering can also be tested, such as the services themselves.

It is considered best practice to include a benchmarking clause and process in long outsourcing transactions. However, benchmarking may not always be appropriate, in particular where it could undermine the overall pricing model (typically, in fixed-price projects), and where the time and cost of the exercise are considered as limiting its interest. Benchmarking is rarely triggered in practice, although it can increase the bargaining position of a customer.

Having said that, benchmarking provisions are often hotly negotiated in the context of outsourcing contracts. Typically, battlegrounds include:

- the identity of the benchmarker – must it be agreed, can it be freely selected by the customer, or must it be picked from a pre-set list?
- instructing party – does the benchmarker report solely to the customer, or jointly to the the customer and service provider?
- cost – who pays for the benchmark exercise? Will it always be the customer, will the cost be shared, or will it perhaps be a question left for the determination of the benchmarker?

- the process – is the process left entirely to the discretion of the benchmarker, or will the benchmarker be compelled to consider specific factors?
- scope – must the benchmarker cover the entirety of the services, or will the customer be able to require assessments of discrete elements of the services or charges?
- standard to be achieved – what is the target that the service provider is to be judged against? For example, is it enough to be in line with the average results identified by the benchmarker, or is the requirement to be in the upper quartile?
- outcome – perhaps the most important question of all is: what happens if the benchmarker concludes that the service provider's charges and/or service levels fall short of the targeted levels? Service providers may argue for a form of words that requires any subsequent changes to the pricing or service levels to be subject to mutual agreement (ie, so as to be non-binding). Customers will conversely want automatic adjustments in line with the benchmarker's findings. Potential compromises might include granting the customer a no/low cost exit right if agreements on variations cannot be reached, or inserting some degree of limitations on the maximum amount of variation that the service provider can be compelled to make (eg, no more than 5% from its existing level of charges).

6. Longer-term considerations

A managed services/outsourcing, as recurring services arrangement will need to be either renewed or brought back in house at some point.

Accordingly, when any such deal is signed, stakeholders must immediately diarise a point in time in accordance with the planning of the performance of the contract to extend, or retender, bring back in house and, where appropriate, to organise termination assistance services (see the chapter on renegotiations, retenders and termination assistance), if such phase was agreed upon.

Aside from renegotiations, other issues may arise in connection with the larger/more complicated projects, and in respect of which inputs from stakeholders involved in contract management will be required: many of these will simply be matters of contract interpretation, but in the event that a matter of interpretation seems likely to develop into a dispute, care must be taken to ensure that each party preserve its rights and arguments *vis à vis* any potential litigations (see section 3 above regarding dispute resolution).

Renegotiations, retenders and termination assistance

Tim Lyons
Jan Pohle

1. Introduction

The vast majority of, if not all, outsourcing arrangements have a particular term. Towards the end of the term, the customer must make the decision as to whether to extend the existing arrangement, take back (or insource) part or all of the services or seek a new service provider, whether through a retendering or other market approaches.

Most outsourcing contracts contain an option for the customer simply to extend the contract on its existing terms (eg, usually for a set period or sequence of set periods, such as one or two successive one-year extensions). However, as part of the extension of an existing arrangement, the customer may wish (or be required) to negotiate amendments to the existing agreement to address matters that are out of date, or to incorporate required improvements in respect of the services.

Where a new service provider is to be appointed, there will need to be a process of transitioning to that new provider (which may be far from straightforward). To use an oft-heard analogy, an outsourcing project may be akin to a marriage in the sense of the commitment of the parties and the need for them to work through the problems that might arise, but it is a marriage with a pre-nuptial agreement attached to cater for the near-certainty of an eventual divorce (however amicable it may then be).

This chapter therefore considers some of the key issues that the parties to an outsourcing contract will have to overcome when reaching the critical check point associated with contract exit, transition or renewal.

2. Renegotiation or retender?

Various considerations will determine whether an existing outsourcing arrangement is renegotiated with the current provider or whether a new provider is sought. These considerations can be a mix of practical, legal or commercial; sometimes they can even be based on changes in the customer's strategic thinking.

Practical considerations include whether there is enough time to conduct a tender exercise and whether the procurement policies of the customer require a retendering of the services as will often be the case in the public sector, for example.

There may be regulatory reasons to stay or to move. Thus, a service provider may be implementing plans to offshore all of its data centres, in circumstances where the customer is required to have the services provided from onshore.

From a commercial perspective, poor service or a change in control of the service

Diagram 1 – Factors to a decision as to the future of an outsourcing contract

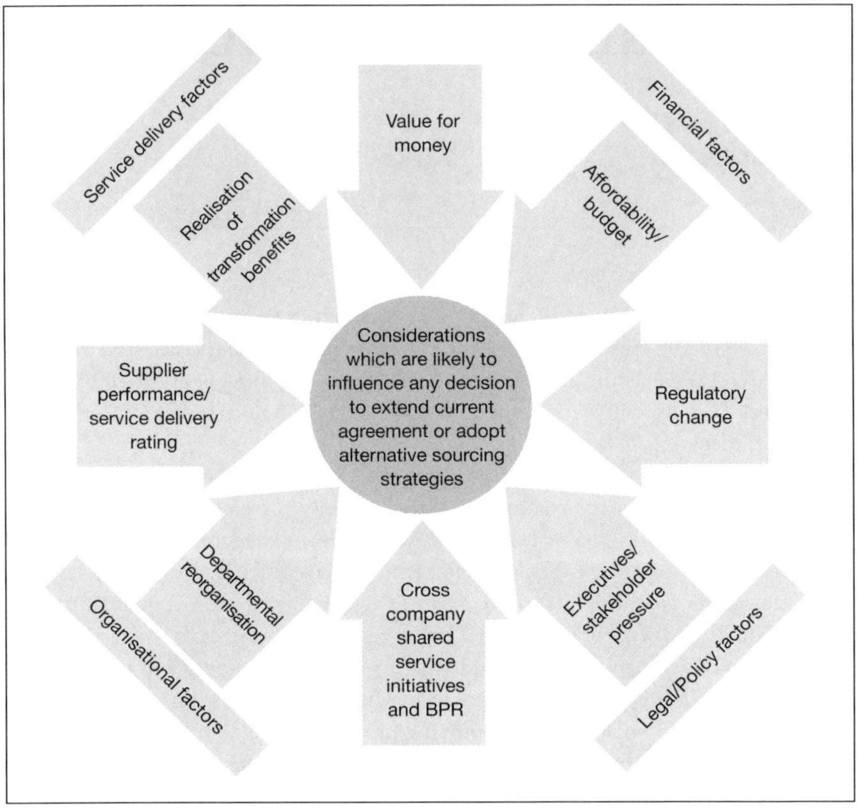

provider may necessitate a change. The customer may simply be unhappy with the level of service provided, or may be constrained by internal policies (or, in the case of public-sector bodies, public procurement-related laws and regulations) to seek competitive bids. Alternatively, the current charges under an existing contract may be too high or inflexible, requiring a market-testing exercise to obtain the best pricing available in the market. Conversely, if the customer elects to stay with its current provider, it must take into consideration the possibility that the service provider will seek itself an opportunity to renegotiate its pricing, especially if any changes are made to the scope of the services or if the provider has been running at a loss or with very narrow margins.

A common reason for a new approach to the market is that there are new or alternative services available in the market and the incumbent service provider may not be the best entity to provide those new services. The introduction of more cloud-based service offerings is a good current example of this, but in the past this would have included the ability of new potential suppliers to leverage more offshore delivery capabilities (with consequent price advantages).

The customer may want to change the scope of the existing services and this may require an approach to the market in order to add services, and to assess who may then be best placed to provide them. For example, an infrastructure-based outsource deal might have Applications Development and Maintenance (ADM) or network-related services added to it.

The transition-out provisions in the existing contract may also have some bearing on whether the contract is extended or retendered, as it may not be possible to transition immediately to a new provider. Indeed, many first-generation outsourcing contracts have had to be renegotiated to include effective transition-out provisions, which were often lacking in the terms originally negotiated between the parties.

A customer may decide to extend and vary an existing contract as part of a longer strategy to be in a better position itself to transition to a new provider at a later date (eg, as part of a potential vendor consolidation exercise). In these circumstances, the extension of the existing contract may be for a shorter, interim term. The customer and the service provider may then also seek to address any perceived deficiencies in the existing contract as part of a contract extension and renegotiation (eg, if the service level regime was not perceived to be working well in the sense that it did not reflect customer priorities, or if the service provider felt that it was incurring significant levels of service credits when, in fact, it was still delivering a relatively high-quality service).

2.1 Contract extension and negotiation

When choosing to seek the renegotiation of an existing contract, the customer must consider what leverage it has in order to negotiate more favourable terms (and of course the service provider will be thinking along the same lines, although suppliers are less commonly able to improve their contractual position significantly in a renegotiation or renewal). For example, if the customer has not yet exercised its option to extend the contract on its existing terms, it may use that option as a fall-back position if renegotiated terms cannot be agreed with the service provider. In addition, if the customer has sufficient time to benchmark or retender the services, it can use the possible retendering as leverage to drive an acceptable offer from the incumbent provider (eg, on the basis that the service provider will then have the advantage of avoiding the costs of a competitive process, and of course will also avoid the risk of losing the work to a competing bidder).

Assuming that the service provider has performed broadly in accordance with the contract and the service levels so that these do not need detailed reconsideration, some key points must still be considered as part of the renegotiation process. They include:

- determining what needs to change in the contract. Is it any of the legal obligations (eg, the provisions relating to service levels, quality of service, intellectual property and/or data)? Are changes to scope required? If extensive changes or even transformation from a 'current mode of operation' to a 'future mode of operation' are required, it may be more sensible to negotiate an entirely new agreement rather than try to work with the existing contract terms. This will also be affected by whether the customer's requirements are the same now as when the customer entered into the agreement or whether things have changed to such an extent that the parties are, in effect, looking at a new deal as opposed to simply tweaking an existing one;

- determining whether the change control provisions in the contract set out a fixed process for any changes to scope, service levels or pricing that must therefore be followed as part of a contract extension. If the contract contains these provisions, the correct procedure in the contract should be followed, unless the parties expressly agree otherwise;
- assessing any legislative and/or regulatory changes that have occurred and need to be addressed in any renegotiated agreement, particularly in more heavily regulated sectors such as financial services;
- diligently checking whether the charging model still meets the customer's needs, and whether this payment model is still in line with best market practice to optimise the commercial value of the renegotiation process (while the service provider is busy analysing whether the past provisions have enabled it to recover a reasonable level of profit); and
- reviewing the contract history and preparing a list of lessons learned, not only from an operational and commercial point of view, but also in legal terms. This analysis should also result in a guideline to optimise the existing agreement with the service provider for future cooperation. Of course, the service provider will be doing the same thing, in reverse.

The customer must always remember any notice periods that apply where it wishes to extend a contract term pursuant to a contractual option. For instance, the customer may have a right to extend the term for a further 12 months on the same terms, but this is subject to giving the service provider a certain minimum written notice (which is reasonable, given the need for the service provider to ensure that it retains its personnel and service delivery capabilities, rather than reallocating them to new clients or engagements).

2.2 Insourcing

A customer may also consider insourcing some functions, so as to start to provide the relevant services again itself rather than via a third party. In doing so, it should consider whether existing areas within the organisation can take over the scope of these services, or whether it will need to recruit new personnel and skills, and/or invest in new facilities or systems to fill the gaps left by replacing what the service provider would have been able to supply.

A key issue in relation to any decision to insource is whether the service provider's staff currently providing the services can be transferred to the customer (eg, pursuant to the EU Acquired Rights Directive for personnel based in the European Union). If staff transfer is not available, this poses a major risk to the customer's continuity of service if the customer has neither comparable resources in house nor an ability to acquire them quickly – a process likely to take several months.

The customer must also consider whether:

- the transition of services in house will require data to be migrated 'as is' from the provider, or whether it must be cleansed or converted prior to delivery back to the customer organisation; and
- any transfer of ownership of software or hardware is required.

As a starting point, the customer should review the transition-out obligations in its existing outsource contract to identify what level of assistance the service provider is required to give (eg, is data cleansing included? Is the service provider required to transfer assets if required by the customer, and if so at what cost?). The customer must then consider whether the transition-out obligations are sufficient to enable the customer to insource the services safely. If the customer then concludes that it does not have the internal skills to provide the services, it will need to appoint an alternate provider of the services, or at least provide for a period of parallel running so as to give it time to get up to speed. A potential timeframe/process for insourcing is set out below.

Diagram 2 – Insourcing process

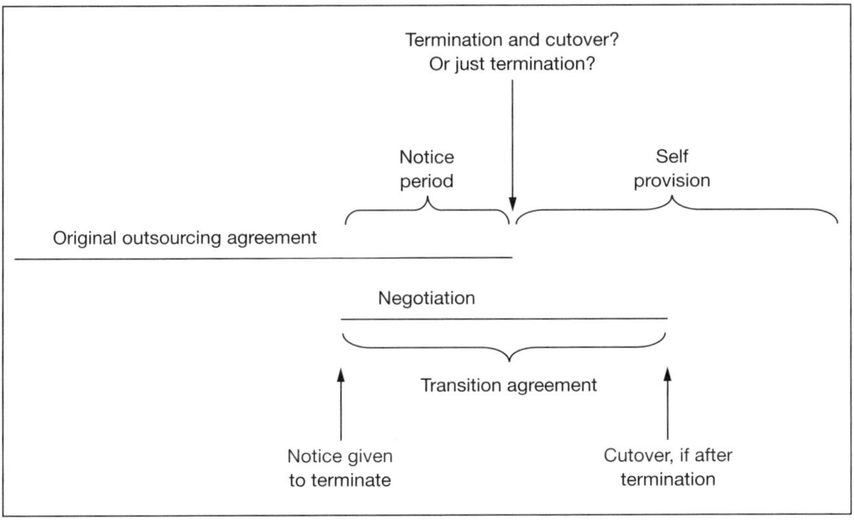

2.3 Retendering

A key consideration in any retendering is whether or not the customer has sufficient information regarding the services as they currently stand in order to put them out to tender.

The incumbent service provider's cooperation will be a key factor in the smooth running of any retendering. Incoming providers will seek access to various pieces of information relating to the existing services (see the chapter on due diligence and transition for more detail). In contrast to a first-generation deal where the customer will previously have been providing the relevant services itself, in a retendering situation the customer may not have ready access to all the information relating to how its current outsource service provider has been operating and, unless its existing contract provides for it, the customer may not be in a position to compel its current service provider to give access to the information sought by the prospective new suppliers. Conversely, the customer should at least have better data regarding performance against specific service levels, as will be apparent from the reports that the current service provider will have been producing month on month (as compared to first-generation deals where – with a few notable exceptions – customers tend not to have comprehensive data regarding their historic performance of internal services).

An inability to provide detailed information regarding the services means that the customer may have difficulty providing an even playing field for bidders. The incumbent service provider will most likely have an advantage over other bidders, as it will necessarily have a greater understanding of the existing services. Disclosure of all relevant information in relation to the existing services will accordingly be required in order to try to remove (or at least mitigate) this advantage.

In order to ensure that all relevant information is available, the customer will need to have included various provisions in its existing contract (the 'pre-nup' clauses referred to earlier in this chapter). The contract should therefore ideally require the incumbent service provider to hand over various pieces of information to the customer, with an express right for the customer to disclose that information to prospective suppliers (if it is subject to confidentiality obligations in favour of the incumbent service provider). Where information comprises material in which the relevant intellectual property is owned by the service provider, a licence will need to be granted in respect of intellectual property subsisting in that material, so that copies can be given to prospective service providers.

Information that the customer will wish to disclose to prospective suppliers will include:

- all technical information relating to the assets used to provide the services. In the case of an IT outsourcing, this will involve architectural/design documentation and configuration data, identification of developed software, scripts, tools, command procedures and the like. For hardware assets, the information that needs to be kept by the service provider and made available would include make and model, date of purchase and whether the asset is used solely for the customer or whether it is a shared asset (see section 3.5 below);
- information as to the relevant versions of software and whether the software is up to date and supported;
- information as to whether hardware is up to date and whether it is the subject of ongoing warranty support from the equipment manufacturer or ongoing maintenance arrangements;
- copies of third-party contracts (or, at least, access to those contracts with certain information redacted, such as the pricing) relevant to the provision of the services. This will include licences of software and maintenance and support agreements. Consideration will need to be given as to whether these contracts may be novated or assigned to a new supplier or whether new contracts will need to be entered into. If the customer wishes to disclose the terms of these

contracts to prospective suppliers, it will need to consider the confidentiality provisions under the contracts and, if necessary, obtain consents from the relevant counterparties to the disclosure of the contract terms;
- the service levels currently being met – an incoming supplier will always seek information on the number of incidents and problems in relation to the existing services and the level of services currently provided (whether by the customer or the service provider). Prospective suppliers will seek access to reports in relation to service level compliance over time, to ascertain any trends in relation to incident and problem volumes;
- transaction volumes (to the extent that the customer does not have this information already);
- data schema and other information relevant to customer data; and
- information in relation to the number and type of employees already providing the services and the terms of their employment. The details that will be given will depend on the jurisdiction in which the services are provided and whether employees are required to transfer with the services (see the chapter on human resources).

In most circumstances, prospective suppliers will also want to have access to the premises utilised by the current service provider in providing the existing services. Where the premises are a shared data centre used by the service provider, such access may be either impossible or limited.

All this information must not only be obtained from the incumbent service provider, but also properly processed and edited by the customer prior to the formal start of the tender process. All this requires considerable time; accordingly, any retender process, which includes a transition to a new service provider, requires substantial time and diligent project planning.

By contrast, the incumbent service provider will be concerned that it does not have to disclose anything that it might reasonably consider to be confidential (eg, details of pricing or margins).

If a new service provider is appointed as a result of this retender process, service continuity for the customer must be ensured. This requires that the outgoing service provider give assistance in transitioning the existing services to a new provider. This is dealt with in more detail in the remainder of this chapter.

3. Termination assistance and transition-out

3.1 Setting the scene for exit

At the end of a contract, whether it has expired or come to an early termination, the customer's priority should be to retain continuity of service during the existing service provider's exit from the contract. A gap in service provision could be disastrous for the customer's business (and potentially attract regulatory sanctions – eg, for financial services entities); equally, the customer will want to avoid a marked deterioration in service quality as one (potentially disgruntled) supplier heads for the exit, while another is struggling to get up to speed.

For the outgoing service provider, the priority will be to ensure an orderly transition-out with minimal downtime for its resources and protection of its financial interests and proprietary rights. By contrast, the incoming service provider will want to get as much assistance and information as possible.

Generally speaking, a well-drafted contract will include a separate schedule setting out what termination assistance the outgoing service provider must offer and a description of the documentation and knowledge that the existing service provider must pass on to the incoming service provider (or to the customer, where services are being insourced). In relation to the types of information that will be provided, see section 2.3 above. The information that is provided as part of the retendering process is usually handed over at the time of transition-out.

The period for transition will depend upon the complexity of the outsourced services. Often services agreements include a maximum term for the provision of transition support by the incumbent provider with limited options for extension. These stipulations must be carefully observed and need to be considered in the overall project planning prior to the start of the tender process. At its simplest, a transition could involve the transfer of some assets, assignment of third-party contracts and the transfer of staff currently employed in the provision of the services. Another option is a complete new set-up of the technical and organisational environment for the provision of the services by the new service provider, with the only remaining transition requirement being the transfer of the relevant data by the incumbent service provider. Once this has occurred, the supplier is in a position to provide the services to the level prescribed by the service levels.

At the other end of the scale (eg, for large, multi-tower and/or multi-jurisdictional deals), extensive knowledge sharing will be required, which may involve the new service provider interviewing and shadowing the incumbent service provider's personnel. In such circumstances, it is not unusual for the termination assistance period to last as long as 12 to 18 months (often also with the option to extend still further, if certain transitional tasks are incomplete by the end of the stipulated transition period).

3.2 Transition-out plan

Under an outsourcing contract, a key obligation for the service provider should be to draw up a transition-out plan setting out the governance and handover requirements for the transition of the services to a new service provider (or to the customer, if the services are to be insourced). The transition-out plan must specify all the activities that must be executed to ensure that there is an orderly transfer of the services, while also providing for continuity of service.

The contract should provide for a draft transition-out plan to be prepared by the service provider and given to the customer within a certain number of weeks or months of execution of the contract. It should then be refreshed from time to time (both on a regular basis, such as every six or 12 months, and following any material changes in scope such as the introduction of a new service). Without the requirement for a draft transition-out plan to be provided early in the contract term, there is a risk that the customer will request a plan only at a time when the relationship between the parties is not as good as it was at the beginning of the contract (and, unfortunately, it is often the case that the obligation – even if included in the contract – is forgotten about until termination is imminent, at which point the parties' views as to what they expect to give and to receive will be more entrenched). If the transition plan is not prepared in advance or kept up to date, it may equally not be readily available if the customer is required to terminate the outsourcing contract early for any reason.

Generally speaking, the transition-out plan is subject to review and comment from the customer and, usually, the service provider is under an obligation to update the plan if requested by the customer (at least to the extent that the customer's requirements are 'reasonable').

3.3 Matters to be addressed during transition-out

A number of items need to be addressed during transition-out. The transition-out plan should refer to all the activities needed to facilitate the following:

- the handover of all architectural/design documentation and configuration data, identification of developed software, scripts, tools, command procedures and the like;
- handover of documented processes, standards, procedures manuals and associated reference material relating to the infrastructure (including hardware and software) used to provide the services;
- a description of all in-flight projects;
- a listing of any open issues or problems;
- transfer of all hardware used in the provision of the services (if this is part of the commercial construct of the deal – eg, a service provider will be unlikely to transfer assets from offshore delivery centres or assets used to support services provided to multiple clients);
- assignment of software used by the service provider in the provision of the services where the service provider is the licensee and where it is envisaged that the customer will still want to use such software in the future;
- novation or assignment of all third-party contracts used by the outgoing service provider where those contracts can be assigned to the incoming supplier;
- identification of employees used in the provision of the services and, where applicable, provision for transfer of those personnel (whether by operation of law or a separate consensual process); and
- arrangements for transfer of all customer data.

The transition-out plan will also need to deal with the provision of information relating directly to the provision of the services by the incumbent service provider. This information is in addition to the information that may already have been provided during the tendering process (see section 2.3 above). This is generally done by requiring that the outgoing service provider attend workshops with the customer and the incoming supplier; it can also be achieved by allowing staff from the incoming service provider to shadow staff from the existing service provider during the transition period. The contract should also provide for key personnel to be available during the course of transition-out services. A form of words may accordingly be:

As part of the Disengagement Services, the service provider must provide to the Customer and the Replacement Provider(s) a copy of all documentation required to be created or maintained by the service provider under this Agreement, including procedures manuals, schedules, usage reports, service issue logs, change information reports, product and service specifications, architecture and system mapping documents and other reference materials and related information. Such documentation must be provided promptly upon request by the Customer and, in any event, unless otherwise agreed, within 10 Business Days of a request from the Customer.

As part of the Disengagement Services, the service provider must provide to the Customer advice and information regarding the Services, and related topics as are required to facilitate the provision of the Replacement Services. This will include responding to all requests for information and advice by the Customer and providing the information and advice to the Customer within 5 Business Days (or such other period as is agreed) of receiving a request from the Customer. Where required, the service provider will make available all Key Personnel providing the Services to attend all meetings requested by the Customer.

It is worthwhile listing in the transition-out plan all items that will be handed over to the incoming service provider. This will limit arguments in relation to what are trade secrets or what intellectual property is owned by the outgoing service provider (and therefore unavailable to other suppliers, which will likely be direct competitors). During the negotiation of an agreement, a service provider may be made to disclose these materials provided that they are disclosed only for the limited purposes of due diligence, are returned at the end of that due diligence period, and are otherwise subject to obligations of confidence so that other prospective suppliers are not entitled to use that material for any purpose other than for the purpose of providing services to the customer; see also the chapter on confidentiality, intellectual property and data in this regard.

A strong governance structure throughout the transition is crucial to ensure that any impact on the customer's existing business is minimised, while at the same time giving the service provider sufficient contact with key personnel and subject-matter experts so that it fully understands the provision of the services.

3.4 Incentives

A customer could consider having separately specified service credits or liquidated damages for failure to provide due diligence materials by the due date specified in the transition-out plan, or at least some deferral of related payments until transition-related milestones are met.

3.5 Asset transfers

Asset transfer may involve the transfer of particular hardware and the assignment of software licenses. It could also involve the assignment of third-party contracts for the maintenance and support of the relevant assets used to provide the services.

An issue that may arise in respect of assets (usually hardware) is whether the asset is used solely in the provision of services to the customer. Where the asset is used by the supplier to provide services to multiple clients, it is impractical for the contract to require transfer of that asset to an incoming service provider.

Where an asset cannot be transferred, the customer (and the incoming service provider) will need to know all relevant details in respect of that asset so that an alternative asset may be purchased and commissioned to replace that asset upon completion of the transition process, should that be necessary to support the ongoing services; often it will be unnecessary, as the new service provider will have its own delivery infrastructure in place (and particularly when customers are increasingly commissioning cloud-based solutions).

Lastly, for assets that will be transferred there must be some form of valuation methodology to calculate the price (if any) payable for those assets. The price may depend on whether the customer has paid for the assets in full (which will normally be the case upon expiry of the contract, but may not be the case on early termination of the contract). If the contract has expired, then presumably the service provider has recouped in full the value of the assets and the incoming provider will not need to pay for them. If the assets have not been paid for, then options for valuation will include net book value and fair market value, but such terms can be subject to debate; recourse to binding third-party determination may be worth considering.

See the chapter on assets and third-party contracts for a more detailed analysis of the likely issues arising in this regard.

3.6 Assignment of contracts

Contracts that an incoming service provider may need to have assigned or novated to it may include maintenance and support contracts, subcontractor agreements and supply arrangements.

Ideally, all contracts entered into by the original service provider specifically in connection with the services should be at least capable of assignment to the incoming service provider. The outsourcing contract will often place a positive obligation on the service provider to ensure that any contracts that it enters into contain provisions permitting the assignment of that contract to another party.

Where this is not the case (and it frequently will not be, especially *vis à vis* larger third-party suppliers and/or those providing commercial, off-the-shelf solutions), and the terms of a particular contract entered into by the service provider prevent it from being assigned to the incumbent service provider, the outsourcing contract will need to contain alternative arrangements in relation to the service provided under that contract. These may include:

- the ongoing provision of that service by the outgoing service provider for a period of time, so as to allow the new service provider (or the customer if the services are being insourced) to obtain replacement services;
- holding of the benefit of that contract on trust for the customer, which allows the customer to receive the benefit of the contract for at least a transitional period; and
- where neither of the above are possible, the provision of assistance by the

service provider in negotiating a new contract in the name of the customer for those services on an ongoing basis.

Where none of the above options are available, the incoming supplier will need to provide alternative replacement services, either from its own resources or by engaging in fresh negotiations with the relevant third party or with someone providing an equivalent service or product. The key will be to ascertain the position early in the process, so as to allow for sufficient time for these steps to be taken, if necessary.

Any contract that transfers should provide for an apportionment of any advance payments made for services not yet provided and for amounts that are yet to be paid for services already provided. In addition, it is common to include provisions ascribing liability for claims made for breaches of the contract or acts or omissions, depending on when the breach, act or omission occurred.

Again, see the chapter on assets and third-party contracts for further details as to third-party contract issues.

3.7 Staff transfer

Depending on the jurisdiction involved, the transfer of staff may be either compulsory or a voluntary process whereby the incoming service provider will make offers of employment to various personnel whom it considers necessary for the ongoing provision of the services.

In any event, a separate schedule will set out the terms applicable to staff transfers (see the chapter on human resources).

Such a schedule will deal in detail with responsibility for financial liabilities for the employees, including any accrued entitlements of the employees.

The schedule will normally contain provisions regulating contact with employees by the incoming provider and the timing of when offers of employment must be made to the transferring employees.

3.8 Data transfer

Where an incoming service provider is not taking over all of the hardware and software used by the incumbent service provider, there will need to be provision for the transfer of the customer's data to the incoming service provider. The contract will need to provide for all other information necessary for the incoming service provider to understand and use the data in conjunction with its own systems. This may require the outgoing service provider to provide the data in a particular format and, if necessary, to provide other information in respect of the data that the incoming service provider may need to migrate and convert.

3.9 Trade secrets, tools and methodologies

One area of contention that arises in respect of the transfer of software and information is the transfer of the service provider's intellectual property. Ideally, prospective service providers will be given all information in relation to the current services. However, some of that information will include the incumbent service provider's tools and methodologies (ie, its way of providing the services), which the supplier likely sees as what differentiates it from other service providers; therefore, it will treat these tools and methodologies as its trade secrets.

The incoming service provider should have its own internal tools and methodologies, and in many if not most cases it will not even want to use the approaches or materials of its predecessor (although it might be interested in seeing them). The grey area is where the documentation relating to the existing services includes the incumbent service provider's method of providing the services (ie, where the customer's internal ways of working have become synonymous with the approach and documentation of the outgoing service provider).

A customer will therefore need to ensure that its contract with a service provider allows for disclosure of all information that an incoming service provider must have access to in order to provide the services on an ongoing basis and without risk to service continuity. In most cases, this need not extend to the incumbent service provider's method of providing the services, but may include materials that have been delivered to (and are used by) the customer.

Where the tools are embedded in software that is provided to the incoming service provider, the contract will need to provide for an ongoing licence of those tools to the customer and to other service providers, for the purposes of providing services to the customer.

See the chapter on confidentially, intellectual property and data for further consideration of these issues.

3.10 Cost of services

The service provider should be paid for any additional services that it provides during transition to the new service provider which are over and above the business-as-usual type of services. Ideally, as part of the transition-out plan, the service provider should give an estimate of its costs for the relevant activities set out in the transition-out plan. One particular issue for a customer to consider is whether some of the service provider personnel who are engaged in business-as-usual services (and who may be covered by the core charges in the contract) could be utilised to provide some or all of the termination assistance services. Depending on the circumstances, this may come at the price of having to relax or even disapply some of the service levels that such individuals would otherwise have been supporting.

About the authors

Paul Allen
Partner, DLA Piper
Paul.Allen@dlapiper.com

Paul Allen is a partner at DLA Piper and leads the firm's IP and technology practice in the Middle East. He has over 15 years of international experience, having worked for extended periods in Asia Pacific, Europe and the Middle East. Mr Allen specialises in information and communications technology projects, with particular expertise in the delivery of large-scale outsourcing, managed service and procurement programmes in technology, media and telecommunications (TMT), financial services, healthcare and the public sector. Mr Allen regularly advises clients on their market strategies and coordinates the provision of a broad range of corporate, commercial and dispute resolution advice and support. He has been recognised by *Chambers Global* as a Band 1 leading individual for TMT in the United Arab Emirates. His clients have commented that he "stands out for his client relations, follow up and problem-solving skills" (*Chambers Global 2015*) and has been referred to by clients as "the best TMT lawyer in the region" (*Legal 500 2015*).

Kai Bodenstedt
Partner, DLA Piper
kai.bodenstedt@dlapiper.com

Dr Kai Bodenstedt is a partner at DLA Piper and heads the firm's German employment practice. He provides legal advice to international corporate clients on all aspects of employment and labour projects and disputes. In particular, he advises international commercial enterprises on reductions in force and restructurings and advises on works council and co-determination issues. He also handles transfers of businesses under the German Acquired Rights Directive implementing legislation, especially in cross-border situations. His work extends to representing employers in labour courts in both works councils and individual employment law issues.

Peter Brook
Partner, DLA Piper
peter.brook@dlapiper.com

Peter Brook has advised on outsourcing contracts over many years. He has advised on a full range of contracts for national and global clients in most sectors. He has particular experience in acting on major outsourcing in the public sector where he has advised on many large and complex government outsourcing transactions.

Kit Burden
Partner and co-head of technology sector, DLA Piper
kit.burden@dlapiper.com

Kit Burden is co-head of DLA Piper's global technology sector. He specialises in outsourcing and complex technology transactions, advising IT users and suppliers, outsourcing services and all aspects of the procurement process. His work ordinarily involves business critical projects frequently valued in the hundreds of millions of pounds. His major clients include UBS, Dixons Carphone Warehouse, RBS, Lloyds Banking Group, HSBC, TUI, John Lewis, HCL Technologies, Allied Irish Banks, Wipro, Red Hat and Infosys, as well as various other large corporations, IT providers and outsourcing services.

Mr Burden is identified as a leading IT and outsourcing lawyer by legal directories – including *Legal 500*, *Legal Experts* and *Chambers* – which variously describe him as "an outsourcing guru" and "a brilliant IT lawyer".

He is a fellow and past trustee of the Society of Computers and Law and chairs its outsourcing group. He is also a member of the Computer Law Group. A frequent speaker at industry and legal conferences both in the United Kingdom and internationally, Mr Burden also writes on information technology and outsourcing for various journals, including *IT Law Today*, *Computers and Law* and the *Computer Law and Security Review*, for which he is on the correspondents' panel.

He is the author of two leading publications, *Computer Contracts* (Sweet & Maxwell) and *Legal Protection of Computer Software*, and is co-author of the "IT Contracts" chapter in the *Encyclopaedia of IT Law* (Sweet & Maxwell).

Kristof De Vulder
Partner, DLA Piper
Kristof.DeVulder@dlapiper.com

Kristof De Vulder heads DLA Piper's technology and source practice in Brussels. He has vast experience in IT contracts, outsourcing, business process outsourcing and offshoring. He was lead lawyer for several global and multi-jurisdictional strategic outsourcing deals (including offshore transactions) in different sectors. His clients include large-scale sellers and buyers of outsourcing services, information and communications technology products and solutions and government companies. Mr De Vulder also provides clients with pre-litigation services and assists them during disputes.

He has received international recognition with respect to outsourcing and IT contracts. Chambers Europe describes him as "an excellent negotiator" with "unmatched" outsourcing experience. Mr De Vulder is a frequent speaker at industry and legal conferences. He also writes for various journals on information technology and is the author of a leading publication on IT outsourcing (Wolters Kluwer).

Anne Friedman
Of counsel – Intellectual Property and Technology (Strategic Sourcing), DLA Piper
Anne.Friedman@dlapiper.com

Anne Friedman focuses her practice on structuring and negotiating large-scale sourcing and technology transactions, concentrating on global and domestic outsourcings in information technology, software development and maintenance and business process outsourcing. Her practice also includes drafting and negotiating transition services agreements in connection with M&A transactions, software licensing, integration and implementation transactions, hosting agreements, distribution agreements and related corporate transactions, as well as handling issues relating to data privacy, data security and IP matters. Ms Friedman's experience spans all transaction phases, including request for proposal and contract development, execution, implementation and maintenance.

Ms Friedman has represented a variety of Fortune 500 and other large companies in various business areas, including financial services, general and investment banking, pharmaceuticals, health insurance, hospitality, food and beverage, mortgage banking and educational groups. Providing *pro bono* legal services is also an important part of Ms Friedman's practice. Her *pro bono* clients include a woman's health non-profit, the Executive Service Corps of Southern California, the IMPACT LA project in the Los Angeles metropolitan area, the Legal Aid Society of the District of Columbia and Bread for the City (Washington, DC).

Peter Jones
Partner, DLA Piper
peter.jones@dlapiper.com

Peter Jones advises clients on a broad range of projects involving complex contracting arrangements and has key sector experience in information technology, telecommunications, financial services, retail, logistics and health.

Mr Jones's involvement in negotiations has included advising both customers and service providers. He has also worked closely with a number of sourcing advisers and consultants. In addition, Mr Jones often works closely with corporate partners on complex acquisition and divestment activities, including long-term transitional arrangements.

Tom Kerr Williams
Partner, DLA Piper
tom.kerrwilliams@dlapiper.com

Tom Kerr Williams is an employment law specialist. He advises employer clients on the full range of contentious and non-contentious issues arising from the employment relationship, with a particular focus on collective rights and the HR aspects of major outsourcing transactions.

Mr Kerr Williams is experienced in advising global service providers and customers through first and second generation outsourcing projects, including negotiating multi-national outsourcing deals involving offshoring to multiple locations. He works with clients on all HR aspects of the sourcing process to ensure smooth consultation, transfer of staff and the integration of staff into a new workforce.

Mr Kerr Williams is a firm believer that the people issues in an outsourcing can make or break the commercial deal. He has worked with clients on shaping their people solutions to ensure that commercial deals make sense, that the people aspects of services are sufficiently resilient to meet business and regulatory requirements, and that exit from the contract is as smooth and pain free as possible.

He is acknowledged by legal directories as "technically superb" and an "expert in traditional labour law matters".

Stéphane Lemarchand
Partner – Global co-chair, IP and technology group, DLA Piper
stephane.lemarchand@dlapiper.com

Stéphane Lemarchand assists IT service providers in litigation matters and strategic projects. He has extensive experience in assisting large companies in international IT outsourcing transactions and business process outsourcing.

He is joint global head of the IP and technology practice and head of the practice across Europe, the Middle East and Africa.

Mr Lemarchand has been named IT lawyer of the year by *Best Lawyers France*, 2014 to 2015.

Tim Lyons
Partner, DLA Piper
tim.lyons@dlapiper.com

Tim Lyons leads DLA Piper's technology and sourcing practice in Australia. He works closely with his partners across DLA Piper's global technology and sourcing practice. Mr Lyons has extensive experience in all areas of information and communications technology law and specialises in advising both government and private sector clients on large-scale outsourcing transactions and upgrade and implementation projects. He has recently been involved in two significant IT outsourcing transactions covering end-to-end computing for more than 50,000 employees. Mr Lyons regularly contributes to information and technology thought leadership, including presenting to in-house counsel of private and public sector organisations on legal issues and current trends in outsourcing transactions.

Gregory Manter
Partner, DLA Piper
gregory.manter@dlapiper.com

Greg Manter represents clients in a wide variety of IT and business process outsourcing transactions and other IT licensing and development transactions.

He has represented customers in numerous software implementation agreements, including several large enterprise resource planning implementation agreements.

John McKinlay
Partner, DLA Piper
john.mckinlay@dlapiper.com

John McKinlay advises a range of businesses and public sector organisations on contractual, technology and IP matters. His core practice is negotiating commercial, outsourcing and technology contracts.

He advises clients in a range of industries, most typically financial services, life sciences and the public sector, and he regularly advises on projects which involve working across a number of international jurisdictions.

Mr McKinlay heads DLA Piper's Scottish IP and technology practice.

Jan Geert Meents
Partner, DLA Piper
Jan.Meents@dlapiper.com

Dr Jan Geert Meents is a partner in the Intellectual Property and Technology Group of DLA Piper and is based in the Munich office. He has over 15 years' experience advising IT companies and national and international businesses. His practice involves a combination of corporate, intellectual property and other legal issues specific to the technology sector. As part of this blend, Dr Meents has focused on complex technology transactions involving the exploitation, leveraging and transfer of IP rights with the focus on transformative technologies and their impact on corporate enterprises. Consistent with this specialisation, Dr Meents' practice involves the representation of customers and providers in sophisticated sourcing and offshoring transactions including large-scale IT and business process outsourcing projects. Furthermore, Dr Meents is extensively engaged in open source aspects on behalf of vendors and users, as well as in data protection and related IT compliance issues.

Duncan Pithouse
Partner, DLA Piper
duncan.pithouse@dlapiper.com

Duncan Pithouse is experienced in non-contentious technology and sourcing matters and focuses on complex international outsourcing contracts.

Mr Pithouse has advised on a wide range of outsourcing transactions relating to business functions and activities, including IT infrastructure, application design, build and support, finance and accounting, human resources, procurement, pension administration and actuarial services.

He advises on all aspects of clients' sourcing requirements, including sourcing strategies, deal shaping, pricing models, service level and credit mechanisms, as well as drafting and negotiating agreements.

Mr Pithouse's clients include investment banks, retail banks, insurers, pharmaceutical companies, consumer products companies and providers of technology and outsourced services.

Jan Pohle
Partner, DLA Piper
jan.pohle@dlapiper.com

Jan Pohle focuses on complex technology-related transactions and day-to-day legal advice to enterprises in the IT and telecoms industry.

His practice includes the legal structuring and management of complex business processes, IT outsourcing and other IT procurement and implementation projects (including drafting related documentation). He also advises on the implementation of emerging online business models, as well as M&A transactions in the IT and telecoms sector. Mr Pohle's practice advises on international and domestic data privacy matters.

Throughout his career Mr Pohle has also advised on complex contentious matters from the IT and telecoms industry and related litigation, including software audits.

Jonathan Rofé
Partner, DLA Piper
jonathan.rofe@dlapiper.com

Jonathan Rofé has extensive experience of working with national and international large-scale organisations on their IT projects. He focuses on drafting and negotiating outsourcing and other complex IT projects and has been lead lawyer for several global and multi-jurisdictional strategic outsourcing deals (eg, business process outsourcing, IT outsourcing and application management outsourcing). He also advises his clients on IP and data protection issues, notably in the outsourcing context, and has developed a specialist cloud computing, internet of things and big data practice. Mr Rofé is seen as an expert providing high-quality, value-added legal support and combining subject matter expertise with considerable knowledge of clients' operational and business constraints.

Sharon Rowe
Partner, DLA Piper
sharon.rowe@dlapiper.com

Sharon Rowe is a Partner at DLA Piper Australia. She specialises in complex technology and telecommunications contracting and procurement projects, working with clients throughout the whole procurement process. Her experience includes advising on the preparation and evaluation of requests for tender and other procurement documentation and drafting and negotiating contracts, including for sensitive, high-value Australian government projects. She also advises on IP protection, enforcement, licensing, commercialisation and management. Her practice includes developing and delivering tailored practical legal training programmes for clients. Ms Rowe was formerly a member of the Australian Capital Territory Guardianship and Management of Property Tribunal. She was also formerly a lecturer at the Australian National University.

Callum Sinclair
Partner, intellectual property and technology (technology and sourcing), DLA Piper
callum.sinclair@dlapiper.com

Callum Sinclair is a UK technology and sourcing partner with DLA Piper. He has 14 years' experience of major information and communications technology and telecoms projects, and specialises in advising clients in the government contracting, utilities, financial services and technology sectors. Mr Sinclair has advised on sourcing transactions worth collectively over £3 billion, and in the past few years alone he has provided pro-active legal and commercial solutions in a lead adviser role to the world's largest arts festival; Scotland's fastest-growing international company; the United Kingdom's leading cider and beer business; three of Scotland's largest banks; the Scottish Government Digital Directorate; one of the world's leading international testing companies; the Scottish Premiership defending football champions and Northern Ireland's three biggest utilities. Mr Sinclair is a prolific article writer in his field and is a board member of ScotlandIS, the representative body for Scotland's digital industries.

Gareth Stokes
Partner, DLA Piper
gareth.stokes@dlapiper.com

Gareth Stokes specialises in advising customer and supplier clients entering into IT, outsourcing and IP-driven contracts. He has particular experience advising on major IT outsourcing and business process outsourcing projects within heavily regulated industries (eg, financial services, life sciences and defence). He also regularly advises clients on public sector projects, working for both governmental bodies and their suppliers.

Mr Stokes's experience spans numerous complex major procurement and sourcing projects. Most engagements involve elements of service delivery onshore, with other elements delivered further afield, whether near shore within newer EU member states or offshore in places like India or China. In many cases these projects have involved innovative contractual structures, including corporate and contractual joint venture arrangements, multi-level framework and call-off structures, trust arrangements and other interlinked multi-contract arrangements.

Scott Thiel
Partner, DLA Piper
scott.thiel@dlapiper.com

Scott Thiel specialises in outsourcing and complex technology transactions, advising IT users and suppliers and outsourcing services relating to all aspects of the procurement process. His work ordinarily involves advising on business critical projects – frequently valued in the tens or hundreds of millions of dollars – to clients across a range of key sectors, including technology, banking, transport, energy and sport.

Mr Thiel also advises a broad range of public and private sector clients on information and data-privacy issues, including developing and implementing outsourcing models which support global data privacy compliance.

Mr Thiel is recognised as a leading IT and outsourcing lawyer by legal directories, including *Legal 500* and *Chambers*. *Legal 500 2014* states that "key strengths are his experience and accessibility", while clients particularly appreciate "the personal attention he provides".

Gregory Tulquois
Partner, DLA Piper
gregory.tulquois@dlapiper.com

Gregory Tulquois handles major projects, business-critical contracts and provides day-to-day advice in commercial and marketing matters over a range of industries, including food and beverage, retail and consumer products.

Mr Tulquois advises all stages of the supply chain on structure and document relationships with suppliers, customers and strategic partners, including in complex multi-party projects spanning multiple jurisdictions. He drafts and negotiates the range of documents necessary to create and preserve these relationships, protect clients' rights and enhance the value of their businesses.

His practice covers all kinds of commercial agreements, including sourcing, procurement and supply, sales, agency and distribution, franchise, logistics and warehousing, facilities management, management arrangements, outsourcing and offshoring, joint ventures, partnerships and strategic alliances. For companies in consumer product sectors, including fast-moving consumer goods, he also advises on all legal aspects of advertising, sales promotions, product regulations and consumer relations.

Joris Willems
Partner, DLA Piper
Joris.willems@dlapiper.com

Joris Willems has more than 15 years' experience advising IT companies and national and international businesses. His practice focuses on complex (international) licensing and commercial contracts, with an emphasis on technology, outsourcing transactions and cloud computing. He has experience across a range of sectors, including financial services and telecoms. Mr Willems has negotiated numerous complex multi-jurisdictional transactions and has extensive experience in operating in various jurisdictions, including China, India, South Korea, the African continent and the United States. Mr Willems is a member of the Global Board of DLA Piper, a member of the global technology and sourcing leadership team and co-heads the technology team in the Amsterdam office. He has also worked at DLA Piper's Hong Kong and Shanghai offices.

Anthony Willis
Partner and head, government sector – Australia, DLA Piper
Anthony.willis@dlapiper.com

Anthony Willis is recognised as one of Australia's leading government commercial, contracting, technology and IP lawyers, having spent more than 20 years advising on some of Australia's largest government commercial and technology transactions. He has led tender and contract development and negotiations for many multi-billion dollar Australian government procurements, including for the departments of defence, finance, human services and health. Mr Willis is recognised as a highly-skilled negotiation strategist and lead negotiator for major projects. He has also advised on the resolution of a number of major contract disputes, as well as leading-edge IP and technology matters arising in major outsourcing projects and significant technology procurements and complex research and development projects.